SYRIAN REQUIEM

Map of Syria

Control on the Ground

- Syrian regime
- Kurds
- Rebels
- Turkish military and Turkish-backed Syrian rebels
- 10km-deep zone patrolled by Turkish and Russian militaries
- Islamic State

TURKEY

IRAQ

JORDAN

ISRAEL

LEBANON

Qamishli
Al Hasakah
Raqqah
Deir ez-Zor
Kobane
Manbij
Afrin
Idlib
Aleppo
Khmeimim Air Base
Hama
Homs
Latakia
Tartus
Palmyra
Al-Tanf
Damascus
Suwayda
Dar'a
Golan Heights

SYRIAN REQUIEM

The Civil War and Its Aftermath

ITAMAR RABINOVICH
CARMIT VALENSI

PRINCETON UNIVERSITY PRESS

PRINCETON & OXFORD

Published by Princeton University Press
41 William Street, Princeton, New Jersey 08540
6 Oxford Street, Woodstock, Oxfordshire OX20 1TR

press.princeton.edu

All Rights Reserved

Library of Congress Cataloging-in-Publication Data

Names: Rabinovich, Itamar, 1942– author. | Valensi, Carmit,
    1980– author.
Title: Syrian requiem : the civil war and its aftermath / Itamar
    Rabinovich, Carmit Valensi.
Description: Princeton : Princeton University Press, 2021. | Includes
    bibliographical references and index.
Identifiers: LCCN 2020017878 (print) | LCCN 2020017879 (ebook) |
    ISBN 9780691193311 (hardback) | ISBN 9780691212616 (ebook)
Subjects: LCSH: Syria—History—Civil War, 2011– | Syria—Politics and
    government—2000– | Syria—Foreign relations—21st century. |
    Syria—Foreign relations—United States. | United States—Foreign
    relations—Syria.
Classification: LCC DS98.6 .R335 2021 (print) | LCC DS98.6 (ebook) |
    DDC 956.9104/23—dc23
LC record available at https://lccn.loc.gov/2020017878
LC ebook record available at https://lccn.loc.gov/2020017879

British Library Cataloging-in-Publication Data is available

Editorial: Fred Appel and Jenny Tan
Production Editorial: Sara Lerner
Text Design: Leslie Flis
Jacket Design: Karl Spurzem
Production: Erin Suydam
Publicity: Kate Hensley and Kathryn Stevens
Copyeditor: Kathleen Kageff

Jacket Credit: Two Syrian men walk among the rubble following recent
airstrikes in the Al-Kalasa neighborhood of Aleppo, Sept. 24, 2016.
Credit: Basem Ayoubi / ImagesLive / ZUMA Wire / Alamy

This book has been composed in Arno Pro with News Gothic display

Printed on acid-free paper. ∞

Printed in the United States of America
10 9 8 7 6 5 4 3 2 1

Itamar dedicates this book to Frank Lowy;
and Carmit dedicates it to Daniel, Mia,
and Emma Rozenblum

CONTENTS

PREFACE

The Syrian civil war and crisis has been a major event in the Middle Eastern and global arenas during most of the second decade of the current century. Unfolding in an important Arab and Middle Eastern country sharing borders with five neighboring states, the Syrian rebellion against Bashar al-Asad's regime has set off a major regional and global crisis. It did not remain a domestic affair for long. The ripple effects of the crisis would reach Europe and, to a lesser extent, even the United States by 2015–16, with important political consequences on both continents. The decisions made by at least two American presidents about America's involvement in Syria have triggered sharp debate and are likely to figure prominently in the discussion of their legacies. And the international community's failure to respond properly to a humanitarian disaster of this magnitude raises important questions regarding the current global international order. Authoritative figures of the casualties, the degree of physical destruction, and the enormity of the refugee problem inside and outside Syria are unavailable, but most sources agree that by the middle of 2020 close to half a million people had died in Syria and close to twelve million Syrians had become refugees or IDPs (internally displaced persons). The United Nations estimates that of the eighteen million people who currently live in Syria, almost twelve million are in need of humanitarian help. Six million Syrian Sunnis now live outside

Syria, and their return is uncertain if not unlikely. The extent of this human tragedy goes beyond numbers and is forcefully described in the writing of several Syrian and other authors.[1]

The Syrian crisis has also been one of the most thoroughly reported on events of this decade. Conventional media coverage was not just supplemented but in some cases overtaken by instantaneous, on-the-ground coverage widely disseminated on the internet and on social media. Events from peaceful demonstrations to barrel bombings and chemical weapons attacks have been recorded on cell phones and sent across the globe. Alongside such wide coverage, academic analysis of the events as well as advocacy have proliferated in many forms, including articles, monographs, essays, think-tank blog postings, and—perhaps especially—tweets. The number of books dealing with the Syrian civil war and the larger Syrian crisis continues to grow, running the gamut from straight histories[2] to memoirs,[3] denunciations of the Asad regime,[4] social science analyses,[5] high journalism,[6] and sui generis books.[7]

The present book is a contribution to the contemporary history of the conflict and crisis. In what follows we seek to provide context and perspective by addressing several major and underlying issues and questions: the structural weakness of the Syrian state, the relationship between state and political community in Syria, the unique role of sectarianism in Syrian politics, the transformation of Middle Eastern and regional politics by the new roles played by Iran and Turkey, along with the United States' diminished role and Russia's return to a dominant role in the Middle East.

Historians engage in critical studies of past events and seek to narrate, explain, and interpret them by putting them in context and perspective. One of the main challenges confronting historians, contemporary historians among them, is the need to combine narrative with analysis of the main themes and issues. The British historian Ian Kershaw in his masterly study of the final phase of World War II explained the approach he chose:

> The chapters that follow proceed chronologically. . . . By combining structural history and the history of mentalities and dealing with German society from above and below the narrative approach has the virtue of being able to depict in precise fashion the dramatic stages of the regime's collapse but at the same time its astonishing resilience and desperate defiance in sustaining an increasingly obvious lost cause.[8]

We attempt to meet this challenge by beginning with two narrative chapters and then moving to three thematic ones. The first chapter offers an overview and interpretation of Syrian history from 1963, when the Ba'th Party came to power, to March 2011, when the Syrian rebellion broke out. An understanding of this history is essential to grasping the major issues at stake in Syria during the past nine years. The second chapter offers a narrative of the civil war and the Syrian crisis from March 2011 to the end of 2018. The next three chapters, the core of the book, take up the roles played by the principal actors: domestic (chapter 3), regional (chapter 4), and international (chapter 5). In the fifth chapter, dealing with the role and policies of the external powers, the reader will note that the section on the United States is significantly longer and more detailed than the one dealing with Russia. This reflects the fact that Russia's policy in Syria has been formulated and carried out in an opaque manner by a group of notoriously secretive cadre of policy makers. For the analyst, there is a lamentable dearth of material. The policy of the United States, by contrast, has been carried out by two administrations and has been discussed and debated openly and at length. Since the debate over Obama's and Trump's policies in Syria is bound to continue, we wanted to provide a rich factual record for future participants in such debates. After discussing the role of key international actors, the book proceeds with a sixth chapter on post–civil war developments in 2019–20 and considers possible future developments. Finally, the book concludes with a set of brief reflections on some of the major questions raised by the most recent chain of events and considers the motivation and drivers currently at play for those principal actors.

We began researching and writing this book in late 2017 when the Syrian civil war was still raging. At that point in time we were focused on the civil war itself. Now, as we are completing our work, we end up dealing also with the significantly new phase of the Syrian crisis: while full-fledged fighting between regime and opposition has ended, a low-intensity civil war continues, and a postwar conflict—domestic, regional, and international—has been exacerbated.

The title we chose for this book reflects our belief that Syria of the years 1963–2011 is unlikely to be restored any time soon. With massive external support, Bashar al-Asad has defeated his political and military opposition. He now controls more than 60 percent of his country's territory and will persist in his efforts to extend his control over the other 40 percent. But this will be an arduous task. The central government's sway over large parts of the country is limited, and a large part of the population does not—and will not—accept Asad's regime as a legitimate government. The process of reconstruction is also likely to be both lengthy and limited. Asad's two patrons, Russia and Iran, intend to stay in Syria. Both are determined to deepen and expand their influence in the country. Turkey and Israel also have important interests in Syria and will pursue them from across the border (Israel) or by occupying Syrian territory (Turkey). Syria's Sunni majority and several Sunni states in the region will not accept the war's outcome and the hegemony of the triad of Syria's Alawi community, Iran, and foreign Shi'i militias.

Syria is likely to remain a focal point of regional and international tensions. Six million Sunnis now live outside Syria, and their return is uncertain if not unlikely; a large part of Syria's Christian population has left for good, and a large part of Syria's cultural elite lives in exile and is unlikely to return any time soon. The aspect of life that the cultural elite in Syria contributed to even under the Asad dictatorship is now glaringly absent.

In researching and writing this book we were assisted by many colleagues and partners whom we wish to thank. Our research assistants, Anat Ben Haim and Arik Rudnitzky, and Dr. Tamar Yegnes were helpful in this as with earlier projects, and Revital Yerushalmi helped with the transliteration of Arabic names and terms. We are also grateful to our literary agent Deborah Harris; the staff of Princeton University Press, headed by Fred Appel; and our editor Hanne Tidnam and copyeditor Kathleen Kageff. We are grateful to the two external readers for their criticism and comments. Numerous individuals, policy makers, and experts generously shared their knowledge with us: Dimitry Adamsky, Zvi Barel, Ofra Bengio, Jennifer Cafarella, Rob Danin, Udi Dekel, Michel Duclos, Robert Ford, Philip Gordon, Major H., Fred Hof, James Jeffrey, Gallia Lindenshtraus, Charles Lister, Meir Litvak, Marko Moreno, Ehud Olmert, Assaf Orion, David Petraeus, Michael Ratney, Dennis Ross, Dror Shalom, Dan Shapiro, Andrew Tabler, Shlomi Weitzman, Bogi Yaalon, Tamar Yegnes, Raz Zimmt, and Eyal Zisser. We are deeply grateful to Elizabeth Tsurkov, who shared with us her profound knowledge of the Syrian opposition. We would like to express our gratitude to several members of the Syrian opposition who cannot be named but who have shared with us both their experiences and their insights.

A note on transliteration. As a rule, we sought to simplify the transliteration of Arabic names and terms rather than apply the rules of academic transliteration. With regard to several names of persons and locations commonly mentioned in Western media we used the common form such as Nasser and Latakia.

SYRIAN REQUIEM

CHAPTER 1

The Ba'th in Power, 1963–2011

Roots and Weakness of the Syrian State

The seeds of modern Syria were sown in negotiations between Great Britain, France, and their other allies during the First World War. When planning the future of the region in the war's aftermath, Britain was especially interested in securing a land bridge from Iraq to the Mediterranean in order to transport Iraqi oil through territory it controlled. France, by contrast, had vaguer goals in mind—primarily the desire to emerge from the war with its colonial empire enhanced.[1] France's claims to the region included an interest, manifest since the 1860s, in protecting the Christians of the Levant, the Lebanese Maronites. The Sykes-Picot Agreement of May 1916 reflected France's desire to control the Levant, namely the area covered currently by Syria, Lebanon, Israel, and the Palestinian authority.

Shortly after the war the League of Nations accorded France a mandate for Syria and Lebanon.

At that stage, the French government opposed the very notion of Syrian statehood, viewing the principal political force in the Syrian heartland—Sunni Arab nationalists—with suspicion and hostility.[2] In French eyes, modern Arab nationalism was actually a British creation, a force and a movement hostile to France's interests and aspirations. So upon taking control of Syria and Lebanon in 1920, the architects of French policy in Syria refrained from creating a unitary Syrian state, forming instead a Syrian federation composed of several statelets characterized by sectarian division and regional rivalries. They also added parts of Syria in southeastern and northern Lebanon to the Lebanese state, seeking to enlarge the entity they viewed as the mainstay of their position in the area. It was only five years later, in 1925, that a Syrian state was established. Two statelets populated by the Alawi and Druze minorities were integrated into that entity in 1945, when in the aftermath of World War II and under American and British pressure Syria was accorded independence. The newly independent Syria was governed by the traditional Arab nationalist elite, composed mostly of urban notables and landlords. This leadership had struggled against French control during the previous decades but failed to mobilize and lead a successful national war of liberation. Thus, France left Syria not as a result of expulsion by a nationalist opposition but rather as a result of pressure from the United States and Britain. These victorious wartime powers concluded that the French claim to Syria and Lebanon had expired, and they sought to absorb the new Syrian and Lebanese states into their spheres of influence.[3]

The Syrian Republic emerged as a weak and fragile state. Through the late 1940s and the 1950s Syria would become synonymous with instability. The traditional Arab nationalist politicians who came to power upon independence failed to form a stable, effective regime; the country was buffeted by internal divisions and conflicts, the intervention of regional and foreign powers, and successive coups d'état. Three military coups were staged in Syria in 1949 alone, and even the return to parliamentary life in 1954 failed to stabilize the chaotic state.

The rulers of a newly independent Syria had to cope with a vast array of challenges, first and foremost the need to engage in nation and state building. The population was diverse, with an Arab Sunni majority of 60 percent, and the rest composed of several religious and ethnic minorities: 10 percent Alawis, 10 percent Christians, 10 percent Kurds, and such smaller groups as the Druze, Ismailis, and Armenians. The Kurds were Sunni but not Arab, and most of them lived in the country's northeastern part close to the Turkish and Iraqi borders. The Alawis and the Druze were so-called "compact minorities," concentrated in mountainous areas, and their separatist tendencies had been encouraged by the French authorities earlier in the century to weaken the Sunni Arab nationalist elite of Syria's major cities.

The fledgling new Syrian state was pulled in opposite directions, between supranational ideologies and identities (Arab and Greater Syrian) and the reality of regionalism and localism. Syria was ruled by staunch Arab nationalists, and Damascus was commonly known as "Arabism's pulsating heart." The Kurdish minority naturally felt alienated in a country defined as Arab, and many Kurds did not actually possess Syrian citizenship. They crossed the border from Turkey and were not accorded citizenship by Syrian Arab nationalist governments, which were uninterested in expanding the ranks of this non-Arab minority. Other minorities, such as Christian and sectarian Muslims (Alawis, Druze, and Ismailis), regarded the dominant ideology of Pan-Arab nationalism to be an essentially Sunni Arab phenomenon in which they were relegated to an inferior position as members of minority sectarian groups. (Christians had played an important role in formulating the ideology of Pan-Arabism, but their hope of becoming equal members in a new political community were frustrated by

Arabism's Sunni tincture.) A new postindependence generation of younger Syrians, defined neither by sect nor by ethnic affiliation but as "a new middle class," felt excluded and exploited by the traditional governing elite. There was also tension between the civilian government and the leadership of the Syrian army, since that army had been built originally on the colonial auxiliary military force formed by the French authorities. As part of their policy of "divide and rule," the French had sought out military recruits from members of minority communities, and army commanders from these groups were treated with disdain by civilian politicians. Syrian politicians, in turn, were divided among themselves by personal and regional rivalries, with individual political actors forming alliances with rival regional and external powers seeking to manipulate Syria's politics. Internal tensions were exacerbated by the unsuccessful war with Israel in 1948–49.[4]

The rise of messianic Pan-Arab nationalism in the region, under Gamal Abd al-Nasser—second president of Egypt—and the impact of the Cold War and Soviet influence in the region in the 1950s further radicalized Syrian politics. In February 1958, Syria's leaders, led by the Ba'th, finally sought refuge by merging themselves with Egypt into what became known as the United Arab Republic (UAR). But the UAR proved to be a failure; the much larger and more assertive Egypt ended up dominating Syria. Paradoxically, the union reinforced a sense of Syrian distinctiveness owing to the bitter experience of Syria's being overwhelmed and overshadowed by Egypt. In September 1961 Syria seceded from the UAR and reestablished itself as an independent state. Egypt's Nasser refused to accept the secession and attempted to undermine the newly formed Syrian state by speaking over the heads of the Syrian government to the Syrian public directly via radio broadcasts. Nasser had retained some lingering support among Syrian politicians and army officers. It was against this backdrop that a group of officers identified with the Ba'th Party staged their coup on March 8, 1963, thus laying the foundation for decades of Ba'thi rule. Ironically, it was a party advocating Arab unity and union that consolidated Syria's existence as a self-standing sovereign state.

The Ba'th in Power

The Ba'th has been nominally in power in Syria ever since the military coup of March 8, 1963—but it has undergone several transformations.[5] Known in Arabic as the "Socialist Party of Arab Renaissance," the Ba'th Party was first founded in the 1940s by two Damascene intellectuals: Michel Aflaq and Salah al-Bitar. The party offered a secular version of Arab nationalism combined with a social democratic ideology. Its secularism attracted members of minority communities, and its social democratic ideology attracted younger men who were critical of the traditional ruling elite and who sought social and political change. In 1953, the original Ba'th founding party merged with another party formed by a politician from the central Syrian city of Hama: Akram Hourani. Hourani had recruited to his party young army officers and mobilized peasants in the countryside against the traditional political elite under the banner of Arab socialism. Hourani brought to the augmented Ba'th Party both voting power and influence in the military. The combined party—which spread beyond purely Syria, to Iraq, Lebanon, and Jordan—did well in parliamentary elections, particularly in the elections of 1954, and played an important role in the ongoing radicalization of Syrian politics, and in championing the ill-fated union with Egypt, aiming for a leading role in Pan-Arab politics. But the party's hopes of genuine partnership with

Abd al-Nasser were to be frustrated; Nasser wanted full mastery of the political sphere. The Ba'th became a hostile critic of the Nasserist regime, and some of its leaders turned to facilitating instead the breakup from the UAR and rebuilding Syrian independence.

The party's rise to power in Syria came about in an unusual way. A group of army officers—members of the party, most of them from minority communities—formed a secret cabal known as "the Military Committee" during the union with Egypt. This was the group that planned and executed the coup on March 8, 1963, quickly forming a partnership with the traditional leadership of the Ba'th to establish the Ba'th regime.

The first phase of the Ba'th regime lasted from March 1963 to February 1966. During this period the new regime consolidated its hold over the country, confronting both Nasser's pressure from outside and the enmity of the Sunni urban elite and middle class at home. It carried out several socialist reforms, including nationalizing large enterprises and an agrarian reform distributing land owned by major landowners to peasants. Consequently, the state and the public sector came to dominate the economy, and the regime enjoyed support in the countryside among the beneficiaries of the agrarian reform. Yet the new regime was also torn by internecine conflicts: between the army officers who had staged the coup and who consequently felt they owned the regime, and the historical leadership of the Ba'th; and between the party's more moderate wing and a new radical, Marxist wing that had emerged during the union with Egypt. The regime as a whole found itself in conflict with the Sunni urban elite, the religious establishment, and the merchant classes. These groups felt dispossessed and alienated: by the large number of minority members (Alawis, Druze, and

Ismailis) in the ranks of the regime's military wing; and by the radicalism and secularism of part of its leadership.

The overrepresentation of minoritarian officers in the ranks of the new regime—particularly its military wing—turned sectarian and communal issues into a major element in Syrian politics. This overrepresentation had its origins, first, in French colonial "divide and rule" practices of recruiting officers and noncommissioned officers from minority communities, and second, in the attraction that young men of these same minority communities, wary of the Sunni orientation of Arab nationalism, had to secular political parties. In the 1940s and 1950s two secular parties, the Ba'th and the SSNP (Syrian Social Nationalist Party), competed for the hearts and minds young Alawis, Druze, Ismailis, and Christians across all Syria, adding them in large numbers to their ranks.

In Ba'thi Syria, sectarian solidarity became a major political force for the first time, particularly as individuals and factions within the regime began to fight over position and influence. In Arabic, the term *ta'ifiyyah* refers to social and political allegiance and conduct determined by sectarian and ethnic affiliation. The term *Ta'ifah* referred to a religious community. In the Ottoman system, the Islamic empire—headed by a sultan, also regarded as a caliph—had no problem giving religious groups known as *millets* a large degree of autonomy in the so-called millet system. But once Arab nationalist sentiment replaced allegiance to the Ottoman caliph, all ultimate loyalty to such primordial groups as sects and tribes came to be seen as retrograde. The prominent role played by members of minority communities in the new regime was therefore unacceptable to many Sunnis, who—in addition to feeling dispossessed—refused to accept Alawis and (to a lesser extent) Druze as proper

Muslims. In 1964, the Syrian branch of the Egyptian Muslim Brotherhood Islamist movement organized an early protest in Hama against the regime's secularist nature; a second outburst against the regime's secularism and socialism broke out in Homs in 1965. A third protest occurred in 1967 following the publication of an atheistic essay in the Syrian army's magazine authored by a radical Alawi Ba'thi intellectual.

The principal challenge to the Ba'th regime, however, remained Abd al-Nasser's refusal to accept Syria's secession from the UAR and the new regime's legitimacy. In 1963, Syria signed a tripartite union with Egypt and the new Ba'th Party regime in Iraq in an attempt to consolidate its hold over the country. This short-lived abortive agreement was never to be implemented because of the underlying hostility between Nasser and the two Ba'th regimes.

In late 1963, in an effort to neutralize Nasser's animosity, the Ba'th regime adopted a radical new strategy vis-à-vis Egypt—a strategy that would play a major role in escalating Arab-Israeli tensions in the years 1964–67, and which would ultimately lead to the crisis of May 1967 and to the Six-Day War. Simply put, Syria threatened to go to war against Israel and to drag Egypt into that war against the latter's will. The Syrian threat was triggered by Israel's completion of an overland water carrier (consisting of both a canal and a pipeline) from Lake Tiberias to the south of the country. In Arab eyes, the completion of the project was seen as a crucial step in consolidating Israel's existence by enabling it to settle the country's arid southern region. When Israel announced the project, the Ba'th regime threatened to go to war in order to abort it. The threat was in fact directed at Egypt rather than at Israel.[6] Implicit behind this was the knowledge that a Syrian-Israeli war would end in Syria's military defeat—which would force Egypt to intervene on Syria's behalf. Nasser had already learned from the Second Arab-Israeli War of 1956 that it was imperative for Egypt not to be drawn prematurely to another war with Israel. So, in order to check Syria, in January 1964 Nasser summoned the first Arab summit conference in Cairo, to develop a comprehensive strategy for dealing with Israel's water project and other core issues of the Arab-Israeli conflict. It would not be the last time Syria's Ba'thi rulers would use the threat of escalation with Israel as a means of pressuring Egypt to recognize Syria's legitimacy as an independent state. Much as Nasser resented the new regime in Syria, he realized that he could not afford to see it militarily destroyed by Israel. The resolutions adopted in Cairo—to divert the tributaries of the Jordan River, to build unified Arab command in support of that move, and to support the establishment of the PLO (Palestine Liberation Organization, an organization created by the Arab League, dominated by Egypt)—would inaugurate a new phase in the Arab-Israeli conflict. Their strategy proved effective, but it also would bring the region to the brink of war in May 1967.

Meanwhile, internecine conflicts within the Ba'th regime in Syria were coalescing by 1965 into a struggle between two coalitions. One was led by the country's president, the Sunni general Amin al-Hafez, along with the Ba'th Party's historic civilian leadership and a supportive military faction; the other consisted of a group of mostly Alawi and Druze army officers, along with the civilian party's radical wing. In February 1966, the latter group—known as the Neo-Ba'th—staged a coup and took control of the regime. The coup of February 23, 1966, would have far-reaching consequences. The new regime in power had a more distinctive sectarian character and a much narrower base of support. The new regime had a difficult dilemma to resolve right off the bat: How could it legitimize its conduct as a

Ba'th regime when it had expelled the party's founding fathers? In an effort to overcome this problem, the regime now argued that the Ba'th Party's *true* founder was Zaki al-Arsuzi, an Alawi intellectual from Alexandretta (the Syrian province ceded to Turkey by France on the eve of World War II). The fact that Arsuzi was Alawi suited the country's new rulers. The Ba'th regime had previously dispossessed and antagonized Syria's urban Sunni elite during its first three years of power, but some of its leaders, including Amin al-Hafez and Salah al-Bitar, still managed to communicate with members of the country's ousted elite, in order to minimize its opposition to the regime and to guarantee broader base of support. After February 1966 these lines of communication were completely severed, and the regime relied on an extremely slender base consisting of radical intellectuals as well as provincial and rural groups. The new regime was supported by Egypt and the Soviet Union; both were worried that it would be toppled and replaced by a regime friendly to the West and to the conservative Arab states, thus changing the regional balance of power in the context of an escalating Cold War.

Between February 1966 and June 1967, the Neo-Ba'th, as the regime came to be commonly called, continued to deal with broad opposition inside Syria to its radicalism. It was also torn by continued internecine conflicts governed by personal rivalries and sectarian loyalties. Alawi army officers who had initially collaborated in ousting Druze and Ismaili ones began to fight each other. Two coalitions were formed around two generals: General Salah Jadid, and General Hafez al-Asad, commander of the air force and acting minister of defense. Beyond the personal rivalry, the conflict between Jadid and Asad and their factions was also about orientation and policy. Salah Jadid was considered to be politically savvier, but at the end of the day

Asad would prove to be more cunning. Jadid allied with the party's radical wing while Asad supported a more pragmatic and moderate line on socioeconomic issues. When Asad seized power, he did manage to build bridges to the urban bourgeoisie and mitigate its hostility to the regime.

The Neo-Ba'th's domestic radicalism was matched by an adventurous foreign policy: a reliance on the Soviet Union and escalation of its antagonistic policy toward Israel. Syria's role in trying to divert the tributaries of the Jordan, its support of the new Palestinian nationalist organizations headed by Fatah (the Palestinian nationalist organization founded and led by Yasser Arafat), and its confrontation with Israel over border and water issues (access to Lake Tiberias) brought the two countries to the brink of war in 1967. The Syrian-Israeli border dispute went back to the armistice agreement signed between the two countries in 1949 at the end of the 1948 war. These agreements were made on the assumption that they would apply to the brief transitional period prior to the signing of a peace agreement. In the event, peace was not made, and the two countries found themselves in almost permanent conflict over border issues. The radicalization of Syrian politics under the Neo-Ba'th and Syria's decision to use these issues as means of pressuring Egypt brought Syria and Israel to the verge of war. Despite Nasser's reservations, Egypt was drawn increasingly into this conflict and finally decided to deter Israel by remilitarizing the Sinai in May 1967. A series of miscalculations by regional and international actors resulted in the outbreak of the Six-Day War. And yet in sharp contrast to its bellicosity prior to the war, the Ba'th regime did not prosecute this war energetically, knowing full well that it was no match for the Israeli army. In the last phase of this war, Israel launched an attack directly against Syria and captured the Golan Heights.

Recriminations about the Syrian army's performance during the Six-Day War exacerbated the conflicts within the Ba'th regime. The factions headed by Hafez al-Asad and Salah Jadid argued over the responsibility for the military defeat. Jadid and his people argued that, as minister of defense, Asad was responsible for the failure. Finally, in November 1970, Hafez al-Asad seized full power in another coup, which he called "the Corrective Movement." This term was meant to signal that Syria's new ruler intended to "correct" the deviations of the Neo-Ba'th and restore the party and its regime to their correct course.

The Hafez al-Asad Regime

"The Corrective Coup" of November 1970 would be a major turning point in the history of the Syrian state, after which Hafez al-Asad would hold onto power for thirty years, introducing profound changes in Syrian politics and society and turning the previously weak state into an important regional and occasionally international actor. He came to power fully ready: Asad had been a senior partner in the Ba'th regime since March 1963, demonstrating his leading position within the regime in 1969 by staging a preliminary coup and biding his time until he was ready to seize complete power. By the time he took command of Syria he had a full plan for building a stable and durable regime.

Asad's strategy was to construct his regime in a series of concentric circles. At its inner core was a neopatrimonial regime built around Asad's immediate family, his Alawi clan, and, in a looser way, the whole Alawi community along with a group of close confidants (who were not all Alawi). This inner core was surrounded by larger circles: the institution of the presidency; the Ba'th Party; the Syrian armed forces; the cabinet and the government; a coalition of "progressive parties" (established in 1972); and a number of popular organizations. Asad's policy of relying on the Alawi community as the true core of his regime was far reaching. Traditionally, the Alawis were a downtrodden community exploited by tribal chiefs and urban Sunni landlords. The community's partnership with the French authorities had enabled some members of the community to do well, particularly in the ranks of the military. Asad recruited large numbers of Alawis, some of them to senior positions, many of them to junior and middling ones. Soon most key positions in the Syrian armed forces and security services were filled with Asad loyalists from the Alawi community. Asad's immediate circle, known as al-Jama'ah ("the group"), included Ali Haydar (commander of the special forces); Muhammad al-Khuly (head of air force intelligence); Ali Duba (head of military intelligence); and Shafiq Fayad, Ibrahim al-Safi, and Adnan Bader al-Din (all three commanders of key divisions). A large number of Alawis was also recruited to lower-level positions in the military, the security services, government bureaucracy, and the public sector. Significant investments were made in the Alawi region, including the establishment of a university in Latakia. Large numbers of Alawis migrated from the mountains and the coast into inner Syria, to Damascus, Homs, and Hama. While most officers and enlisted men in the army were not Alawi, the chain of command was restructured such that every Sunni officer had an Alawi subordinate or superior. The city of Damascus underwent important changes. Its meager Alawi population increased exponentially, and the city was surrounded by military bases and units that were largely Alawi.

This structure enabled Asad to build a stable regime based on primordial loyalty and overlaid with supportive groups and institutions not explicitly Alawi, thus creating the semblance of a party regime resting on a broad base of the rural population and minority communities other than the Alawis who were distrustful of Sunni domination, and elements of the Sunni Arab majority.

Over time Asad's success in providing Syria with a stable government built genuine support among broad groups in the Syrian population. While his strategy was adopted in order to guarantee absolute loyalty to Asad and the regime, its negative effects were mitigated in a number of ways. Asad made sure to place Sunnis in several senior military and civilian positions: for example, Hikmat al-Shihabi as chief of staff of the Syrian army; Naji Jamil as commander of the air force; Mustafa Tlas as minister of defense; and Abdallah al-Ahmar as his chief lieutenant in the Ba'th Party. Asad also cultivated the Sunni religious establishment and appointed the cooperative Sheikh Ahmad al-Kaftaru as the country's mufti instead of the hostile Hasan Habanake.[7] He took care to participate in Friday prayers and other occasions of a religious nature. And Asad also sought rapprochement with the Sunni bourgeoisie in Syria's major cities; he did not share power with them but gave them space and enabled them to do well economically. In time, a new economic elite composed of Sunni-Alawi partnerships emerged. Such partnerships rested on collaboration between senior members of the regime and businessmen, directly or through their offspring. Asad also recruited to his regime a large number of Sunnis from the Houran area. He enabled the bourgeoisie in Damascus and Aleppo, and the country's small but impressive intelligentsia, to operate within a well-defined space.

While the public sector remained dominant in the Syrian economy, Asad's economic reforms enabled members of the private sector to do well and develop a stake in the regime's durability. Prominent academics and intellectuals such as Sadiq al-Azm and members of the country's impressive theater community were allowed to pursue their professional life as long as they did not cross well-defined red lines to engage in what the regime regarded as "politics." Political opposition, needless to say, was not tolerated. Asad's Syria was a brutal dictatorship, but it was not Saddam Hussein's "Republic of Fear."

Asad's strategy was successful in that during his thirty years in power, his country's Sunni Arab majority came to accept, however reluctantly, the rule of a handpicked Alawi elite. There was a militant minority to whom this state of affairs remained unacceptable, but the majority was willing to accept the status quo because of the stability and foreign policy achievements provided by the regime. And yet on several occasions the majority's unhappiness with Alawi control bubbled up to the surface. For example, when a new constitution was drafted in January 1973, Asad decided it was time to formalize his position as Syria's president. Syria's original constitution stipulated that Islamic law would be the chief source of legislation and that the country's president must be a Muslim. Since Alawis were not considered proper Muslims by conservative Sunnis, Asad tried to skirt the issue by omitting this stipulation. This triggered massive demonstrations that forced Asad to step back. He tried to resolve the issue by having Lebanon's chief Shi'i imam recognize the Alawis as part of the Shi'i community. His close alliance with Iran after the 1979 Islamic revolution was also motivated in part by the fact that Islamic legitimacy could be provided by the endorsement of the ayatollahs. Both moves met with limited success and the discontent of Syria's Sunnis.

Sunni discontent with the regime's Alawi nature reignited once again in 1976 when Asad intervened in the Lebanese civil war on the side of the Christian camp against a Muslim-Palestinian coalition. Asad's intervention was chiefly motivated by his fear that a Muslim-Palestinian victory could lead to another war with Israel, but his Syrian critics interpreted his stance through a sectarian lens: an Alawi ruler helping members of another minority, Lebanon's Maronites, against the country's Sunnis. This criticism was shared, notably, by members of the Syrian branch of the Sunni Muslim Brotherhood, which led a revolt against Asad's regime in the late 1970s.

The Muslim Brotherhood, the most militant and effective Sunni organization in Syria, had organized earlier demonstrations against the Ba'th regime in 1964, 1965, and 1967 that threatened but failed to topple it. But in the mid-1970s the organization underwent a transformation when members of a radical wing called the Fighting Vanguard (al-Tali'ah al-Muqatilah) took over the movement. The members of this team were an early version of movements such as the Egyptian Jama'at al-Hijra wal-Takfir and Al Qaeda. They criticized the movement's traditional leadership for being much too passive, even compliant, and argued that violence alone would accomplish their mission. The Fighting Vanguard launched a terrorist campaign against senior Alawis and other members of the regime. In one of the worst incidents, one of their members perpetrated a massacre in the Syrian army's Aleppo Artillery School in 1979, killing some sixty Alawi cadets (this grim massacre was a rare opportunity to realize the disproportionate number of Alawis prepared for high military office).

It took three years for the regime to defeat this Jihadi insurgency, culminating in February 1982, when the Ba'th artillery destroyed a whole quarter in the city of Hama, putting an end to the Islamic rebellion but killing more than twenty thousand civilians. This bloody episode was never forgotten, even if the memory of it slipped into dormancy in the decades that followed.

The other severe crisis faced by Asad occurred in 1983–84, when he suffered a major health crisis due to a cardiac illness.

Asad was bedridden for several months, and his brother, Rif'at, took advantage of the situation by attempting to seize power. Rif'at was the commander of the Defense Detachments (Saraya al-Difa'), one of the special units created by his brother to protect the regime (another such unit was the Presidential Guard, headed by his brother-in-law Adnan Makhluf). Rif'at was an undisciplined, corrupt man who represented the most egregious aspects of a family- and clan-based regime. The crisis ended when Hafez Asad recovered, asserted himself, and sent his brother into exile.

Asad's success in reconciling diverse and contradictory elements in his domestic policies was also replicated in the conduct of his foreign policy. In one respect, he was the ultimate Arab nationalist, representing Arab resistance (*muqawamah*) to the United States and Israel. An ally of the Soviet Union, he remained Moscow's major asset in the region. Asad also became a close ally of the new Iranian regime after the Islamic revolution in 1979, sharing its radical anti-American and anti-Israeli (as well as anti-Iraqi) positions. He led the Arab opposition to Sadat's peacemaking with Israel and sought to keep his patronage of Palestinian nationalism and resistance despite his dislike of Yasser Arafat.

Asad pursued a policy of building not just a Syrian state but an enhanced Syrian nation, seeking to extend his country's geographic reach. In 1976, with the encouragement of the Ford administration and the tacit agreement of Israel, Asad sent his army into Lebanon. His initial purpose was to prevent a radical victory in the Lebanese civil war, but the initially modest foray led to the establishment of Syrian hegemony in Lebanon. His cultivation of the Palestinians and efforts to extend his influence over Jordan were parts of the same policy. These expansionist policies attracted significant internal support for the regime from those who shared Asad's quest for enhanced regional power.

Asad's adroitness in the conduct of his foreign policy was demonstrated by his ability to balance conflicting interests. For example, while it may have been risky to support a non-Arab country, Iran, in its war with its Arab neighbor, Iraq, in the early 1980s, this effort to outflank a regional power rival (Saddam Hussein) by building a partnership with Iran was largely successful. And Asad's close relationship with the Soviet Union did not prevent him from cultivating diplomatic ties with the United States. In the aftermath of the October 1973 Arab-Israeli war, he conducted long negotiations with Henry Kissinger, who was hoping to repeat his success with Egypt. Asad's ambition was to become the regional power that both Moscow and Washington would have to work with in order to accomplish their Middle Eastern aims.

But Asad's foreign policy universe was complicated by the collapse of the Soviet Union and Saddam Hussein's invasion of Kuwait in 1989–90. The adroit leader lost the support of his biggest external patron and had to adapt to the international reality of the US-led coalition against Saddam Hussein. Asad was invited to join the coalition. For the United States, having Syria and its leader representing "resistance" in the ranks of the coalition would be a great asset. For Asad, joining a Western-led coalition against another Arab country presented yet another risk, but he accepted the invitation in order to cultivate a relationship with the last remaining superpower while enabling the defeat of his arch enemy, Saddam.

In the aftermath of the Gulf War, the Bush-Baker administration in the United States decided to launch a massive effort to resolve the Arab-Israeli conflict and persuaded Asad and Israel's right-wing leader, Yitzhak Shamir, to take part in a peace conference in Madrid in October 1991. Entering into direct negotiations with Israel was a far-reaching decision for the leader who fourteen years earlier had denounced Sadat's trip to Jerusalem and the subsequent Egyptian peace negotiations with Israel as an act of treason. Yet Asad ended up joining the US initiative. The Madrid conference inaugurated a two-decade-long period during which Syria and Israel negotiated peace. The negotiations were intermittent and difficult. The difficulty was due in no small part to the continued hostilities between the two countries—Syria, notably, continued to collaborate with Iran in supporting Hezbollah, the main violent opposition to Israel's lingering presence in south Lebanon in the aftermath of the 1982 war. Five Israeli prime ministers (Rabin, Peres, Netanyahu, Barak, and Olmert) conveyed a conditional hypothetical willingness to withdraw from the Golan in return for peace, with conditions attached. On several occasions, Asad—and his son after him—indicated a willingness to sign a full peace agreement with Israel on that basis. In the end, it all came to naught. Both sides were ambivalent in their approach to peacemaking, and there were several decisive moments when either an Israeli leader or the Syrian president refrained from making a bold, unequivocal decision.

As Asad's health began to deteriorate during his final years in power, his energies were poured into an effort to ensure his succession by his son, Bashar. Asad's original heir apparent, his other son Basel, was killed in a car accident in 1994. After Basel's death Bashar was brought back from London, where he had been training as an ophthalmologist, and spent the next six years being groomed by his father, who died in June 2000.

Hafez al-Asad's legacy was complex. After thirty years in power he left behind a relatively strong and stable Syrian state and had turned his country into an important regional player. But the regime's stability rested on shaky foundations. Asad was successful in building a complex dual system based on a family-sectarian core surrounded by a complex structure of a military security establishment, state and party institutions, and the support of broad strata of the Syrian population. But the delicate balance that held this system together depended on the extraordinary skills of the man who built it—and exacted a heavy price. Asad's large governmental bureaucracy and the public sector were corrupt and inefficient. Syria was in urgent need of administrative and economic modernization and re-form. Asad recognized the need, but he also realized that there would be massive opposition by vested interests to any change and reform.

At different phases of Asad's tenure Syria's economy was boosted by minor economic changes and reforms: revenues from higher oil prices, cheap oil from Iran for local consump-tion, remittances from Syrian workers abroad, and financial aid from Saudi Arabia and other gulf countries after the First Gulf War. Such income helped Asad and his regime get by but were insufficient to address the country's underlying problems. A broad-reaching political reform—demanded by the opposition and indeed vital for modernization of the country—was never contemplated.

Bashar al-Asad: A Crisis Foretold

In the summer of 2000, when Bashar succeeded his father as president,[8] he was an unknown quantity; his ability to master the system built by his father had yet to be demonstrated. The transition from a revolutionary Arab republic to a hereditary one could be problematic, but rival factions and individuals within the Ba'th regime calculated that it was safest for them to respect the father's wish, and transfer power to his son rather than run the risk of internecine strife. Initially, Bashar seemed to represent progress and change. He was young, with a deceptively mild and self-deprecating manner, a trained ophthalmologist who had spent three years studying in London and was the president of Syria's computer society. His first speech promised change, reform, and modernization. He allowed an unprecedented degree of political freedom, a so-called Damascus Spring, in which intellectuals, artists, and political activists were suddenly allowed to demand reform and offer criticism. The winds of change were blowing. Bashar was well aware of the effervescence in Syria and was seeking to offer the regime's critics a measure of political freedom.

In September 2000, a group of civil society and political activists released the "manifesto of the 99," a call demanding the lifting of the state of emergency and martial law imposed in 1963; an amnesty for all political prisoners; the return of political exiles; and freedom of expression, freedom of the press, and the freedom of public life in general. Among the signatories were Syria's greatest poet, Adonis, and its most prominent public intellectual, Sadiq al-Azm. In short order, a more radical petition signed by one thousand intellectuals was published, demanding free elections and the end of the Ba'th Party's monopoly of political power. The two manifestos were followed by the resurgence of political activity, first and foremost through informal forums. Non-Ba'thi members of the parliament and other political activists joined the fray by demanding greater freedom.

The initial response of Bashar's regime to these manifestos was surprisingly mild and sanguine. Hundreds of political prisoners were pardoned, political parties were granted permission to publish their own newspapers, and the activity of hundreds of discussion forums was tolerated, at least initially. Then the regime suddenly changed its mind and decided to crack down on opposition activity and arrest activists. By September 2001 the Damascus Spring was brought to an end.

Why the about-face and seemingly contradictory approaches to political change? One explanation was that the suppression of the Damascus Spring was forced on Bashar by the old guard of the regime. Undoubtedly, key figures in the regime were worried by the extent of criticism and opposition exercised by Syria's civil society and political opposition, and in all likelihood they impressed their concern on the young president. He himself was initially uncertain of his position and policies. It took him time to acquire firsthand experience and self-confidence, to remove several of his father's confidants, and to plant in key positions younger men with whom he felt more comfortable. By 2007–8, Bashar would emerge from a period of formidable challenges, domestic and external, with a bolstered sense of confidence. And he revealed to the world that he was less a forward-looking liberal modernizer than a quintessential product of the system he inherited.

External and Domestic Challenges

The presidency of George W. Bush, the crisis of 9/11, and eventually the 2003 US invasion of Iraq posed a daunting set of challenges for Bashar. Shortly after his assumption of power, Syria's foreign policy environment underwent significant changes. In the United States, the Clinton administration was replaced by the harder-line George W. Bush's administration. Any hope that the moribund Syrian-Israeli peace process would revive was shattered when Ariel Sharon—an opponent of any withdrawal from the Golan—became Israel's prime minister. Moreover, the outbreak of the second Palestinian Intifada in the fall of 2000 led to increased pressure on the Syrian regime to show enhanced support for the Palestinian cause. Bashar responded to such pressure by enhancing his sponsorship of Hezbollah in Lebanon and the Palestinian Islamic Jihad organization. This strategy was met with retaliation on both sides. Israel penalized Syria for its support of Palestinian Islamic Jihad's activity by bombing an Islamic Jihad base in Syria. And in Lebanon, the Sunni leader Rafiq al-Hariri created significant opposition to Syrian hegemony with Saudi backing. Meanwhile, in Iraq, Saddam Hussein's maneuvers vis-à-vis the United States created both opportunities and risks for Bashar. As the specter of an American military attack on Iraq grew closer, Bashar tried to maintain his opposition to US military presence east of his border without unduly antagonizing the Bush administration.

The impact of the American invasion on Syria was immediately evident. Opposition groups in Syria were encouraged by the fact that one Ba'th regime had just been toppled by the United States. Like Qaddafi, Bashar suspected that his country might be the next target of a US president determined to change the face of the Middle East. In May 2003, US secretary of state Colin Powell visited Damascus and exerted pressure on Asad not to interfere with US policy in Iraq, to stop his support to such terrorist groups as Hezbollah and Islamic Jihad, and to cease the development of weapons of mass destruction (chemical weapons in particular). Powell did not have to use explicit threats against the background of the administration's recent invasion of Iraq and the calls for further action against other hostile regimes in the region. Asad promised to respond but in fact did not deliver; when asked why he did not close the offices of Islamic Jihad in Damascus as promised, the answer was vague: "operational offices were closed and only media spokesmen were allowed to continue."[9]

This line of conduct was met with disapproval in official Washington, particularly inside a Bush administration divided between those who thought one had to cooperate with Bashar and others who argued that only a hard line and an iron fist could effect any change in Syria's conduct. Republicans in Congress pushed through the legislation of the Syria Accountability and Lebanon Sovereignty Act in April 2003; President Bush signed the act into law in December 2003. The text denounced Syria for supporting terrorist groups, allowing armed volunteers to slip into Iraq, developing weapons of mass destruction, and occupying Lebanon. The act also banned all export to Syria of military and dual-use items, and it offered the president a menu of sanctions to choose from, including a complete ban of exports to Syria, a prohibition of US businesses operating in Syria, restrictions on Syrian diplomats in the United States, limits on Syrian airline flights, a downgrading of US diplomatic representation, and a potential freeze on Syrian economic assets.

Syria's role in facilitating the transit of Islamist volunteers to the Sunni insurrection against the US military occupation of Iraq came to dominate the American-Syrian relationship during this period. Bashar not only facilitated the transit of Islamists into Iraq but created a whole infrastructure with his intelligence service in northeastern Syria that was responsible for the safe crossing of thousands of anti-American warriors. For Asad, the US presence in Iraq and on his eastern border was a threat that he was determined to reduce, if not eradicate. When the United States exerted pressure or disapproval, the regime tried to placate Washington with occasional cooperation. So, for example, Syria extradited Saddam's half brother Sabawi Ibrahim al-Tikriti to the Iraqi authorities—who in turn handed him over to the United States. But such occasional cooperation failed to placate Washington, where anger against Bashar and his regime mounted.

Syria's regional and international standing was also buffeted during this period because of its deep and controversial involvement in Lebanese politics. Tensions flared over the issue of whether to extend the Lebanese presidency of the Christian Maronite Emile Lahud. Lahud was close to the Syrian intelligence services, and Syria considered the extension of his term essential to their control over Lebanon. Such an extension required an amendment of the Lebanese constitution. The anti-Syrian political opposition in Lebanon was led by the Sunni prime minister Rafiq al-Hariri, a wealthy businessman who made his fortune in Saudi Arabia and who was close to the Saudis as well as to French president Jacques Chirac. With the active support of Hariri, who despite pressure from Bashar opposed extending the Syrian-backed presidency of Lahud, the French and the Americans collaborated at the UN Security Council to pass Council Resolution 1559 on September 2, 2004, calling for the departure from Lebanon of all foreign (namely, Syrian) forces.

When Hariri was assassinated in Beirut in February 2005, the murder created domestic and international outrage. Suspicion fell on Syria and Hezbollah. The UN launched an investigation headed by the German prosecutor Detlev Mehlis. Mehlis submitted two reports in October and December 2005—carefully drafted and pointing a clear finger at Syria and Hezbollah. The aftermath of the report was messy but inconclusive. An Alawi officer and head of Syria's security apparatus in Lebanon, Ghazi Kan'an, who had been in charge of the Lebanese portfolio, died mysteriously in October 2005. Kan'an's death was described as a suicide, but it is quite possible that he was killed or forced to kill himself, thus becoming a sacrificial lamb.[10] The international investigation was never consummated. The whole affair contributed to darkening the image of Bashar's regime, and to the undermining of Syria's position in Lebanon.

Syria's position in Lebanon was directly assailed on February 21, 2005, by an unusual rallying of internal Lebanese opposition to Syria and Hezbollah when masses of opponents demonstrated in Beirut demanding an end to Syrian occupation. The combined Lebanese and international pressure persuaded Bashar that Syria's military presence in Lebanon had become untenable. On April 27 of that same year, Bashar withdrew his forces from Lebanon.

It was a major blow for the young president. Syria's hegemony in and control of Lebanon was one of his father's major achievements, in line with his view of Lebanon as part of Greater Syria. It also led Bashar to rely more heavily on his relationship with Iran and Hezbollah. Hafez al-Asad had built a close partnership with Iran that essentially was a partnership of equals. Yes, he had cultivated Syria's relationship with Hezbollah; but for him Hassan Nasrallah, the organization's leader, was a client and not a partner. Hafez al-Asad never gave Nasrallah an audience and dealt with him through his underlings. Under Bashar, the nature of the relationship with Hezbollah changed to more of a partner relationship. Bashar not only met with Nasrallah; he even made public his admiration for the Hezbollah leader.

These foreign policy setbacks were reflected in Bashar's domestic position as well. Bashar now had to contend with opposition from inside the regime *and* a new wave from Syria's civil society. Inside the regime, criticism by major figures from within and of his father's reign became more evident. The chief critic was Abd al-Halim Khaddam, Syria's Sunni vice president. The clash between Bashar and his intra-Ba'thi critics came to a head during the party's regional conference in June 2005, when Bashar asserted himself over Khaddam—who was then ousted from his position. Asad also removed his former minister of defense, Mustafa Tlas, and Abdallah al-Ahmar, both close collaborators of his father from their party positions. Syria's civil opponents of the regime were given a boost by the external pressures, and in October 2005 they published the "Damascus Declaration," signed by 250 opposition figures. The declaration—organized by two prominent civil society activists, Michel Kilo and Riad Seif—criticized the Syrian government as "authoritarian, totalitarian and cliquish," and called for "peaceful, gradual," reform "founded on accord, and based on dialogue and recognition of the other."[11] Signatories included both secular and Islamist critics of the regime and Kurdish as well as Arab names. The publication of the declaration in turn boosted opposition activities. Abd al-Halim Khaddam left Syria; in March 2006, he announced in Brussels—along with the Muslim Brotherhood—the formation of the National Salvation Front, composed of seventeen groups of political exiles.

These were significant challenges, but Bashar managed to overcome them. The year 2005 was an important one in the evolution of Bashar al-Asad's regime as he was able to overcome the criticism and opposition of members of the old guard and to impose his control over the Ba'th Party. A new, the tenth, five-year plan was approved. The slogan "social market reform" was adopted by the regime in an effort to strike a compromise between the original ethos of the Ba'th revolution and the need for economic reform and modernization. Khaddam's removal and departure from Syria enabled Bashar to tighten his grip over the regime. Opposition activists were jailed. In 2007 Bashar was elected for a second term as president. It was hardly surprising, in a country that had not had a free election in a long time, that he won the election by massive majority, but the reelection still gave Bashar a much needed dose of self-confidence.

A series of external developments also helped to facilitate Bashar's way out of the crisis. The war between Israel and Hezbollah in the summer of 2006—and the inconclusive fashion in which it ended—was seen overall as an achievement for the Tehran-Damascus-Hezbollah axis. There were also indications of a shift in US policy. The Iraq Study Group, a bipartisan group headed by former secretary of state James Baker and former chairman of the House Committee on Foreign Relations Lee Hamilton, was formed against the background of dissatisfaction with US policy in Iraq and examined ways for dealing with the issue. In March 2006 the committee published its report; one of its key recommendations was for the United States "to engage with Iran and Syria."[12] These recommendations were in stark contrast to the position of the Bush administration, which felt there was no point in talking to Syria. Next came Democratic Speaker of the House of Representatives Nancy Pelosi's visit to Damascus in April 2007; this was another indication of growing opposition in the United States to the Bush administration's Middle Eastern policy, in this case specifically its Syrian component. Bashar was invited to Paris by France's new president, Nicolas Sarkozy, in July 2008; July 2008 saw also the launch of a Turkish mediation between Syria and Israel. In short, by 2008, Bashar seemed to have overcome his immediate domestic and external problems and to have consolidated his rule.

A Futile Quest for "Social Market Reform"

Bashar al-Asad inherited both the system and the need to reform it.[13] A study published in 2004 by the International Crisis Group (ICG) was prescient in this regard:

Syria urgently needs domestic change. Its economy is plagued by corruption, ageing state industries, a volatile and under-performing agricultural sector, rapidly depleting oil resources, an anachronistic educational system, capital flight and lack of foreign investment.

The study recognized the regime's resistance to any fundamental reform:

> The elites that have navigated repeated domestic and foreign crises for three decades, providing the country unprecedented stability are wary of change and attached to a formula that so far has served them well. They will be hard to persuade of the merits of a course change. Nor should their fears of an Islamist take-over, sectarian or ethnic conflict, and renewed and prolonged instability be taken lightly. Even assuming Bashar wishes to take bold steps, it would be unrealistic to expect a rapid transformation.[14]

As the ICG's report makes clear, Bashar was incapable (or unwilling, or both) to introduce substantive changes in Syria's political and economic systems and address all the concerns expressed.

Some of the difficulties facing the new president were directly inherited from his father's era: like his father before him, Bashar found it impossible to reconcile his regime's minoritarian coalition with economic liberalization. There was an inherent antagonism between the ethos of the Ba'th regime and Syria's private sector, and one simply could not reform the government bureaucracy in a serious way, as the public sector served as the chief depository for the network of cronies that formed the bedrock of regime support. Nevertheless several economic reforms were introduced such as the establishment of private banks (2004) and the introduction of holding companies (2007) into the Syrian economy.

The pace of reform was dramatically expedited in 2005 in the aftermath of the tenth regional conference of the Ba'th Party, when Bashar managed to get rid of several senior members of the old guard and reinforced his hold over the party and the regime. He put Abdallah al-Dardari, as deputy prime minister, in charge of economic reform and development, and he launched a five-year plan. As we saw, the slogan "social market reform" was broadly used in order to signal a middle way chosen by the regime: modernization and liberalization, while keeping the policy of social welfare in support of the poorer strata of society.

Six years later, although the record was far from impressive in terms of economic growth and development and modernization of the system, Bashar's efforts did have some impact. By 2010, Syria's GNP had grown, the private sector's share in the economy and in external investment had grown, and the business sector had become a bit more autonomous. But on the other side of the equation was a dramatic expansion of inequality. In 2008, almost 70 percent of Syrian employees earned less than one hundred dollars a month, almost 40 percent of public sector employees took a second job, and the average salary was between US$225 and US$270 a month. These figures starkly contrasted with the ostentatious lifestyle of the small elite that was the principal beneficiary of the president's policies.

The reality of Syrian politics was such that the opening of the Syrian economy was used and abused by a new elite composed of the president's own family and clan, heads of the military and security services, and their partners in the private sector. These groups managed to either block reforms that threatened their interests or take advantage of such reforms in order to further enrich themselves. Bashar was obviously aware of this state of affairs but was himself a beneficiary of it and unable to undermine the position of the very group on which he relied for his political survival. The US Embassy's reports from Damascus—made available through WikiLeaks and cited by Alan George—are very illuminating. In January 2006, a US Embassy cable entitled "Syria's Corrupt Classes" affirmed that:

> Syria continues to be dominated by a "corrupt class" who use their personal ties to members of the Asad family and the security services to gain monopolistic control over most sectors of the economy while enriching themselves and the regime beneficiaries. Contacts state that the corruption which starts at the top filters down to all levels of business. Contacts among Damascus' Sunni business elite, many of whom have an axe to grind with the regime because of their class's diminished role, complain that the predominantly Allawite [*sic*] "corrupt class" has become entrenched over the past thirty years and in using the corrupt system to dominate all level[s] of business. . . . The corrupt classes have a symbiotic relationship with the Asad regime—both profit from their relationship and neither could function without the other. As contacts among Syria's Sunni community are quick to point out, the corrupt classes are preventing more progressive elements . . . from fully participating in the economy. The Asads run Syria as a family business and the corrupt classes are the ones that make the business function.[15]

Abdallah al-Dardari, the architect of Bashar's reform policy, lost his position in 2011. He left Syria for Beirut, where he took up work for United Nations Economic and Social Commission for West Asia (ESCWA) and ran a project on Syria's economic

future before moving to Washington, where he has been employed by the World Bank. He has since explained how, for example, certain businessmen would press for a certain sector of
the Syrian economy to be opened up for private investment,
and after being granted a license would press for the sector to
be closed for competition: "I refused to close the door. . . . They
would then use their influence with the bureaucracy to hinder
the issue of licenses to competitors. . . . Verbal opposition came
from the Ba'th party and groups such as the popular organizations, the peasants' organization and so on. The ultimate
sabotage came from the 'money-power alliance.'"[16]

So the economic impact of Bashar's reforms was limited.
And yet its political repercussions were far reaching. In fact,
Bashar distanced himself from one of the main strategies of his
father's regime—reliance on the rural population—and shifted
his regime's basis of support to the much narrower new economic elite. In order to implement his policies, Bashar weakened the Ba'th Party itself, as well as the popular organizations
such as the trade unions and the peasants' union. In doing so,
his regime lost the ability to penetrate society and mobilize it
in the service of the regime. A drastic reduction of subsidies
as well as inflation drove down the standard of living of the
popular classes. These developments were reinforced by the
steady demographic expansion and by the drought of the years
2008–11. One significant outcome of these developments was a
large-scale migration of displaced peasants to the cities and the
creation of shanty towns around Damascus and other Syrian
cities.

The explosive potential of these developments was magnified by a trend that the regime either failed to notice or greatly
underestimated: the proliferation of radical Islamist currents.
The regime itself contributed to this development by opening

the door to radical Islamist ideas from the gulf as part of a Faustian bargain with countries like Saudi Arabia and Qatar in return for the flow of cash and investments. The Ba'th regime's preference for Wahabi (Saudi-style Islamism) influence over that of its Muslim Brotherhood foes was not new and went back to the days of Hafez al-Asad. More significant was the expansion by the regime of the space for such faith-based groups as the Qubaysiyat.[17]

Bashar and His Regime

By the end of 2010, after more than a decade in power, both Bashar and the regime he had inherited from his father had been transformed. The American academic David Lesch, who has interviewed Bashar several times and written about him extensively, registered the changes of these years as he watched Bashar "grow more comfortable as president—perhaps too comfortable." In their first meetings early in Bashar's presidency, he was still "unsure about the world around him," mostly about the United States. During those early meetings Lesch saw "an unpretentious, even self-deprecating young man." He was not "a commanding figure at first glance: soft spoken, gregarious and with a childlike laugh." By 2005 he was "defensive and angry"; in 2006 "he began to feel more secure in his position and more sure of his future." Later that year, in the aftermath of the Lebanon war, Bashar's self-confidence was elevated; in 2007 during the election campaign for his second term, Lesch noticed "self-satisfaction, even smugness"; and finally in the election's aftermath his impression was that Bashar had begun to "believe the 'sycophants' who surrounded him."[18] Michel Duclos, former French ambassador to Damascus and a keen observer of Syrian politics, has presented a more complex assessment of Bashar al-Asad's persona. "Some consider him to be a weak and hesitant man who lacks authority even over his own family, ultimately overshadowed by his own father and convinced he has to imitate his pitiless toughness. However, his close circles describe him as a confident man who does not question his personal superiority over his entourage or the leadership of the regime and who has faith in his own luck."[19]

Sam Dagher describes in detail how a pale, insecure Bashar, dominated by his older brother and sister, Basel and Bushra, was transformed once selected by his father to replace Basel as heir apparent and acquired self-confidence and a streak of toughness disguised by a pleasant, almost shy demeanor.[20] Once in power Bashar was determined to demonstrate that he was a worthy successor to his father who could act in a brutal fashion when this was deemed necessary.

Clearly the mild, soft-spoken demeanor is a deception. Underneath it lies an ambitious, resilient, determined man with the stamina to stay the course—a man who can be ruthless, deceptive, and cruel. Like all of us, Bashar is complex; he genuinely admired Hezbollah's leader Hasan Nasrallah, the revolutionary zealot, the quintessential incarnation of the notion of *muqawama* (resistance), but was also anxious to liberalize Syria's economy, connect to the global economy, and build a different relationship with the United States. Bashar's Israeli counterparts have been struck by the same complexity: a willingness to launch a risky and high-stakes project (that his father avoided) by partnering with North Korea to build a secret nuclear reactor, twinned with an ability to display coolheadedness and self-control and refrain from any retaliation when Israel destroyed that reactor. Bashar displayed the same self-control when he assumed that it was Israel that eliminated his righthand man,

Muhammad Suleiman, on the Syrian coast, and Hezbollah's head of operations, Imad Mughniyyah, in Damascus.[21]

Bashar's sustained effort to replace most of his father's old guard in the regime's core with his own men, to reform (in a limited way) Syria's government and public sector, to weaken the Ba'th Party, and to liberalize and privatize the Syrian economy created far-reaching changes in the makeup of the Ba'th regime and its base of support. While the core of Hafez al-Asad's regime could be described as a series of concentric circles, Bashar's system is better described as "hub and spokes," a looser system of individuals connected directly to the president. Bashar's own circle was made up of several dozen men, members of his own family and clan, heads of the security and intelligence services, and the commanders of the armed forces' key units. This circle included or was closely connected to key members of the country's new economic elite, a product of the economic reforms. Networks of Alawi officers and Sunni businessmen had existed under Hafez al-Asad, but they were expanded and grew dramatically richer under Bashar.

As Bashar cultivated this group as the mainstay of his regime, he weakened the organizations and groups that had served his father well in penetrating and mobilizing large segments of Syrian society—the Ba'th Party's "popular" organizations, such as trade unions and peasants' organization. In governmental bureaucracy and public sector, power was transmitted at least in part to the technocrats who were designated to modernize the Syrian system. And while the new elite were getting richer and engaged in ostentatious consumption, the lower middle class and the poorer elements of society were pushed further down the ladder with dramatic declines in salaries and income and the abrogation or shrinking of subsidies on food and oil. The impact of these developments was exacerbated by irresponsible management of water and a severe drought in eastern Syria—the impact of which was described poignantly by Abdallah bin Yahya, representative of the UN's Office for Coordination of Humanitarian Affairs, when he asked the US Embassy in Damascus for emergency help for the rural population in that part of the country and told UN officials in July 2008 that "economic and social fallout from the drought was beyond our capacity as a country to deal with." Yahya was worried by the potential for what he called "social destruction" that would accompany "erosion of the agricultural industry in rural Syria." Yahya predicted that close to fifteen thousand smallholding farmers would be forced to depart the Al Hasakah province to seek work in cities such as Damascus and Aleppo. This migration "would add to the social and economic pressures presently at play in major Syrian cities. A system already burdened by a large Iraqi refugee population may not be able to absorb another influx of displaced persons . . . particularly at this time of rising costs, growing dissatisfaction of the middle class and the perceived . . . weakening of the social fabric and security structures that Syrians have come to expect and—in some cases—rely on."[22] Yahya's dire prediction was fully vindicated in the spring of 2011.

The Inner Core

We have a very clear picture of the nucleus of Bashar's regime on the eve of the 2011 rebellion's outbreak.[23] At its very core were the Asad family and clan, Bashar's brothers and sister, their maternal and paternal cousins, and their networks—an extended family with its own share of internecine squabbles. Bashar's younger brother Maher was a commander of the praetorian guard, the Republican Guard and the Fourth Armored

Division. His marriage to a Sunni wife resulted in close association with several Sunni business families, first and foremost the Hamsho family, which controlled a large number of Syrian and international companies. In 2009, according to a State Department report, the US government intended to target Hamsho for sanctions "for engaging in and facilitating public corruption by senior officials within the government of Syria."[24] Action was delayed by the difficulty in obtaining from the Canadian government information as to whether Hamsho was a Canadian citizen. But in 2011 Hamsho and his company (and Maher al-Asad) were sanctioned by the United States and the EU as part of the international community's response to the violent repression of the antiregime demonstrations.

Bashar's older sister, Bushra, married (after initial opposition by the family) Asef Shawkat, who as director of military intelligence wielded considerable influence. He was removed from that position in 2010 after colliding with his brother-in-law Maher (possibly also as a concession to international public opinion owing to his alleged role in the Hariri assassination) and was appointed to the position of deputy chief of staff of the Syrian army. As early as 2006, he was defined by the US government as an SDN (Specially Designated National), a category that enables the authorities to freeze his assets. This action was taken because he has "been a key architect of Syria's domination of Lebanon as well as a fundamental contributor to Syria's long standing policy to foment terrorism."[25]

Hafez al-Asad's wife came from the Makhluf family. Her brother Adnan was entrusted at the time with command of the president's praetorian guard. Under Bashar, members of the family came to control mutually reinforcing networks of security and economic positions. Bashar's cousin Hafez Makhluf headed the General Intelligence Directorate, where another member of the family, Iyad Makhluf, was employed as well. Cousin Ihab and his father, Muhammad, are chairman and vice president respectively of SyriaTel, one of Syria's two cell phone companies, in which Rami Makhluf is the largest shareholder. Ihab's brother also had a stake in that company and in numerous other lucrative businesses. Rami Makhluf was considered at the time the richest man in Syria and never shied away from displaying his wealth and political clout. In 2006 Rami Makhluf, who acted as the family banker, funded together with Bashar a corporation named Ash-Sham, which played an important role in enhancing and managing the family's wealth.

The same pattern on a more modest scale was evident in the roles assigned to members of other branches of the family: Dhu-al Himma and Riad Shalish (cousins through Hafez al-Asad's sister). Dhu-al Himma was head of presidential security, and Riad director of military housing, and both managed to privatize part of these activities and build their own businesses.

Another important group were Bashar loyalists who were given key military and security positions: Ali Mamluk, director of the National Security Bureau; Muhammad Dib Zaytun, head of the General Intelligence Directorate; Abd al-Fattah Qudsi-yyah, deputy chief of national security; Jamil Hasan, head of air force intelligence, and the commanders of the army's elite and major units.

Other officers had a direct relationship with the president and were used for special assignments. Hasan Turkmani, the highest-ranking Sunni in Bashar's system, served as minister of defense and then as special adviser and envoy with the title of vice president. The Alawi Muhammad Suleiman served in the shadows and was entrusted with the relationship with Iran, Hezbollah, and North Korea. In that capacity he was in charge of constructing the nuclear reactor in Al Kibar destroyed by Israel in 2007. Muhammad Nasif, a former intelligence chief, served as close mentor and adviser to Bashar.

Bashar had a special relationship with the two sons of his father's close partner and minister of defense, the Sunni Mustafa Tlas. The young president replaced Tlas as minister of defense but struck up a friendship with and promoted his two sons. Manaf became a brigadier general and served in the Republican Guard; Firas became an important businessman and an embodiment of the regime's pursuit of crony capitalism, and he owned MAS, a group of agriculture and service companies. It was indicative of the changes in the social base of the regime that both Manaf and Firas married into prominent Sunni families in Aleppo and Damascus. Firas was a prime example of what Syrians called "Awlad al-sultah" (the children of power), namely the sons of major regime figures who relied on their family connections in order to promote their business interests. When Lafarge, the French cement company, built a large plant in northeastern Syria in 2010, it partnered with Firas Tlas— who was given 30 percent of the project.[26] Other members of the Tlas clan who held senior positions were Ahmad Tlas, commander of the First Army deployed in the Syrian Golan, and Talal Tlas, the deputy minister of defense. Vice President Faruq al-Shara, Foreign Minister Walid al-Mu'allem, and minister and adviser Buthaina Sha'ban played the chief roles in implementing the regime's foreign policy. Of the three, Shara was the only one who was possessed of a political dimension on top of his professional capacity.

The net effect of Bashar's choices was to create a new, coherent governing elite with a stake in the regime's survival and prosperity—but that elite rested on a very narrow base of support. Bashar was aware of this inherent weakness and employed several strategies to expand his basis of support. He gave civil society more space and invested a particular effort to deal with the growing influence of Salafi Islam over large segments of the population. The regime fought public manifestations of Islamism, forbidding, for example, schoolteachers to cover themselves with the niqab; but he also cultivated Sufi orders and other groups that advocated personal piety. In the end, however, as the events of 2011 were to show, these measures were to no avail.

CHAPTER 2

The Syrian Civil War and Crisis, 2011–18

The Syrian civil war and the larger crisis it produced has been unfolding for more than nine years now. It has been compounded, exacerbated, and prolonged by the interplay between four subconflicts: the domestic civil war; the conflict's regional and international dimensions; and the war against the Islamic State. This dynamic has been central to the evolution of the Syrian crisis from the initial antiregime demonstrations in March 2011 to the present. As the conflict between regime and opposition continued, early manifestations of the main themes of the rebellion's next phases began to appear: militarization, sectarianism, Islamization of the opposition, and external criticism of the regime's conduct.

Outbreak and Initial Phase

In the early months of 2011, Syria seemed to be an island of stability in the midst of the turmoil produced by the Arab Spring. In January 2011 in an interview with the *Wall Street Journal*, Bashar al-Asad insisted that his country and regime were immune to the upheaval that had toppled the Tunisian regime and rattled Mubarak's regime in Egypt. Syria, he claimed, was different.[1] The reassuring message was echoed in the February 2011 edition of *Vogue* magazine in a feature on Asma al-Asad, Bashar's wife, entitled "A Rose in the Desert." The article played up the theme of a glamorous former London investment banker busy alongside her husband modernizing a formerly revolutionary Arab country.[2]

Asad clearly overstated his regime's sense of security. In fact he and his underlings were fully aware that Syria was in ferment, that large segments of the population were unhappy with the regime and tuned to the events of the Arab Spring, and that radical Islamism (seeking to shape public and political life according to Islamic law) was spreading in the country. There were also several instances of violent protests, some of them in Damascus, that worried the regime. It initiated a series of measures designed to defuse the mounting tension, such as a rise in state subsidies for fuel.[3] Recent developments in the country—demographic explosion, drought, the water crisis, impoverishment of the lower and middle classes by the transition to a neoliberal economy of sorts—had created a large population of disenchanted Syrians, particularly in the countryside and on the fringes of its major cities. The events of the Arab Spring provided a pretext for public expression of this discontent.

The fact that the revolt of 2011 broke out in the southern region of Houran reflected the changes that Syria had undergone under Bashar. The Houran had once been one of the Ba'th regime's strongholds and bastion of popular support, but years of drought and deprivation had turned a large part of its population against the regime.

The initial protests against the regime in Dar'a (a city in southern Syria close to the Jordanian border) began modestly and developed gradually. In mid-March, a group of young boys sprayed antiregime graffiti on the walls of a local school. Clearly inspired by the texts used in Tunisia and Egypt, the graffiti stated, "freedom . . . down with the regime . . . it's your turn doctor." They were arrested by the police. Requests by their families to release them were ignored or rudely rejected. When two of them were finally released it transpired that they had been tortured, and that their companion—a thirteen-year-old—had been mutilated and killed. The effect of the torture and killing was magnified by the high-handed conduct of the Alawi army officers, led by Bashar al-Asad's cousin Atef Najib, who commanded the local security apparatus and forces. The local population responded on Friday, March 18, with a massive demonstration at the end of the Friday prayers. A wave of demonstrations followed in other towns in the Houran and then spread to the cities of Latakia and Banyas on the coast and Deir ez-Zor in the northeast. Violent crackdowns by the regime—which included shooting at demonstrators, arrests, torture, and murder—failed to quell the protests and only inflamed them further.

Unlike the course of events in Tunisia and Egypt, protest in Syria swelled gradually without the equivalent of a major event on the scale of Cairo's Tahrir Square demonstrations. The sectarian issue that would become a major dimension of the Syrian civil war was still marginal during this period. Demonstrations were held in Sunni cities and in the Sunni areas of mixed cities. Alawis, Druzes, and Christians played a minor role in the protest, although members of these communities did take part in antiregime demonstrations in largely Sunni cities. Only later did conflict morph into one between an essentially Alawi regime and a provincial Sunni opposition. By contrast, the country's two largest cities, Damascus and Aleppo, remained quiet in these early days, with the bulk of the new Sunni bourgeoisie in these areas preferring stability to a revolution led by provincial, rural, and Islamist elements. And with few exceptions, the Druze and Christian communities preferred Alawi predominance to the prospect of an Islamist Syria.[4]

The regime's response to the early demonstrations was two-fold. On the one hand, the government cracked down violently with arrests, torture, and murder and adamantly opposed the significant political reforms demanded by the demonstrators. On the other, it did try to placate the public with a series of modest, limited reforms and symbolic concessions such as raising salaries to some certain low-wage earners and offering Syrian citizenship to a large number of Kurds residing in northeast Syria.

Such measures proved to be futile and in fact exacerbated the public's frustration. On March 24, 2011, government spokesperson Buthaina Sha'ban announced a series of additional reforms to address these frustrations that had no real effect. The very next day, which came to be known among antiregime demonstrators as "the Friday of Glory," the largest protest yet took place when tens of thousands assembled in Dar'a. By this time significant demonstrations were also staged in Damascus. In Dar'a, demonstrators now called for toppling the regime, and pictures of Asad were torn up. Security forces fired at the demonstrators and dispersed the protesting crowd. The gravity of the situation was not entirely lost on the regime. Three days later Asad fired his cabinet. Prime Minister Naji al-Atari and his deputy, Abdallah al-Dardari, the architect of Bashar's economic reforms, resigned.

Three days later, and almost two weeks after the outbreak of these spring 2011 mass protests, Asad delivered the first of three public speeches to address the unrest. The first speech presented the narrative developed by the regime that remained consistent throughout the conflict: Syria was not affected by genuine protest, he insisted, but was the victim of a conspiracy hatched from outside (primarily the United States, Israel, and conservative Arab states all hostile to the regime).

The speech was widely deemed a failure. The public was disappointed by the absence of a real response to its grievances and expectations for change. The demonstrations continued and expanded. In April they spread to larger cities such as Latakia, Hama, and Homs but still did not reach Aleppo and Damascus, where the opposition was entrenched in the suburbs and the capital's periphery but not at the city's center. The regime's dual-track policy continued: violent suppression of the demonstrations alongside further mild concessions such as the lifting—at least on paper—of the state of emergency that had been in force since 1963 and further economic measures such as the lowering of fuel prices, the freezing of the cost of electricity, the establishment of a fund for supporting needy families, and the launching of a program to reduce unemployment. One concession made in April 2011 was specifically designed to placate the conservative Sunni population: the ban on the wearing of the hijab by women schoolteachers was lifted. On April 16, with protests still persisting, Asad delivered a second—and equally disappointing—speech, offering a few additional concessions and expressing sorrow for the losses sustained by the public. In June, the regime decided to call in the army (as distinct from the security forces) to quell the demonstrations, and soon tanks and artillery, fighter jets, and helicopter gunships were being used against civilian protesters.

By the time Asad gave his third speech in the spring of 2011, in June, his views had become clear. Asad saw any significant political concessions to the burgeoning opposition as a slippery slope. He repeatedly put forward the view that he was facing not genuine popular protest but rather a foreign conspiracy that

needed to be quashed. He depicted himself as a defender of secular Arab nationalism and a bulwark against terrorism and Jihadi
Islam. In line with this argument the regime then resorted to a
radical measure: the release of several hundred Jihadi prisoners.
Asad was willing to take the risk of their joining the opposition
in order to prove the veracity of his allegations.

By May 2011 the political character of the Syrian opposition
began to take shape. What had begun as a series of spontaneous
demonstrations was now being coordinated by a network of
Local Coordination Committees (LCCs). These were made up
of young people—unknown to the regime or to the public—
who took to social media to launch and coordinate demonstrations nationally.[5] There was a paradox inherent in the very character of these committees: their anonymity provided protection
from the regime but in the longer run impeded the ability of the
leaders to build the reputation and stature required to become
credible alternatives to the regime. In addition to the LCCs,
two other groups assumed active political roles in the opposition. One was made up of the traditional civil society groups
that had been active during the previous decade. The other was
composed of regime critics who resided abroad. Members of this
external group organized the first large-scale meeting in Antalya,
Turkey, from May 31 to June 3. The traditional opposition to the
regime that had been active during Bashar's first decade in power
was well represented in these two groups, markedly different
from the LCCs. Their membership was largely composed of intellectuals and professionals from Syria's major urban centers,
while the LCCs' membership was mostly made up of unknown
younger persons from smaller towns and the countryside.

The very fact that the Turkish government allowed this
meeting of three hundred delegates under the title "The Syrian
Conference for Change" was a clear indication of the Turkish

shift of policy toward Syria. Turkey's leader, Recep Tayyip Erdogan, who had been mentoring Bashar just a few years earlier, had initially invested a major effort in persuading him to offer his people genuine political reform. When he realized that Bashar had no intention of doing so, Erdogan turned against him.

And yet Asad continued to make small gestures toward reform, including institutional reforms and the formation of a committee for a national dialogue. He also offered to issue pardons to all political crimes committed before May 31, 2011. The regime followed these measures with mild constitutional reforms and a draft of a new political party law that would end the monopoly of the Ba'th Party.

The opposition's response to these measures exposed the divisions within its own ranks. Some opposition members rejected the notion of a direct give-and-take with a regime they regarded as illegitimate. Others agreed to take part in a dialogue, which led to a meeting on July 10, 2011, at the Sahara Hotel in Damascus between the regime and certain members of the opposition. The regime was represented by Vice President Faruq al-Shara, a Sunni considered more acceptable to the Sunni majority. Shara was able to persuade Asad to abandon his initial attempt to choose the opposition's representatives in the meeting. In his opening remarks Shara stated, "we hope . . . at the end of this comprehensive meeting to announce the transition of Syria to a pluralistic democratic nation where all citizens are guided by equality and participate in the modeling of the future of their country."[6] The meeting ended with a call for peaceful transition to democracy, but in fact the dialogue went nowhere, and there were no additional meetings. The Local Coordination Committees and the external opposition—not represented in the meeting—criticized the participants for playing right into the regime's hands.

July 2011–December 2012:
Transition to Civil War

July 2011 to December 2012 marks the period in which the Syrian uprising morphed into a full-fledged civil war. The first serious military action by an opposition group against the regime's security forces occurred in Jisr al-Shughur, near the Turkish border. Local citizens who were probably aided by defectors from the Syrian army killed several dozen members of the security forces. On July 29, the Free Syrian Army (FSA) was formed as the main military arm of the opposition. News of the FSA's formation was broadcast over the internet by Colonel Riad al-As'ad, a defector from the Syrian army. Initially formed to provide protection to peaceful demonstrators, the FSA had no political goals other than the toppling of the Asad regime.[7] It incorporated the Free Officers' Battalion, which had been founded in June by another defector, Colonel Husein Harmush. The battalion had shown some initial success in confronting and defeating Syrian army units but was terminated when Syria's intelligence services abducted Colonel Harmush from southern Turkey. The FSA would reach its pinnacle of power in 2012, when units affiliated with it seized control of a large part of Syria.

The Syrian National Council (SNC), for its part, was designed to serve as the political backbone of the mainstream opposition. The SNC's first president, Burhan Ghalyun, was a Syrian expatriate professor at the University of Paris who quickly resigned in May 2012, exasperated by incessant intrigue and internecine bickering. His successor, Abd al-Baset Sayda, a Syrian Kurdish academic, resigned in turn in November 2012. From the outset the SNC failed to bring the opposition's major political factions together into one coherent political entity. In light of this failure, the SNC's external supporters—which included the United States, Saudi Arabia, and Qatar—initiated in November 2012 the formation of an alternative umbrella organization named the National Coalition for Syrian Revolutionary and Opposition Forces (or the Syrian National Coalition) headed by Muaz al-Khatib, the former imam of the Umayyad Mosque in Damascus.[8] This organization, known in Arabic as al-I'tilaf, operated in parallel to the SNC.

On the military front, the FSA's efforts against the regime were challenged by the emergence of several Salafi militias (such as the Syrian Islamic Front, Jaysh al-Islam, and the Islamic Front). These groups merged in December 2011 into one organization, known as Ahrar al-Sham. Of these groups Jaysh al-Islam maintained the strongest presence particularly in the eastern suburbs of Damascus. The Salafi movement—with the long-term goal of replacing Asad's regime with an Islamist government—was initially led by Hassan Aboud, one of the Salafi prisoners released by the regime in March 2011. The Salafi movement represents a particularly radical current of Islamism seeking to restore Islam to the greatness of the days of Muhammad and his immediate successors. Ahrar al-Sham was the largest and most effective Salafi group. It collaborated on and off with other Salafi groups and was also supported by Turkey, Saudi Arabia, and Qatar, all of them champions of Salafi Islam. These Islamist groups were soon outflanked by the appearance of radical Jihadi formations. In December 2011, Al Qaeda's leadership dispatched Abu Muhammad al-Julani from Iraq to officially found Jabhat al-Nusrah in January 2012 (see chapter 3).[9]

Despite the fragmentation of the military opposition these factions managed to score several significant achievements and gain control of large segments of Syrian territory. These successes were due to a large extent to the weakness of the regime's armed forces. The regime suffered massive defections and was in fact unable to use most of its units against demonstrators and armed rebels. Although Alawis dominated elite units and the security and intelligence services, the rank and file were Sunnis, and the regime—for good reason—hesitated to employ them against Sunni rebels. Instead, the regime depended on a limited number of loyal elite units and, increasingly, on such Alawi militias as the Shabiha (*ghosts* in Arabic). These militias had begun as semicriminal gangs prior to the outbreak of the civil war and began to play a role in support of the regime against the opposition in 2011. That role would become increasingly more prominent and notorious in the coming years and would play an important role in exacerbating the sectarian dimensions of the Syrian conflict.

It was perhaps inevitable that a predominantly Sunni revolt against an Alawi-dominated regime would acquire that sectarian dimension, despite the fact that the uprising had begun not as a sectarian conflict but as an outburst against repression, corruption, and deprivation. As the conflict continued to unfold, both regime and opposition played the sectarian card. The Ba'th regime sought to consolidate support from both the Alawi community and other non-Sunni groups, while the opposition mainly sought to rally the Sunni population. As time passed and as both the regime and the radical Islamists resorted more and more to sectarian incitement, mutual animosity between Sunnis and Alawis spiked, a development reinforced by the refusal of Islamist and Salafi groups to recognize the Alawis as proper Muslims. Religious fanaticism from leaders like Sheikh Qaradawi, a radical preacher on the Qatari television channel Al Jazeera, inflamed further with systematic incitement against Alawis, calling them "worse infidels than Christians and Jews" and referring to them by the pejorative term "Nusayris."

Qaradawi went so far as to explicitly call for a Sunni Jihad in Syria.[10]

The military action of the armed opposition escalated in September 2011, when rebel units, most of them operating under the umbrella of FSA, occupied the city of Rastan, strategically located on the main south-north axis just above Homs. In January 2012 the Free Syrian Army scored similar successes in Al-Zabdani—just thirty kilometers northwest of Damascus—and in other areas closer to the capital. At that point the Syrian army, under pressure, began to use heavy armor and airplanes. Rebels could not cope with the firepower of the Syrian army and could not hold captured territory over time—but they could act simultaneously in multiple locations, and force the regime to spread its forces thin.

The battle over control of the city of Homs in central Syria in the fall of 2011 was of particular importance in the escalating military conflict. Occupying a crucial position on the main axis between Damascus and Aleppo and its Sunni community (into which Bashar and his brother Maher had married), Homs was politically and symbolically important to the regime. It was hardly surprising that a massive effort was invested by the regime after February 2012 to regain control of the city. The regime employed the air force, tanks, and artillery, destroying big swaths of the city and inflicting heavy civilian casualties. In February 2012, the FSA decided to withdraw from Homs in order to save it from further destruction. The battle over Homs was thus won by the regime, though armed resistance continued in parts of the city and in the surrounding rural areas. Homs was not decisively taken by the regime until 2014. Parts of the city were under siege for three years. The regime's success had the further effect of weakening the FSA and playing into the hands of the Islamist militias.

Homs notwithstanding, the opposition scored victories in other arenas such al-Qusayr (near Homs) and Saraqib (near Idlib). One result of these successes for the opposition was the UN's decision, in July 2012, to formally declare the conflict in Syria to be a civil war. The armed opposition was able to penetrate Damascus and Aleppo, despite the fact that those populations had chosen early on to support the regime or stand by on the sidelines—although the regime was able to maintain normalcy (or a semblance of normalcy) in the capital's central area, some opposition groups embedded themselves in a number of Damascus suburbs and in the rural area surrounding it. During the following months the rebels scored new successes, taking control of al-Raqqah in the northeast in September, and Ma'arat al-Nu'man near Idlib in October 2012.

The decision by the UN to call this a Syrian civil war reflected the growing sense that the regime was facing a real prospect of defeat, given the opposition's successes in Damascus and Aleppo, the control it took of the border crossings to Turkey and Iraq, the weakening of the Kurds' neutrality, and a new wave of defections (most notably of General Manaf Tlas, son of the former minister of defense and a former personal friend of Bashar). Moreover, some months earlier, in July 2012, the leadership of the army was seriously weakened after senior members of the regime's military and security core—including Minister of Defense Daud Rajha, his deputy and Bashar's brother-in-law Asef Shawkat, former minister of defense and chief of staff Hasan Turkmani, and head of the National Security Bureau Hisham al-Ikhtiyar)—were killed by an explosive charge during a meeting held at the headquarters of the National Security Bureau. The FSA and the Salafi group Liwa' al-Islam took credit for this operation, but a different version of events suggested that the explosion was carried out by Asef

Shawkat's rivals, within the ruling family and the regime. According to that latter version, Shawkat advocated a more conciliatory line and supported some form of compromise with the opposition; the more radical wing of the family, headed by Bashar's brother Maher and the two Makhlouf cousins, were adamantly opposed to any compromise and are still suspected to this day in Syria of being responsible for eliminating their domestic opponent.

Regional and International Responses

As the uprising continued to unfold, the international response to it also took shape. The ruling Ba'th regime was supported by Russia, Iran, and Hezbollah. Russia's support at that phase consisted of military aid and diplomatic support. China could also be counted on as a supporter of sorts. In the UN Security Council it tended to vote on such issues with Russia and expressed strong and consistent opposition to the notion of international intervention in any country's domestic affairs. Russia blocked even the mildest Security Council resolutions regarding the events in Syria. To some extent, Russia's position was affected by the developments in Libya, where the United States exploited Security Council resolutions in order to legitimize its military intervention against Qaddafi's regime. Iran and Hezbollah, alarmed by the threat to the Asad regime, began their military intervention in Syria in 2012. Initially modest, it would eventually grow to massive proportions.

On the other side of the equation, the United States and its European allies and the majority of the Arab states denounced the Asad regime and its brutal conduct during the early weeks and months of the uprising. The first major international response to the events in Syria, and specifically to the regime's

harsh crackdown on unarmed demonstrators, occurred on
May 16, when US president Barack Obama announced personal
sanctions against Bashar al-Asad and several senior members of
his regime. Obama called on Asad to lead a process of reform
or abdicate. Washington's action was followed a few days later
by similar steps taken by the European Union.

The Arab League followed the United States and the EU in
November 2011. On November 2, the Arab League released a
peace initiative. When it transpired that Syria would not honor
its terms, the league suspended its membership on November 22. On December 11 and through January 2012, the Arab
League initiated and pursued a second mediation effort. The
league crafted a plan that called for the withdrawal of both the
army and the demonstrators from the streets, the release of political prisoners, the deployment of Arab League observers, and
the opening of talks between the regime and the opposition.
The regime responded by agreeing to the deployment of the
fifty observers. When Asad obstructed their activity, the league
pulled out its observers and imposed sanctions. In short order
Turkey's leader Erdogan joined the chorus of condemnation,
as Bashar's evasiveness finally turned him against the Syrian
regime.

During the latter half of 2011 and through 2012 an internal
debate took place inside the Obama administration over the
policy that the United States should adopt toward the Syrian
rebellion. Should the United States offer help to the unfolding
revolution, or should it limit itself to criticizing the regime? And
would the basis for intervention in Syria be humanitarian, an
expression of support for the cause of democratic expansion, or
a way of pursuing American's geopolitical influence?[11] The administration's criticism of Asad and his regime was manifested
publicly on several occasions. In July 2011, the American and

French ambassadors to Syria, Robert Ford and Eric Chevallier, traveled to Hama to demonstrate their support for the antiregime demonstrators. As early as August 2011, in a statement released by the White House, President Obama openly denounced Asad's conduct and explicitly demanded that he step down: "For the sake of the Syrian people, the time has come for President Asad to step aside."[12] The same call was made shortly thereafter by the EU, and by the leaders of Great Britain, France, and Germany. In May 2012 several countries, including the United States, Great Britain, France, Spain, Canada, Australia, and Turkey, recalled their diplomats from Damascus and expelled their Syrian counterparts. Curiously the effort to mobilize Western public opinion and to build a lobby arguing intervention on humanitarian grounds failed to gain momentum.[13] The Canadian intellectual and politician Michael Ignatieff explained why the Syrian opposition in the second decade of the current century, like the Yugoslavs in the 1990s, face such difficulty in mobilizing international liberal support:

What they both lack is time, the experience of democracy, and the opportunity—it can take generations to forge political alliances across confessional, sectarian and clan lines. This was the legacy of dictatorship that Tito bequeathed to Yugoslavia and its poisonous gift to Syria. No wonder then that it has proved agonizingly difficult for the Syrian opposition to create a common front against the dictator and the political program for the country after Asad is defeated, killed or driven into exile. No wonder that the chief casualty of . . . Asad's regime might just be Syria itself. . . . When Western governments consider Syrian pleas for intervention, it is not Bosnia that comes into their mind but Iraq, Afghanistan and Libya.[14]

It was apparently the Ba'th regime's military weakness and the difficulty it had in defending Damascus itself that led Bashar to the decision to use chemical weapons against the rebels and civilian populations in rebel-held areas. The first indications of the preparations to use the regime's chemical arsenal were evident in 2012. On August 20, 2012, Barack Obama made a spontaneous significant statement in the course of a press conference. Against the backdrop of reports that had surfaced about Syrian preparations for using its chemical weapons arsenal, he stated, "We have been very clear to the Asad regime, but also to other players on the ground, that a red line for us is we start seeing a whole bunch of chemical weapons moving around or being utilized. That would change my calculus. That would change my equation."[15]

On February 23, 2012, the UN's secretary general, Ban Ki Moon, and the Arab League's secretary general, Nabil al-Arabi, announced that the UN's former secretary general Kofi Annan was appointed as the UN's and the Arab League's special envoy to the Syrian crisis.

By March 21 Annan had prepared a six-point proposal to put an end to the violence in Syria. According to the plan, the parties (regime and opposition) were "to commit to work with the envoy in an inclusive Syrian led political process to address the legitimate aspirations of the Syrian people and to this end commit to appoint an empowered interlocutor when invited to do so by the envoy." The points were that (1) the Syrian government was to cease troop movements and use of heavy weapons in population centers, and to begin to pull back military concentrations in or around population centers; (2) under the supervision of a UN mechanism, all parties were to put an end to armed violence; (3) measures were to be taken in order to ensure humanitarian aid; (4) political prisoners were to be released or information provided about their whereabouts; (5) access and freedom of movement to journalists was to be guaranteed; and (6) freedom of association and the right to demonstrate peacefully were to be legally guaranteed.[16]

This first effort at devising a political solution (as distinct from ending the violence) during Kofi Annan's tenure, since known as Geneva I, was made in June 2012. Representatives of the five members of the Security Council, along with Turkey, Iraq, Kuwait, and Qatar, met in Geneva. Under Annan's chairmanship, the group known as the Action Group for Syria put together a document calling for the formation of a transitional government composed of representatives of the two parties to the conflict. That government was to seek a peace agreement and lay the foundations for a new political order in Syria. Like several subsequent efforts to find a political solution to the crisis, the plan foundered owing to a fundamental disagreement on the role assigned to Bashar al-Asad. The US secretary of state, Hillary Clinton, insisted that Asad not remain in power during the transition while her Russian counterpart, Sergei Lavrov, rejected the American demand. A compromise was found by using language that finessed the fate of Asad. The plan remained a dead letter.

Annan complained that neither side was complying with his plan, and in August 2012 he resigned from his post. In September 2012 the Algerian diplomat Lakhdar Brahimi was appointed as Annan's successor. He began his mission with a proposal for a cease-fire that was to take place on Eid al-Adha on October 26. The government and most of the opposition accepted Brahimi's initiative, but in practice the cease-fire collapsed in a matter of days. Both sides blamed each other for the initiative's failure.

In 2012, international and regional critics of the Syrian regime launched a forum named the Friends of Syria. The initiative was taken by French president Nicolas Sarkozy as a direct response to the Russian and Chinese veto cast in the Security Council on February 4, 2012, in order to deny the Western powers a legal basis for intervention, blocking a resolution denouncing the conduct of the Syrian regime. The first meeting of the group was held on February 24, 2012, in Tunisia and was attended by over seventy states, among them the United States, Great Britain, France, and Turkey, as well as the Syrian National Council. Russia and China did not attend. The group met five times during 2012, in Tunis, Istanbul, Paris, and Marrakech. It adopted a large number of resolutions criticizing the regime, but these resolutions, lacking the legal power of a Security Council resolution, failed to have a real impact.

The Marrakesh meeting did in fact produced a declaration of the Friends of Syria recognizing the Syrian National Coalition as the legitimate representative of the Syrian people. The declaration proved empty: no effort was made to build a governance alternative to the regime.

2013–14: Escalation

In the absence of either decision or settlement, the Syrian civil war and conflict expanded, grew in depth and intensity, and acquired new dimensions during the years 2013 and 2014. It was during this period that the number of civilian casualties and refugees—who crossed into Turkey, Jordan, and Lebanon, and who moved into safer areas inside Syria—reached the proportions of a major humanitarian disaster. By the first half of April 2013, the estimated number of refugees had crossed the threshold of one million. At the year's end that rose to 2.3 million. The death toll exacted by the civil war at this point was also estimated to be close to one hundred thousand.

The toll rose steeply owing to an intensification of the regime's use of military weaponry on civilians, notably chemical weapons but also conventional methods such as aerial bombardments and barrel bombs (large cylinders filled with explosives and pieces of metal), which exacted a horrific toll. The massive use of chemical weapons led in August 2013 to one of the most important turning points in the Syrian conflict; estimates as to the number of civilians killed in that attack vary, but the number seems to be in the hundreds. The Obama administration grappled with the idea of a punitive raid against Asad's regime, which had crossed the "red line" drawn in August 2012, and finally decided to opt for a diplomatic solution brokered by Russia.

There were several key developments that shaped the contours of the crisis during this phase. These included the new saliency of the regional dimension of the Syrian crisis. As Iran and Hezbollah raised their profile in the fighting and became the mainstay of Asad's regime, their Sunni rivals, Saudi Arabia, Qatar, and Turkey, increased their support to Islamist and Salafi groups. These developments served to portray the Syrian conflict as a Saudi-Iranian (or, even more broadly, Sunni-Shi'i) conflict by proxy.

Meanwhile, it became increasingly difficult to follow the battle lines. For a while, the formation of the Free Syrian Army as the principal military force of the opposition, operating at least to some extent as the military arm of an umbrella political organization, had given the impression that there was a pattern and some coherence to the war between regime and opposition. By 2013, a large number of Islamist and Jihadi organizations and groups, local, national, and transnational, and the eruption of fighting between some of them had emerged. These developments and complications during this time were supplemented by the entry into the war by the Kurds in north-eastern Syria, and the full-fledged role undertaken by Hezbollah.

Of particular importance was the further Islamization of the opposition with the emergence of new Salafi groups, and the role played by the two main Jihadi groups that joined the fray by moving from Iraq into Syria: Jabhat al-Nusrah and the Islamic State (IS). The dramatic successes by the Islamic State in both Syria and Iraq added a new dimension to the Syrian conflict that for some time overshadowed the original conflict between regime and opposition in Syria, threatened the stability of the Middle East, and generated a new wave of terrorism and terrorist threats in Europe and in the United States.

Jabhat al-Nusrah had first appeared in Syria as early as July 2011, when Abu Muhammed al-Julani—dispatched into Syria by al-Nusrah leader Abu Baker al-Baghdadi—crossed the border in northeastern Syria, in the area of Al Hasakah, and established contact with a Jihadi network that had been founded after 2003 by Syria's intelligence organizations in order to facilitate the transition of Jihadi volunteers to join the Sunni insurrection against the US forces. By December 23, 2011, the group perpetrated its first suicide attack near a regime intelligence facility in Damascus, killing some forty security agents. On January 23, 2012, Jabhat al-Nusrah formally announced its formation and called for the establishment of a new regime founded on the principles of Islamic law. Until March 2012 it conducted a limited number of operations and invested efforts in establishing partnerships with Islamist and Salafist groups in different parts of Syria. It first met with initial resistance by its Syrian counterparts, who viewed it as an alien terrorist group, but gradually its leadership succeeded in persuading its prospective Syrian partners that it wanted to be a genuine part of the Syrian opposition. Al-Nusrah fighters proved to be highly effective on the battlefield, and their partnership with other opposition groups led to several military successes against the regime during the winter of 2012–13. On January 11, 2013, they took control of the Syrian air force base Taftanaz in Idlib, taking with them helicopters, tanks, and rocket launchers. A month later, they took control of the city of al-Thawrah near al-Raqqah in northeastern Syria, and of al-Tabaqah Dam, the largest dam in Syria. In early March 2013 they finally managed to capture the large city of al-Raqqah. During the same time, they carried out several successful military operations in Damascus.

As Jabhat al-Nusrah established itself in Syria, it also broke away from the leadership of Abu Baker al-Baghdadi in Iraq. Al-Baghdadi in turn focused his efforts on building the Islamic State (known also by its Arab acronym Da'esh—the Islamic State in Iraq and the Levant; the organization is also referred to as ISIL). Da'esh's initial activities in Syria were not directed against Asad's regime but against other Islamist and Jihadi groups, such as Jabhat al-Nusrah, and were conducted with a view to establishing control over territory on the Syrian side of the Syrian-Iraqi border.

The appearance of the Iraqi Jihadi groups in Syria drove several Islamist and Salafi Syrian groups to close ranks. In December 2011 several such groups combined to establish Ahrar al-Sham. In September 2013, some fifty opposition groups converged around an organization called Liwa' al-Islam ("Islam's Flag") to form Jaysh al-Islam ("Islam's Army"). The commander of Liwa' al-Islam, active in Syria since 2011, was Zahran Alush—one of the several dozen Islamist prisoners released by Asad's regime during the first weeks of the Syrian rebellion in order to depict the insurrection as a terrorist, Islamist rebellion against his secular-nationalist regime. Jaysh al-Islam had major support from Saudi Arabia and did not form part of the Syrian National Coalition. By the end of 2013 both groups, Ahrar al-Sham and Jaysh al-Islam, had overshadowed the Free Syrian Army as the major opposition force.

The Islamic State conducted its first military operation in Syria in September 2013, when it captured the town of A'zaz from the Free Syrian Army. It then fought against Jabhat al-Nusrah and its Syrian allies over the city of al-Raqqah. At the end of the day IS managed to capture al-Raqqah and Palmyra. The Islamic State used its military success in Syria to divert its main effort back to Iraq, where its major exploit was the conquest of the large city of Mosul. Its control of large areas on both sides of the Syrian-Iraqi border led it to announce the abrogation of that border and the formation of a Caliphate, a territorial state, with its capital in al-Raqqah.

During the early phase of the Syrian rebellion the Syrian Kurds sat on the fence and declined to join the revolt against the regime. It was the military pressure of the Jihadi groups that led the Syrian Kurds to join the fighting, under the leadership of YPG (People's Protection Units), the military arm of PYD (Democratic Union Party; the Syrian affiliate of the Kurdish Turkish PKK, the leading Kurdish opposition party in Turkey). They did so first as a defensive measure against the Jihadi groups, and later in order to capture large areas. They did not become a distinctively antiregime force, but their military exploits turned them into an important actor in the context of the Syrian rebellion.

In April and May 2013, the battle of al-Qusayr would bring the Lebanese Shi'i organization Hezbollah into its full-fledged, overt participation in the Syrian civil war. The town of al-Qusayr is strategically located near Homs, on the important road connecting Damascus to the coast. The Syrian army was unable to defeat the rebels holding al-Qusayr, which led to the strategic decision—probably by Iran—to dispatch thousands of Hezbollah's soldiers to fight the rebels. The battle of al-Qusayr marked the transition from Hezbollah's limited involvement to a direct and massive participation on the side of the regime. By that time, defections, the losses it sustained, and the need to deploy itself across the country had all reduced the Syrian army's capacity to a point where it could not have stood up to the rebels without Hezbollah's direct participation. In May 2013, Hezbollah captured and held the town of al-Qusayr.

Meanwhile, the first indication of actual use of chemical weapons was identified by Israeli intelligence just beforehand, in April 2013. At first the Obama administration refused to acknowledge the veracity of these reports, but on August 21, when massive use of chemical weapons against civilian population took place in the al-Ghouta rural area around Damascus, it became difficult for the administration to ignore it. President Obama and his team agonized over how to reconcile his use of the term "red line" with his reluctance to actually use military force in Syria. Obama finally decided to turn to the US Congress in order to obtain authorization for military action, and he came to an agreement with Putin to resolve the issue by dismantling the regime's chemical weapons arsenal. This was to be one of the most important turning points of the Syrian crisis. Obama's decision to refrain from penalizing the regime under these circumstances paved the way for Russian military intervention and inflicted a deadly blow on the more pragmatic elements of the Syrian opposition.

The most important component of the opposition, the FSA, went through several ups and downs during the war years, and the aftermath of the "red line" episode was clearly one of its lowest points.[17]

During this period all efforts to seek a political diplomatic resolution to the Syrian conflict failed for same reason that such initiatives had been blocked during the previous two years: Russian and Chinese vetoes at the Security Council and the regime's refusal to make any substantial concessions to the opposition's demands, first and foremost the regime's rejection of the opposition's insistence that political reform in Syria would be based on Asad's departure. The Friends of Syria held four additional meetings in 2013. Prior to the May 2013 meeting in Amman, Jordan, the United States and Russia tried to reach an understanding that would lay the foundations for yet another major effort to resolve the conflict. Following a day of negotiations between US secretary of state John Kerry and Russian foreign minister Sergei Lavrov, the parties announced that "they would seek to convene an international conference within weeks aimed at ending the civil war." A statement by Lavrov created expectations that Russia could possibly have abandoned its commitment to Bashar al-Asad: "I would like to emphasize that we are not interested in the fate of certain persons. . . . We are interested in the fate of Syrian people."[18]

At the Amman meeting, the Friends of Syria discussed and endorsed the new Russian-American initiative, but it still took several months before a second Geneva conference could be convened. By the end of 2013, both regime and opposition had abandoned their refusal to meet with each other, so that when the second Geneva summit met on January 22, 2014, it was attended by representatives of the regime and of the National Coalition headed by Ahmad al-Jarba, a member of the Shammar tribe in eastern Syria and a Saudi ally. The split between the different opposition groups persisted, and the Syrian National Council decided to withdraw from the National Coalition, refusing to break its commitment not to negotiate with the regime as long as Asad was in power. The Kurds sent their own delegation to Geneva rather than be represented by the National Coalition. Two rounds of talks were held in January and February but failed to produce results. It was decided to hold a third round but without setting a date.

Several months later, in July 2014, the UN secretary general appointed the Italian diplomat Staffan de Mistura as his special envoy to Syria, replacing Lakhdar Brahimi. Brahimi's most important contribution to peacemaking in Syria had been his role in the drafting and acceptance of the Geneva communique. De Mistura proved to be a persistent, creative diplomat and, unlike his predecessors, stayed the course for four and a half years.

2015–16: The Turning of the Tide

By this time the Syrian civil war had grown into a full-blown regional and international crisis.

Russia's military intervention in Syria, in partnership with the Iranians, began in September 2015, turning Russia into the dominant political and military actor in the Syrian arena, enhancing its position and prestige elsewhere in the Middle East, and helping tip the scales in the conflict.

In fact, plans for this intervention had actually been made several months earlier, during the spring and summer of 2015.[19] In July, when the prospect of the regime's collapse seemed a real possibility, the late Qasem Suleimani, the commander of the Quds Force, flew to Moscow and persuaded the Russians to dispatch their air force, promising to take charge of the fighting on the ground. It was justified by a formal request by the Asad regime and was implemented through the dispatching of warplanes and auxiliary units to the Khmeimim air base. By deploying squadrons of fighter jets and advanced air defense systems,

Russia obtained control of Syrian airspace, matched by control of the Syrian coast through naval units operating out of the Russian naval base in Tartus. This new reality was not challenged by the United States. After downing one Russian jet fighter in November 2015, Turkey apologized and made amends. Israel, for its part, reached a modus vivendi with Putin. In October 2015 Russia supplemented its direct intervention in Syria by launching cruise missiles from the Caspian Sea against IS targets. This spectacular action reinforced the sense that in addition to saving his protégé Bashar al-Asad from the brink of disaster, Putin was seeking to demonstrate Russia's capabilities and status as a global military actor. In March 2016 Putin made his "mission accomplished" statement and announced that Russia's forces would be returning home. In reality, though, as has been the case with so many other Russian statements, only some troops were recalled from Syria, and they were subsequently replaced and reinforced by a larger Russian contingent.

With effective, ruthless Russian aerial support, the regime and its allies took to the offensive. In October 2015 the regime began to recapture territory that had been previously lost to rebel groups: in the northwest, in the south, near Damascus, and, of great symbolic importance, in the center—the city of Palmyra (Palmyra was subsequently recaptured by IS and then liberated once again). The major difference was made by Russia, in the battle of Aleppo. In the ebb and flow of the fighting the city's eastern part was held by the rebels, the FSA and Islamist groups, while the western part was controlled by the regime and its allies, who were aided by Hezbollah and other Shi'i militias. Once Russia joined the fray, its air force made a catastrophic difference with massive, and often indiscriminate, bombing. Destruction and loss of civilian life in Syria's second largest city were massive. The regime and its allies managed to encircle and besiege the rebel-held area; in December 2016 they would capture the whole city.

The complexity of the crisis further expanded when Syria's Kurdish minority became embroiled in the conflict. In its quest for local allies in the ground war against IS, the United States discovered that the Syrian Kurds were its most effective partners in Syria. The United States collaborated primarily with the YPG (People's Protection Units), the military wing of the PYD (Democratic Union Party), the Syrian branch of the Turkish Kurdish PKK (the leading Kurdish opposition party in Turkey). As a result the PYD came to control a sizable part of northern Syria and expanded both to the south and to the west. This development alarmed Turkey, which sees the PYD as a dangerous enemy and is determined to prevent Kurdish contiguity on its border and Kurdish expansion toward the Mediterranean. With a Kurdish minority of some 20 percent, Turkey views Kurdish military assertiveness and territorial expansion in either Iraq or Syria as a mortal threat. This outlook has led to Turkish-American tensions and to Turkish-Russian collaboration in northern Syria. (The twists and turns of Turkish policy are described and analyzed in depth in chapter 4.)

While the US organized a large international coalition against IS, the organization was still in control of Mosul in Iraq and Al-Raqqa (the capital of its "Caliphate") in Syria, continued to fight in both countries, carried out barbaric executions, promoted international terrorism, and attracted volunteers from Europe and other parts of the world. The wave of terrorist attacks in Paris and Brussels in 2015–16, and the threat of new terrorist acts by European citizens who returned from Syria and Iraq, as well as the pressure of Syrian refugees seeking to reach Europe helped prompt the wave of right-wing populism that continues to manifest itself in Europe today.

The Fighting

The most prominent arena of fighting in Syria during this period centered on the war against IS, conducted by the international coalition organized and led by the United States. The Global Coalition, as it was called, was put together by the United States in September 2014. The United States however remained determined to refrain from participating in the fighting on the ground and limited its role to bombing IS targets and dispatching a small number of special forces to help with the fighting on the ground through instruction and intelligence sharing. The United States was also determined not to be drawn into the Syrian civil war, namely the conflict between regime and opposition. In order to expand the ranks of the Kurdish militia YPG—the most effective fighters on the ground—and prevent that force from being seen as essentially Kurdish entity (to appease Turkey), the United States subsequently initiated the formation of a larger entity named the SDF (Syrian Democratic Forces), which also included Arab (mostly tribal) and other ethnic elements (Turkemans, Assyrians, and Armenians) and reflected the ethnic diversity of northeastern Syria. The most ferocious fighting between YPG and IS was waged in the town of Kobane on the Turkish border and concluded in January 2015. After a series of further military successes against IS, the SDF announced in September 2016 that it was launching a campaign to conquer the city of al-Raqqah.

Although in earlier phases the organization had primarily been interested in creating its territorial base and fought primarily against opposition forces, IS began to wage new campaigns against the Syrian regime, in addition to defending its Syrian territorial possessions (as well as its Iraqi ones) against the coalition. Islamic State captured the historic city of Palmyra, executed Syrian soldiers, and destroyed priceless antiquities. It then captured the town of al-Qaryatayn, situated just thirty kilometers east of the major city of Homs. By capturing al-Qaryatayn and several nearby sites, IS now presented a major potential threat to the regime.

In the ranks of the Syrian armed opposition, the FSA continued to lose ground that was picked up by radical Islamist paramilitaries, first and foremost Ahrar al-Sham. In addition to its familiar endemic problems and internal splits, the FSA was hit in October 2015 by the Obama administration's decision to end its US$500 million program in support of the moderate armed opposition: Ahrar al-Sham, estimated by this time to have some twenty thousand fighters and in possession of a fairly effective chain of command, now collaborated openly with Jabhat al-Nusrah, despite the reservations of the United States in seeing the Jabhat al-Nusrah as a Jihadi organization, part of the Al Qaeda network and, ultimately, a threat to itself and its European allies. In July 2016 Jabhat al-Nusrah announced that it had severed its ties with Al Qaeda and changed its name to Fath ash-Sham,[20] but the US government and many others were not impressed by these moves. In March 2015 Ahrar al-Sham joined an umbrella organization, Jaysh al-Fath, that was formed in the region of Idlib with the encouragement of Turkey, Saudi Arabia, and Qatar, which sought to enhance cooperation between Islamist organizations. The move proved effective, and Fath al-Sham scored several military successes in northwestern Syria whose impact was felt in Aleppo, Latakia, and Homs. The reverses it sustained in the northwest of Syria and the significance of that region led the regime to dispatch one of its elite forces, Colonel Suheil al-Hasan and his "tiger forces," to join the fray. But, typically for the Syrian opposition, factionalism proved more powerful than loyalty to the common cause, and Jaysh al-Fath disintegrated in January 2017.

The one front in which the mainstream armed opposition registered significant successes was in the south, around the city of Dar'a, the rebellion's birthplace. Here, owing to the location's symbolic significance, the regime fought back, furiously and mercilessly. In 2015 barrel bombs had already been used by the regime elsewhere as a particularly brutal and effective weapon, thrown at rebel fighters and civilians on more than a hundred occasions. Their impact is deadly and their use considered a war crime. Western powers had tried in vain to pass a Security Council resolution denouncing the regime for using them.

Diplomacy

During this period, the futility of the international efforts to resolve the severity of the Syrian crisis and its ripple effects became increasingly apparent. These efforts were channeled through two meetings of the Friends of Syria in Vienna in continuation of the Geneva process and supplemented by bilateral American-Russian negotiations. In a visit to Moscow on December 15, 2015, US secretary of state Kerry succeeded in persuading his Russian counterparts to agree to support UN Security Council Resolution 2254, on December 18, which dealt with the fundamental issues of the Syrian civil war. The text made references to the need for a transition, a new Syrian constitution, and free and fair elections under UN supervision, but in keeping with Russia's insistence, it did not include even the vaguest reference to Asad's departure. Diplomatic efforts produced a brief ceasefire in February 2016, but this achievement proved to be short-lived. Whatever was agreed on at the UN in New York certainly did not prevent the Russian air force from massive bombing in Aleppo and other locations over the next few months.

On September 10, 2016, the United States and Russia signed in Geneva an agreement on reducing the level of fighting in Syria and collaboration in fighting the Islamic State. In a characteristic expression of optimism Secretary of State Kerry stated that the new plan would reduce violence in Syria and lead to a period of political transition. He defined the agreement as "a potential turning point in the conflict" provided that the Syrian government and the rebels respect it.[21] But it was to no avail. In response to the heavy bombardment of Aleppo by the Syrian and Russian air forces, the State Department announced on October 3, 2016, that it was suspending the talks with Moscow regarding the cease-fire in Syria and shutting down the center for operational coordination against the Islamic State that Washington and Moscow had set up during the previous month. Taking its direction from a US administration that was unwilling to implicate itself more deeply in the civil war, State Department spokespersons could only vent their frustrations with statements such as this:

> The United States spared no effort in negotiating and attempting to implement an arrangement with Russia aimed at reducing violence, providing unhindered humanitarian access, and degrading terrorist organizations operating in Syria, including Da'esh [IS] and al-Qaeda in Syria. In backing away from bilateral talks, the United States will for now scrap plans to share intelligence and cooperate militarily with Russia to defeat the enemies they can agree on: IS and the Al-Qaeda spinoff, the Al-Nusra Front.[22]

2017–18

By 2017 and in particular after the regime's victory in Aleppo there was a growing perception that Asad had emerged victorious, without any accompanying decline in the level of violence throughout the country.

The years 2017–18 in the Syrian arena were shaped by several major trends and developments, including the regime's campaign—backed by Russia and Iran—to capture the remaining opposition strongholds across the country, the outbreak of a direct Israeli and Iranian conflict in Syria, Turkey's military intervention in the north of the country, and the transition from the Obama to the Trump administration and the resulting fluctuations of Washington's policies in of the region.

The transition from the Obama to the Trump administration produced some changes and several shifts in Washington's policies in Syria. As in other areas of its foreign policy, Washington's conduct toward and in Syria under the Trump administration was characterized by fluctuations and lack of order. During his first trip abroad, which began in Riyadh, President Trump used strong language to express his determination to contain Iranian expansionism in the Middle East. His rhetoric was seen as an indication that the new administration was willing to invest effort and resources to contain Iran. But then, in December 2018, President Trump announced the withdrawal of the two thousand US troops from eastern and northeastern Syria. The presence of that small force in Syria was considered essential for completing the war on IS, supporting Kurdish control of nearly 25 percent of Syria's territory, and sending a message of US commitment to check Iran's ambitions in Syria and to maintain bargaining chips in its give-and-take with Russia. Trump's decision seemed to signify an abandonment of these policy goals. It was followed by a Trump statement that he planned to evacuate the remaining two thousand US troops stationed in northeastern Syria along with their Kurdish partners.

Eventually, Trump's national security bureaucracy was able to persuade him to keep the US troops in Syria at least temporarily and to keep control of the Al-Tanf border crossing as a crucial stronghold in any effort to prevent the construction of an Iranian land bridge to the Mediterranean. The Syrian issue was also an important component of Trump's Russian agenda because it was widely assumed that in any Russian American give-and-take, Syria was an arena in which Russia could make concessions that would be matched in other arenas such as Ukraine. In the event, much was not accomplished in that give-and-take (for detailed description and analysis of the Trump administration's Syria policy, see chapter 5).

This was a period of intensive diplomacy conducted along several tracks, but the volume of meetings produced little substance. With Russian backing, the regime was determined to translate its military success into political success by reestablishing its rule over the bulk of the national territory. Russia was the dominant actor in the diplomatic arena without a serious American challenge. The opposition remained weak and divided; Turkey's Kurdish agenda added another compounding element to the efforts to seek full or partial agreements.

On January 23, 2017 (three days after Trump's inauguration), a meeting with the leaders of Russia, Turkey, and Iran was convened in Astana, the capital of Kazakhstan. Its immediate purpose was to consolidate the cease-fire between Russia and the Syrian rebels, agreed on in Ankara with Turkish mediation on December 30, 2016. But the Astana forum was also designed beyond this immediate purpose, to create a new framework for conducting a political diplomatic process in Syria without the participation of the US and Syrian opposition elements still interested in toppling the Asad regime. Eight rounds of meetings were held in Astana during 2017. Most important among them was the May 5 meeting, which produced a "memorandum of understanding for the creation of de-escalation zones in Syria."[23] This was yet another attempt to establish in Syria a durable cease-fire, this time through four "de-escalation zones": in Idlib and other parts of northern Syria; in the enclave between Hama and Homs; in an enclave east of Damascus; and in southern Syria. The agreement called for, among other things, an end to fighting between the regime and opposition (except the Jihadi groups), suspension of Syrian air force activity, humanitarian aid, and return of refugees. The three sponsors of Russia, Turkey, and Iran also sent military units in order to supervise the implementation of the agreement (although, as we saw, this did not prevent either Russia or the regime from launching offensives in the deescalation zones).

Alongside the Astana process, the Geneva process and focus on short-term arrangements continued in an effort to reach a more comprehensive settlement. The third Geneva session in February to April 2016 failed. A fourth session was convened on February 23, 2017. This time, too, a breakthrough was not achieved—but a common agenda was put together, and the parties did not abandon the meetings. In practice Staffan de Mistura prior to ending his term tried to merge the Astana and Geneva tracks in order to convene a constituent assembly that would draft a new Syrian constitution. In parallel to the Astana meetings, Turkish president Erdogan also hosted the Russian and Iranian presidents for two trilateral summits, with a view to preventing the deterioration of relations given Turkey's military activities in Syria.

On November 18, 2017, Russian president Putin announced his intention to host in Sochi a "Syrian Congress for National Dialogue," in an effort to bring an end to the war in Syria and to lay the foundations for a new political order by drafting a constitution and holding municipal, parliamentary, and presidential elections in Syria by 2021. The Russian plan included an offer to the Kurds to discuss a federal structure of sorts that would enable them to support the regime. This was an example of an ambitious Russian initiative that in fact went beyond the regime's own wishes. A second Sochi meeting was held on January 30, 2018, and dealt primarily with the formulation of a new draft constitution. Again, the meeting did not prevent Russia from engaging in massive bombing in Syria at the same time. It was yet another manifestation of Putin's dual strategy of using massive force in order to leverage his policy.

Throughout this period, bilateral Russian-American discussions over Syria were held primarily in meetings between Trump and Putin. This was done most notably in the controversial Helsinki summit on July 16, 2018. Little is known about the discussions held by Trump and Putin in Helsinki, but Trump's performance at their press conference drew massive criticism. The prospect of an Israeli-Iranian war in Syria motivated both presidents to agree to seek a limitation on the deployment of Iranian and pro-Iranian troops and installations in southern Syria.

CHAPTER 3

The Domestic Scene

As crucial as the actions of regional and international actors have been in shaping and perpetuating the crisis, Bashar al-Asad's survival in power cannot be attributed strictly to these outside forces. It is also important to understand the internal reasons for the regime's resilience, and the opposition's weakness.

The Regime: Resources and Supporters

Bashar al-Asad may have made errors of judgment, particularly in the early stages of the crisis, and may have been overly influenced by the radical members of his family and entourage, but he has provided his loyal supporters with single-minded, cool-headed, and ruthless leadership, which he has displayed through the most difficult hours of the protracted conflict. In early 2011 Asad is reported to have told his confidants, "My father was right: the 30,000 deaths in Hama ensured us thirty years of stability."[1] This horrific perspective—the belief that brutal suppression guarantees survival, and that compromise with the political opposition is a slippery slope to be avoided—typifies Bashar's governing philosophy and is the rationale for his regime's massive use of violence against both enemies and innocent bystanders through shelling, barrel bombs, missiles, and chemical weapons.

Supporting the man and his unyielding governing philosophy, there are several million Syrians who have never abandoned him. These supporters include, crucially, core members of the armed forces and the intelligence and security community, and of the Ba'th Party and its satellite organizations. These supporters are drawn from the Alawi community and, to a lesser extent, from parts of the Christian and Druze communities and parts of the urban Sunni bourgeoisie. Although the armed forces, estimated at three hundred thousand strong at the outset of the crisis, lost up to one-third of its personnel in the early years of the crisis owing to defections, and the army's effectiveness was diminished because of the need to keep predominantly Sunni units in their barracks, there were almost no senior defectors and no defections by whole units.[2] Several attempts by Western powers to recruit one or several senior Alawi officers into the ranks of the opposition failed to sway their loyalty.[3] The armed forces have remained a functioning entity fighting alongside its foreign and domestic partners. The same can be said about the different security services that were weakened but not incapacitated by the rebellion. As for the governmental and party apparatus, the only senior figure to defect was former prime minister Riad Hijab. Even former vice president and foreign minister Faruq al-Shara, sometimes mentioned as a potential replacement for Bashar, did not defect but was kept under house arrest.

As for the Syrian state bureaucracy, it has continued to function, albeit in only parts of the country (the central and western parts of the country), referred to by the regime as "essential Syria." The regime continued to provide services and pay salaries, though not on a full scale. And most important of all is the fact that during most of the civil war, life in the center of Damascus kept up the appearance of normalcy. The Alawi-dominated coastal region and the Druze town of Suwayda are the other areas where more or less normal life continued.

Alawi Power and Sectarianism

"Sectarianism" is the term used most often as the English equivalent of the Arabic term *ta'ifiyyah*. It is not a precise translation. The essence of the term *ta'ifiyyah* is best conveyed through the French "confessionalisme," often used in academic literature on Lebanon to describe a system based on the political distribution of power through religious communities. Lebanon is the only country in the Arab world in which it is used in a neutral rather than pejorative sense and where politics is practiced routinely along sectarian lines. In the rest of the Arab world, particularly the Levant, it is more commonly held that everyone is an Arab and that differences among religious communities and sects are artificial. Sectarian politics are seen as a device used by internal and external enemies to sow dissension. Secular Arab nationalism of this sort was the core ideology of the founders of Syria's Ba'th Party in the postwar period. Founded by Christians and Alawis, as well as Sunnis, the party was intended as a counterforce against Sunni dominance, and as such it attracted a disproportionate number of minorities into the party's ranks.[4] Sunnis were attracted to the party primarily by the socialist component of its ideology.

It was Bashar al-Asad's father, Hafez, who, after taking power in November 1970, adopted a deliberate systematic policy of mobilizing and recruiting the Alawi community into the party as the mainstay of his regime, and as a tool of exercising power and maintaining allegiance.

Syria's Alawi community as a whole benefitted significantly from the thirty years of Hafez al-Asad's rule. The number of Alawis in Damascus grew during the last decade of the twentieth century from a few thousand to nearly half a million.[5] Investments were made in the Alawi region, and a university was built in Latakia. But benefits have not been enjoyed by all Alawis equally. A small elite, the Asad family and clan, their loyalists, and a relatively small number of members of the regime's elite have been enriched. Some of them, most notably Bashar and his brother Maher, married Sunni women and helped create a new Alawi-Sunni political and economic elite. Other Alawis did less well; tensions became manifest between those who remained at the coast and in the mountains, and those who improved their standard of living by moving to Damascus and other major cities.

In the years preceding the outbreak of the Syrian rebellion, there were Alawi activists in the ranks of the opposition and Alawi participation in the Damascus Spring manifestations of opposition. Aref Dalila was the most senior Alawi participant in the Arab Spring. Dean of the Faculty of Economics at the University of Damascus and an adviser on economic affairs to Hafez al-Asad, Dalila was arrested during the regime's suppression of the Arab Spring and given in 2002 a longer jail sentence than those of his Sunni and Christian colleagues. Clearly the regime viewed opposition by Alawis as particularly dangerous. Dalila was released from jail in 2008, and in 2011 he joined the protest against the regime and the ranks of the opposition.

In 2011 several Alawi intellectuals protested the regime's policy of identifying the Alawi community with the regime, most prominently the actress Fadwa Suleiman, whose antiregime activities compelled her to go into hiding, and eventually into exile.[6] But the regime proved to be successful in endowing the

conflict in Syria with a significant sectarian dimension, depicting it as a Sunni-Alawi clash and persuading most of the Alawi
community that a victory by the opposition would lead to a
large-scale massacre of Alawis. This campaign was bolstered by
radical rhetoric from a number of opposition leaders and their
supporters. Alawi opposition to the dominance of the Asad clan
continued to erupt but was on the whole obscured by the regime's success in keeping the bulk of the community in its
camp.[7]

Beyond being a crucial component of the regime's support
base, the Alawi community's most important contribution to
the war effort was made through its participation in proregime
militias. These militias, rather than the police or the regular
army, were typically responsible for confronting street demonstrators and Sunni insurgents in mixed areas during the rebellion's early phase. Their unofficial status enabled the regime to
deny knowledge or involvement in the atrocities they perpetrated. In later phases of the conflict, they released the army
from the need to carry out tasks more suited for paramilitaries,
such as keeping control of territory captured by the regime,
manning roadblocks, patrolling, and so forth. But at the same
time the militias reinforced the disintegration of state institutions and the undermining of public order.

The most notorious of these militias were the Shabiha
(ghosts), who committed some of the war's worst atrocities.
The term does not refer to a specific group but to the activities
of criminal and semicriminal elements affiliated with the extended Asad clan and its allies in the Alawi community. The
origins of the Shabiha go back to the 1980s, when members of
the Asad family closest to Hafez's brothers Rif'at and Jamil
began to engage in criminal activities such as smuggling and
drug trading. The Shabiha phenomenon was curtailed but not

fully eliminated in the 1990s by Hafez al-Asad through his son
Basel. It was revived after the rebellion's outbreak by businessmen close to the regime, headed by Rami Makhluf.[8] The most
notorious of the Shabiha's massacres were perpetrated in Houla
in central Syria in May 2012 and, two weeks later, in the village
of Qubeir, near Hama.[9]

Similar missions were carried out by smaller paramilitaries
known as "popular committees," which in addition to Alawi
fighters also contained Christian and Druze volunteers. It became common to refer to such groups as "shabiha" despite the
fact that they were quite different from the original Shabiha
phenomenon. The local committees were subsequently organized together into an entity called "The Popular Army" and
subsequently into the NDF (National Defense Forces), in order
to eliminate tensions that had arisen over time between the
army and some paramilitary units. Iran also played an important role in financing and training these paramilitary organizations. Bashar himself lauded these gangs as "citizens fighting
alongside the army to defend their communities and regions"
and complained that the Western press did not give them due
credit for battlefield successes.[10]

To add to the complex field of proregime combatants, still
other paramilitary units were created in order to make up for
the depletion of the army and to better cope with the challenge
of guerrilla warfare. Affiliated with different branches of Syrian
intelligence (mukhabarat), two of these groups are of particular
interest. "The Tiger Forces" (Quwat al-Nimr), created and commanded by the Alawi colonel Suheil al-Hasan in the fall of 2013
and funded by businessmen such as Rami Makhluf, acquired a
reputation for brutality and atrocities but also for battlefield
exploits. Hasan's military prowess was overstated since several

of his battlefield victories derived from his ability to call in air strikes by Syrian and later Russian warplanes. Hasan, whose nickname was the Tiger, began his career as an officer in the regular air defense units. In the course of the Syrian rebellion al-Hasan distinguished himself as a particularly brutal yet creative field commander and has been credited with developing the technology behind the notorious barrel bombs that have been used against civilians.[11] His public image was enhanced by his penchant for writing poetry and by his popular Facebook page. His reputation and that of his paramilitary were buoyed when they broke the three-year siege of Kuweires airfield near Aleppo in December 2015. When Putin arrived at the air base of Khmeimim in December 2017, Hasan was most notably and warmly greeted by Vladimir Putin and given a Russian medal. At the time it seemed that Putin treated Hasan even more cordially than Bashar, leading to widespread speculation that the Russians were grooming Hasan as Bashar's replacement. This impression was reinforced when Putin assigned bodyguards to Hasan. This surely must not have pleased Bashar. Hasan himself made a point of regularly paying tribute to Bashar, but after the Khmeimim episode he seems to have lowered his profile either by choice or through some action taken by Bashar.

A second significant Alawi militia known as "The Desert Hawks Brigade" (Liwa' Suqur al-Sahra) is a private group funded by the Jaber brothers—Muhammad, a retired Syrian army general, and Ayman, a Syrian tycoon heavily invested in oil and TV business—who form part of the new elite that has emerged under Bashar al-Asad. It was hardly surprising that the militia formed and financed by the Jaber brothers was particularly active in the Syrian desert areas where Ayman's oil assets were concentrated.

Other Communities

During the Syrian crisis the Sunni community has been divided between active opponents and passive supporters of the regime. The Christians and Druze, for their part, have tended to lend support to the regime, and the Kurds have pursued their own interests without joining the opposition.

The Sunni population of the Syrian periphery formed the core support of the rebellion when it erupted in 2011, while the Sunni business class in Syria's two main cities, Damascus and Aleppo, failed to join the struggle. This was due to some extent to the symbiotic relationship created by Hafez al-Asad with parts of the urban bourgeoisie. That symbiosis kept power in the hands of the Alawis but gave the commercial classes an opportunity to enrich themselves and to live comfortably as long as they refrained from crossing red lines. When the rebellion broke out, this group calculated that the Asad regime was preferable to a radical, Islamist alternative. This attitude is key to understanding the regime's ability to keep a semblance of normalcy in its capital. The fighting that did occur in Damascus took place mostly in or around the city's outskirts (the Ghouta). Aleppo, too, remained quiet during the rebellion's early phase, drawn into fierce and devastating fighting only when the city's eastern side was taken over by rebels from its immediate periphery. This discrepancy between the position of these Sunni elites and the militancy of the more devout Sunni population in the countryside and in smaller towns has been an important aspect of the Syrian civil war.

The Druze are a heterodox sectarian Muslim community that branched off from Shi'i Islam. Numbering approximately seven hundred thousand, or 3 percent of Syria's general population, they, like the Alawis, are territorially concentrated, a so-called compact minority.[12] The Syrian Druze live in four areas: the largest group (approximately 375,000) lives in the Druze Mountain around the city of Suwayda in Syria's southern province; another large group (250,000) in Damascus neighborhoods; and two smaller groups near Mount Hermon in the Syrian Golan (30,000) and in Jabal al-Soumak in the province of Idlib (25,000). Again, like the Alawis, the Druze were favored by the French during the colonial era and as potential allies against the Sunni Arab nationalists of the big cities and were given a statelet of their own (it was less elaborate than the Alawite statelet and could better be described as an administrative semiautonomy). The Druze were less hostile to the Arab nationalist elite of Syrian major cities but were ultimately rejected by it. Alongside the Alawis, the Druze joined the Syrian army and the Ba'th Party in large numbers. Druze senior officers were partners in the early phases of the Ba'th regime until their ousting in the late 1960s by their Alawi colleagues in the internecine conflicts during the Ba'th regime's early years. No longer partners to power, they nonetheless maintained a reasonably good relationship with Bashar al-Asad's regime. Syria's Druze community maintains close contact with the Druze communities in Lebanon, Israel, and the Israeli Golan. Their closeness to the capital and to the Jordanian and Israeli borders and their ability to mobilize the community, or at least large parts of it, endowed the Druze with considerable potential and actual influence.

Druze attitudes toward the uprising have varied according to region. In the south and the north, there has been a tendency to resist the regime owing to closeness to the Jordanian and Turkish borders, and to the depth of the opposition in the country's north and south. In the Syrian Golan, by contrast, Hezbollah's proximity tilted the Druze toward the regime. And yet tensions with the Asad regime arose from the refusal of many young Druze to enlist in the army or in proregime militias. The tensions became manifest after a July 2018 attack against the Druze population in Suwayda that killed some two hundred civilians. While the regime blamed IS, it was in fact widely suspected and speculated that the attack was provoked by the regime as a means of pressure against the Druze refusal to join the Syrian army. In the larger scheme of things, the Druze have by and large come to terms with the regime's victory and survival, but the aforementioned massacre reinforced their conviction that they must be equipped and organized to protect themselves.

As for Syria's Christian communities, who constituted, on the eve of the rebellion, approximately 10 percent of the country's population, they remain divided into several sects and ethnic groups, including Arabs belonging to several Christian denominations (the largest being Greek Orthodox), Armenians, and Assyrians. Their number has been declining owing to immigration over the last few decades, a process now greatly expedited by the civil war. As a rule, Syrian Christians have supported the regime, preferring it to some variety of Sunni fundamentalism that loomed large as the only likely alternative (Sunni demonstrators used to chant "al Alawi ala al taboot wal masihi ila Beirut," or "The Alawi in the coffin and the Christian to Beirut"). The new Syria that many Sunni fundamentalists had in mind would be a Sunni-Muslim-Arab state with no or little space for minorities or other communities. It was hardly surprising that the patriarch of the Greek Orthodox Church, Ignace IV, let it be known in Damascus that he shared the Maronite patriarch's view[13] that Christians should refrain from taking part in the fighting. Many of them chose to leave Syria and emigrate to the Christian West.

As the tide of the conflict turned in the regime's favor, it made great efforts to cultivate the Christian community while signaling to the West that Asad offered the best protection to Syria's Christians. The following excerpt from the *Economist* from June 2018 is telling:

> In Homs, which Syrians once dubbed the "capital of the revolution" against President Bashar al-Asad, the Muslim quarter and commercial district still lie in ruins, but the Christian quarter is reviving. Churches have been lavishly restored; a large crucifix hangs over the main street. "Groom of Heaven" proclaims a billboard featuring a photo of a Christian soldier killed in the nine year conflict. In their sermons Orthodox patriarchs praise Mr. Asad for saving one of the world's oldest Christian communities.[14]

The Tribes

A large portion of Syria's rural population is tribal, held together by kinship. The tribal population is Sunni, but Islam has traditionally played a limited rule in tribal society. In large parts of eastern Syria, semiarid steppe and tribal societies can be found close to several of central Syria's larger cities. Under Hafez al-Asad the regime was able to build a partnership with the leaders of these tribes as part of a strategy of broadening the basis of support of a minority government. Like other components of Hafez al-Asad's domestic policy, these efforts withered under his son. The effects of this neglect were magnified by the drought of the years preceding the 2011 events and by the penetration of Salafi influences from the Arabian Peninsula.

In the early days of the Syrian rebellion, the clash between the regime and the population of Dar'a (as recounted in chapter 2) had a distinct tribal dimension. The parents of the youth arrested by the regime had tribal affiliations, and their response to the humiliation inflicted by the security services reflected the traditional values of a society that puts a high premium on dignity and the duty to seek vengeance.

During nine years of civil war Syria's tribes have not shared the same stance toward the regime. Some have remained loyal to and cooperated with the government while others have collaborated with the opposition, Jihadi or not. The picture is further compounded by tensions, splits, and conflict within each tribal group. Eastern Syria has been the major arena for the competition for tribal support between IS, Jabhat al-Nusra, the opposition, and the regime. The tribal dimension of the struggle over eastern Syria was magnified by traditional cross-border tribal relationships with the Arabian Peninsula, Jordan, and Iraq. The projection of Saudi influence into Syria through traditional tribal relationship was illustrated by the election in July 2013 of Ahmad al-Jarba as head of the SNC. Jarba hails from the Shammar tribe that had migrated from the Arabian Peninsula and keeps an affiliation with the important Saudi Aneza tribe. In this context IS's success in harnessing the tribal population in the territory under its control (and in exploiting internecine conflicts) was most significant. It derived from several sources. One was its ability to fill the vacuum created by the disappearance of the state by providing services and resources. Another was the use of terror, most notably the massacre of the al-Shu'eitat clan, who had supported Jabhat al-Nusrah in return for control of an oil field. Al-Nusrah's founder, Abu Muhammed al-Julani, comes from al-Shuhail near Deir ez-Zor, and he brought into the competition with IS his own tribal connections. The Islamic State in turn arrived in Syria equipped with a rich experience of working with the tribes in fomenting the insurgency.

At present, the tribal scene in Syria is shaped by several actors. The regime in its drive to reestablish control has built through its intelligence services a number of new tribal militias. The United States and the YPG when they constructed the SDF (Syrian Democratic Forces), in an effort to add an Arab component to the Kurdish militia, did so by recruiting tribal elements. And more recently, the Russians, the Turks, and the Iranians have also been investing efforts in building influence in this important sector of Syrian society.[15]

The Opposition

Just as the single-mindedness of the regime's main allies, Russia and Iran, have given them an advantage over an ambivalent America, so has the largely unified Syrian regime had the upper hand over a deeply divided opposition.

The Political Opposition

The endless game of appointments, resignations, and formations of new entities that became a hallmark of the Syrian opposition has been a sad reflection of the opposition's failure to provide a unified leadership to the Syrian rebellion—and to project to the outside world the existence of a viable alternative to Bashar al-Asad and his regime. A large part of the international community came to see the Asad regime as illegitimate but has been constrained by the failure of the fractured opposition to mount a credible alternative that could provide Syria with a viable, stable government. This failure came not just from the deep divisions of Syrian society, but also from the ceaseless meddling and intervention by the opposition's international and regional supporters. Turkey, Qatar, and Saudi Arabia all had their favorite opposition groups and individuals that they tried to promote regardless of the damage it inflicted on the struggle against the regime. The one outside power that could have imposed a united front on the different opposition groups was the United States, but this was a task Washington declined to undertake. Also glaringly absent from the scene was one dominant Syrian opposition leader who could impose order on the different components of the opposition and provide international public opinion with a concrete figure who would represent and symbolize the Syrian resistance to the Asad regime and be perceived as a credible alternative to Bashar al-Asad.

The initial phase in the formation and evolution of the political opposition to Bashar al-Asad's regime was deceptively auspicious. As described in chapter 2, the Syrian uprising broke out spontaneously and consisted initially of peaceful protest and demonstrations led by local coordination committees (LCCs, or *tansiqiyyat* in Arabic). An entity called SRGC (Syrian Revolution General Commission) was briefly in charge of coordinating the protests on the national level. One of its more effective contributions was a widely distributed manual entitled *Pointers for Demonstrations*. But like so many of the other opposition groups, this group would evaporate over time as violent repression led to rudimentary armed resistance and Sunni defections from the Syrian army. These developments had little to do with the individuals and groups that had led the opposition to Bashar's regime during its first decade in power. Part of this opposition, however, remained in Syria and served as a basis for "the mild opposition" that engaged in a brief abortive dialogue with the regime. During the rebellion's early phases a structure of sorts emerged whereby LCCs operated on the local level while ephemeral National Coordination Committees operated, as the name implies, on the national level.

With the passage of time the national committees lost their influence while the local committees preserved their relevance by serving, among other things, as the channel for distributing aid money sent from abroad. Others stayed abroad or left the country to form the backbone of the political opposition externally. By October 2011, this segment of the opposition was able to organize itself in Turkey as the Syrian National Council (SNC). The SNC defined its goal as "toppling the regime and building a democratic, pluralistic system in Syria."[16] Its proposed program included the formation of a provisional administration; the drafting of a comprehensive national covenant; holding elections to a constituent assembly within a year in order to author a new constitution; and holding free elections to a parliament; as well as the formation of a national reconciliation committee. An important achievement for the SNC was the cooperation agreement it reached in January 2012 with the Free Syrian Army (FSA). For a time, the FSA served as the informal military arm of the SNC, and together the two groups presented themselves as the backbone of a secular, moderate opposition. But in practice the SNC never exercised real authority over the FSA. It was during this time in August 2012 that Burhan Ghalyun, the Syrian French professor at the Sorbonne in Paris, was elected as the council's first president

The SNC's initial success would be torn apart by internal divisions and pulled in different directions by its external supporters. The politics of the external Syrian opposition were full of the dissension and intrigue characteristic of the politics of so many other exiled opposition movements. Secularists complained that the Muslim Brotherhood had excessive influence in the council and over its president. There were disagreements over the position of minorities, particularly the Kurds. There were policy disagreements, including over the issue of foreign involvement in the Syrian rebellion. Initial cooperation with the groups fighting the regime in Syria was marred by the complaints among the armed opposition inside Syria about the pretensions of the political activists living in relative comfort abroad. The slogan "We are in the trenches, and they stay in the hotels" (*Nahnu fi al-khanadiq wa-hum fi al-fanadiq*) reflected these sentiments. This tension reflected also a class difference between members of the Damascene elite who had been the backbone of the political opposition and the demonstrators and rebels who came from provincial towns and the countryside. These were the difficulties that led Burhan Ghalyun to resign, as did in short order his successor, Abd al-Baset Sayda, a Kurdish Syrian academic.

The formation of the National Coalition for Syrian Revolutionary and Opposition Forces (a.k.a., the Coalition, or al-I'tilaf in Arabic) was born in November 2012, when American secretary of state Hillary Clinton stated that the SNC "could no longer be viewed as the visible leader of the opposition" and called for an opposition leadership structure that could "speak to every segment and to every geographic part of Syria."[17] The Coalition grouped together seven major components: members of the SNC; representatives of the FSA; a variety of Syrian movements and parties operating in and outside Syria; minority Kurdish, Assyrian, and Turkeman groups; and prominent individual opponents and critics of the regime. The Coalition announced two major principles: toppling the Syrian regime, and absolute refusal to negotiate with it. The Coalition was also representative of the LCCs and won the endorsement of the Supreme Military Council (SMC) of the FSA. It did *not* include representatives of the National Coordination Committee (NCC/NCB), the "loyal opposition" group inside Syria. In March 2013, the Coalition formed the Syrian Interim Government (SIG) headed by Ghasan Hitu (a Syrian Kurd), who was considered close to the Muslim Brotherhood and to Qatar.

The Coalition's formation did not spell a transition to a more effective political opposition. The efforts by the SIG to provide municipal services in areas controlled by the opposition in Syria failed. The SNC began to agitate against the Coalition and against the SIG's willingness to participate in the Geneva peace efforts with the regime. In January 2014, the SNC formally withdrew from the Coalition. The squabbling in the ranks of the opposition continued when a few months later, Muaz al-Khatib resigned his position as the chairman of the Coalition, as did Ghasan Hitu from the leadership of SIG. Following a Saudi-Qatari conflict over control of the Coalition, Ahmad al-Jarba was elected to replace al-Khatib. The Coalition, like other opposition groups, continues to participate with limited effect in the diplomatic efforts to seek a political solution to the Syrian crisis.

One last effort to create a functioning framework for the Syrian revolution and opposition forces was made in December 2015, when a meeting in Riyadh of thirty-four opposition groups led to the formation of the HNC (High Negotiations Committee). The purpose of the meeting was to create a Syrian entity that would participate in the implementation of the 2012 Geneva Resolution, which called for the creation of a transitional government in Syria. The meeting was well attended by a large variety of groups, including militant Islamic opposition groups. The Kurds were not included because of Turkish opposition. But unsurprisingly, the HNC's effectiveness was also hampered by infighting, as well as by the challenge of two new groups to the HNC, the Moscow and Cairo platforms, small groups perceived as less hostile to Russia and the regime, in an effort to undermine the opposition. The Moscow group was opposed to the armed struggle and advocated compromise with the regime; it was therefore perceived by the HNC as a hostile element. The Cairo group was composed mainly of secular, leftist intellectuals and was more acceptable to the HNC. The HNC stood out among the opposition groups mostly owing to the fact that it included also real representatives of the armed factions. But during the Astana talks, given the failure to accomplish real progress, it disintegrated.

The Armed Opposition

The armed opposition posed the most serious threat to the existence of the Asad regime. While peaceful demonstrations continued, the conflict militarized, and it was up to the armed opposition to escalate the struggle. And yet the divisiveness that characterized the political opposition also afflicted the military one. The armed struggle against the regime was shaped by ever-increasing Islamization, rapidly shifting alliances and coalitions, and a transition—over time—from a national struggle to local conflicts over control of territory and resources. But despite this and other flaws, the military opposition came close to significantly threatening the regime in 2015, to the point that Russia's military intervention was required on the regime's behalf.[18]

At first glance, the number of military opposition groups in Syria is staggering, but most of the groups counted were in fact small local groups, and the number of effective groups was much smaller. These groups can be divided into four categories: moderate/secular, Islamist, Salafi, and Jihadi (this categorization should, however, be taken with a grain of salt given multiple rapid changes of orientation and alliances by different groups, the need to respond to changing local circumstances, and the need to accommodate regional supporters).

Moderate/Secular Groups

The principal moderate/secular group, somewhere between a militia and an army, was the Free Syrian Army. The FSA was a mainstream entity seeking to topple the regime and replace it with a democratic nationalist government. The FSA—founded in 2011 by Sunni officers who defected from the Syrian armed forces—went through several ups and downs between 2011 and 2018 but managed to maintain itself as the single most important framework for moderate/secularist forces. When declaring its establishment, Colonel Riad al-As'ad stated that "the Free Syrian Army works hand in hand with the people to achieve freedom and dignity, to bring this regime down, protect the revolution and the country's resources."[19] The FSA enjoyed Turkish, Jordanian, and Qatari logistical support, Saudi financing, and (albeit limited and intermittent) American logistical support and European and American political support; in practice, the FSA also collaborated with a variety of other groups, including Islamist and Jihadi ones. As noted in the previous section, in the summer of 2011 the FSA positioned itself as the military arm of the SNC. At a high point in 2012, it counted some forty thousand fighters in its ranks. But it never was a single unified hierarchical entity—rather it was a loose structure with limited authority over local units. Scholars are still in disagreement over the ultimate effectiveness of the FSA; some have viewed it as a resilient organization whose loose structure enabled it to adapt itself to changing circumstances and to survive over time, while others consider the looseness of the FSA to be a drawback rather than an advantage, which denigrated its real contribution to the struggle against the regime.[20]

It is moot to speculate how the FSA might have developed had the Obama administration decided in 2012 to extend to it massive support and turn it into the main arm of the effort to topple the Asad regime. But the administration decided to reject the CIA plan to train and equip the FSA, and the "red-line crisis" of 2013 inflicted deadly blows on the FSA and on the orientation it represented. A second enormous challenge came with the assertiveness and greater effectiveness of Islamist groups that took charge of the armed opposition in 2013. The FSA faced a crisis in December 2013 when its commander, Colonel Salim Idris, escaped from Syria to Qatar after Jihadi fighters took control of his logistical base on the Turkish border. At that point the United States and Britain suspended arms delivery to the rebels, fearing that they could fall into Jihadi hands. The FSA's crisis was also exacerbated by Hezbollah's new active role in the fighting, and by the absence of steady foreign support.

In 2014 an effort was made by the United States and its regional partners to try to rebuild the FSA and its position. The new strategy was predicated on the assumption that the FSA should be treated not as a unitary organization but rather as a decentralized entity. The group known as Friends of Syria decided to build training centers in Jordan (MOC, Military Operation Center) and in Turkey (MOM, Joint Operation Center). This was given substance in 2015 when the US Department of Defense started a "train and equip" program. The centers located in Turkey and Jordan did not cooperate with the FSA as such, but with specific groups affiliated with the FSA that had been vetted by the CIA. The decision to supply some of these groups with TOW missiles proved to be crucial. The new equipment enabled the rebels to neutralize the regime's tanks and to register military successes that seemed to threaten the regime's very survival. Some of the groups affiliated with the FSA created regional coalitions such as the Syrian Revolutionary Front (SRF), Jaysh al-Mujahidin, and the Southern Front. The two centers (the southern one in particular) were quite effective in coordinating the opposition's activity, but they were terminated in December 2017 in line with the Trump administration's overall policy in Syria.

After the regime's takeover of southern Syria, the remnants of the FSA found refuge in Idlib along with other rebel groups. As part of its anti-Kurdish campaign, Turkey created units of Turkish-affiliated FSA, which operate in the service of Turkish policy. These Turkish-supported groups were first known as TFSA (Turkish FSA), and later as the National Army. As an instrument of Turkish policy, these groups were and remain engaged in fighting Kurdish militias rather than the regime.

Islamist Groups

The Islamist groups in Syria can be conveniently divided into three categories: political Islamist, Salafist, and Jihadi. It is comparatively easy to define the first and third groups. The Islamist groups and militias were largely identified with the ideology of the Muslim Brotherhood and were therefore supported by the organization's regional supporters, Turkey and Qatar, and not by Saudi Arabia. This Islamist orientation seeks to control the political system and to fashion political and public life according to Islamic law and tradition. Jihadis, by contrast, are radical Islamists who believe in resorting to violence in order to impose the rule of Islam under a strict understanding of Islamic law. Salafis, too, advocate a strict application of Islamic law and a return to the ways of original Islam, but they tended to place emphasis on personal piety and social activism rather than on politics (their formation of the Al Nur Party as an arm of the

Egyptian Salafists in 2011 was seen as an egregious exception).
In the context of the Syrian civil war, most Salafi groups have
been supported by Saudi Arabia.[21] The most prominent Jihadi
groups operated in Syria were the Islamic State (though not
taking a real part in the Syrian opposition) and Jabhat al-Nusra
and its later incarnation, Hay'at Tahrir Alsham.

The three most prominent representatives of Muslim
Brotherhood–affiliated political Islamist trend were

1. Harakat Nur al-Din al-Zenki. This organization, which
   enjoyed Turkey's support and was one of the recipients
   of American antitank missiles, as part of a short-lived
   cooperation that ended in 2015, operated mostly in
   northern Syria and played an important role in the battle
   over Aleppo. In February 2018 the movement merged
   with Ahrar al-Sham to create the Syrian Liberation
   Front (JTS, Jabhat Tahrir Surya).[22] These changes in
   orientation reflect the open-ended character of most
   rebel militias in Syria.
2. Jaysh al-Mujahidin. This group was estimated to have at
   one time between five thousand and twelve thousand
   fighters. It fought against both the Islamic State and the
   Asad regime in the provinces of Aleppo and Idlib.
   Founded in January 2014, in addition to fighting, Jaysh
   al-Mujahidin also engaged in an effort to administer the
   area under its control. It eventually merged into Ahrar
   al-Sham organization.
3. Faylaq al-Sham (Legion of Syria). This was a coalition of
   nineteen groups who were active and fighting in western
   Syria. In May 2018 the coalition eventually came under
   dominant Turkish influence as part of the NLF (National
   Liberation Front).

Owing to their close relationship with Turkey, these groups had their largest impact on the fighting in northern and northwestern Syria.

Salafi Groups

Salafi groups in the Syrian opposition broadly aspired to turn the country into a theocracy based on the Sharia. They were focused on Syria and devoid of any global aspirations. The main group in this category was Ahrar al-Sham al-Islamiyyah, founded in December 2011 in an effort to create an umbrella organization for a variety of Salafi militias. Its founder was Hassan Aboud, a former prisoner released by the regime in 2011 as part of its effort to portray the opposition as radical Islamist. Most members were Syrian, but the organization was also joined by foreign fighters. It started its operations in Idlib and later expanded to other parts of Syria as far as Dar'a in the south. Aboud was killed in Idlib in September 2014. His successors were elected by the organization's Shura (legislative) Council, an entity composed of twenty-two members, thus providing an example of Islamic democracy. Ahrar al-Sham al-Islamiyyah was estimated to have twenty thousand fighters in its ranks. Some of them remain in Idlib, the opposition's last stronghold in Syria.

Jaysh al-Islam was the second largest Salafi organization in Syria. It operated mostly near Damascus. Its first leader was Zahran Alush, one of the other Islamist prisoners released by the regime in the spring of 2011 in order to "prove" the Islamist character of the opposition. Alush was killed by Russian forces in December 2015. In February 2018 the Ahrar merged with Harakat Nur al-Din al-Zenki to form the new JTS (Syrian Liberation Front).

Jihadi Groups

The course of the Syrian rebellion was radically altered by two Jihadi groups that originated in Iraq: Jabhat al-Nusrah and the Islamic State in Iraq and the Levant (ISIL or IS). Both groups originated with Al Qaeda in Iraq and like their mother organization believe both in a return to an original, pristine Islam and in waging Jihad against the West and the "apostate regimes" in the Middle East. Despite their common ancestry, they assumed very different roles in Syria.

Jabhat al-Nusrah Li'ahli al-Sham (the Front for the Support of the People of the Levant), while being essentially part of the Al Qaeda universe, became an integral part of the Syrian rebellion and owing to its military effectiveness played a major role in fighting the Asad regime. It was established by Al Qaeda as its official extension in Syria at the end of 2011 when Abu Mohammed al-Julani was dispatched across the border from Iraq in order to start its Syrian operation. In July 2011 Abu Baker al-Baghdadi made a decision to take advantage of the fact that the Asad regime released Jihadi and Islamist prisoners in order to reinforce its argument that the rebellion against it was an Islamist terrorist campaign against a secular regime. The effect of Asad's decision was the revival of the dormant cells of Al Qaeda in northeastern Syria that had been tolerated by the regime in the previous decade as part of its campaign against the US military presence in Iraq. After several months of preparation, in January 2012 Jabhat al-Nusrah started its activities in Syria.[23] Al-Nusrah enjoyed financial support from Qatar and from private donors in the gulf and early on distinguished itself as one of the most effective fighting forces of the opposition. In Al Qaeda terminology, it focused its efforts on the "near enemy" (namely the Asad regime) rather than the "far enemy" (namely the West). The strategy crafted for the organization in Syria by Al Qaeda's leadership was to seek collaboration with other opposition groups and to avoid anti-Western activity.

Jabhat al-Nusrah remained identified with Al Qaeda despite its genuine efforts to separate itself from Al Qaeda and to be perceived as part of the Syrian opposition. This led the United States, once it launched its campaign against the Islamic State, to include Jabhat al-Nusrah in its target list. Jabhat al-Nusrah's partners in the Syrian opposition and the coalition partners tried to persuade the US that Jabhat al-Nusrah was not part of global Jihad, but the US authorities remained convinced that some hard-core Jihadi elements continued to operate in the organization's ranks and persisted in bombing al-Nusrah's targets.

For its part, Jabhat al-Nusrah established cooperation with the Islamist opposition group Ahrar al-Sham. In March 2015 both organizations joined forces under the umbrella of Jaysh al-Fath (the Army of Conquest) with the support of Turkey, Qatar, and Saudi Arabia. It was a very effective military collaboration. The new entity captured significant areas in the regions of Idlib and Hama. The threat that they presented to the regime played an important role in promoting Russia to intervene militarily in September 2015. In July 2016 the United States and Russia decided to collaborate against Jabhat al-Nusrah. While the United States viewed the organization as part of the global Jihadi threat, Russia was mostly interested to weaken its anti-Asad edge. The decision had little practical impact. Jabhat al-Nusrah persisted in its effort to redefine itself as a Syrian Jihadi organization rather than a global Jihadi one and to create the impression (if not the substance) of a real separation from Al Qaeda. Its leader, al-Julani, appeared on July 28 on Al Jazeera television announcing that the organization reconstituted itself as Jabhat Fath a-Sham (the Front for the Conquest of the Levant), and that it had severed its relationship with Al Qaeda. These steps may well have been motivated by Qatari and other gulf states' pressure, as well as from internal developments in the organization's ranks and a desire to avoid US attacks.

But the union between al-Nusrah and Ahrar a-Sham would dissolve in January 2017. Al-Nusrah (now under its new name, Jabhat Fath al-Sham) changed its name once again to Hay'at Tahrir al-Sham (the Organization for the Liberation of the Levant), better known under the acronym HTS. For a while HTS, operating mostly in northern Syria, became the largest opposition force in that area counting (temporarily, prior to Harakat Nur al-Din al-Zenki's splitting) more than thirty thousand fighters.

The Islamic State pursued a different mission: the establishment of a territorial Caliphate on both sides of the Iraqi-Syrian border. For the Islamic State, the struggle against the Asad regime was a secondary effort and, in many respects, not an integral part of the opposition to it. The magnitude of the challenge posed by the Islamic State both to the conservative regimes in the region and to the West created a subconflict within the Syrian conflict that for two years overshadowed the conflict between regime and opposition.

The Islamic State in Syria and the Levant (ISIL) originated with the organization Jama'at al-Tawhid wal-Jihad (the Organization of Monotheism and Jihad) established by Abu Mus'ab al-Zarqawi in Iraq in 2003.[24] Later ISIL's leader Abu Baker al-Baghdadi seceded from Al Qaeda. In April 2013, having realized that the most promising arena for its area would be Syria, he tried to unify his organization in Syria with Jabhat al-Nusrah.

Having been rejected by al-Nusrah, the organization went out on its own and scored immediate and spectacular successes, mostly at the expense of the opposition. Aside from its military effectiveness and political acumen, the organization resorted to the most brutal methods that it advertised through a savvy media strategy. With its territory in the capital Syrian city of al-Raqqah, the Caliphate occupied a sizeable space in Iraq and Syria and imposed in these areas its version of Islamic law and (often brutal) Islamic justice. Since the organization's priority was to build a territorial Islamic Caliphate on both sides of the Syrian-Iraqi border, fighting the Asad regime was not always a priority, and there were even areas of collaboration between the organization and the regime—such as purchase by the regime of oil products in areas captured by IS.

The Islamic State distinguished itself by developing into a self-sufficient, wealthy territorial organization. Its sources of income were Syrian oil (sold to the Syrian regime and in Turkey and Iraq), taxation imposed in its areas of control, slave trading, sales of antiquities, and expropriation of money from banks in territories under its control. The US military estimated that in its heyday the organization had between US$500 million and US$750 million in its coffers. The Caliphate became a magnet for mostly Muslim volunteers from across the world that reached its territory through Turkey. Some of them returned to Europe as sleeping cells of terrorists and were responsible for the massive attacks in France and Belgium in 2016. Others ended up being disillusioned with IS. At some point the organization seemed to threaten not only the Iraqi state but also Jordan; it also became engaged in the fighting against the Asad regime, capturing the city of Palmyra in central Syria and establishing itself in other parts of the country.

The threat presented by IS in the region and as a global terrorist organization and the flow of refugees to Europe caused by the Asad regime, were the two dimensions of the Syrian crisis with the greatest impact on the international political system. The threat led the United States to organize a coalition and a military campaign launched in September 2014, which reached its zenith in October 2017 with the capture of al-Raqqa, and which continues to date, as the anti-IS coalition is preoccupied with the need to prevent IS's resurgence. Building and leading the coalition against ISIL became the dominant component in Washington's policy toward the Syrian crisis, completely overshadowing the opposition's struggle against Bashar al-Asad and his regime.

That these two organizations originating in Iraq, Jabhat al-Nusrah and the Islamic State, came to play such an important role in Syria, reflects the intricate interplay between Iraqi and Syrian politics in the first two decades of this century as well as the depth of the Sunni-Shi'i rift in the Arab world. As we saw, the Asad regime played an important role in the Sunni insurrection against the US occupation in the early 2000s by providing access to Iraq to thousands of Syrian and foreign volunteers. But Al Qaeda in Iraq fought not just against the United States, but against the Shi'i takeover of a country dominated for centuries by the Sunni Arab minority. During the second decade of the century, these Sunni Al Qaeda partisans saw the struggle against an Alawi regime in Damascus supported by Iran as another dimension of their own struggle. They also wisely identified the potential created for them by the Syrian insurrection. The Islamic State used its successes in Syria in order to move back to Iraq, capture the city of Mosul and additional territory, and threaten Baghdad. The temporary abrogation of the border between Iraq and Syria and the role played by the same organization on both sides of the Iraqi-Syrian border, reinforced the feeling that the political order created after World War I had come to an end. A century later, the catchphrase

"the end of Sykes-Picot"—a code name for the order stipulated by the British-French agreement of May 1916—became
fashionable at the height of the Islamic State's success in 2014–
16 as a term designating this change. The very use of the term
al-Sham (Greater Syria or the Levant) implied the challenge
to the borders created by Britain and France at the end of
World War I (Greater or Geographic Syria refers to the area
covered by Syria, Lebanon, Jordan, Israel, and the Palestinian
Territories).

Syrian Kurds

There is not a single history of the three million Kurds who live
in Syria.[25] At the end of World War I, a million Kurds were estimated to live in Aleppo, Damascus, and other Syrian cities,
many of them fully or partially Arabized. A small number of
Arabized Kurds played an important role in Syrian politics and
military affairs during the French mandate and in the 1950s.
Two of Syria's military dictators (Husni Za'im and Adib
Shishakly) and the notable Barazi family in Hama were of Kurdish descent. So was Khalid Bakdash, who for many years was
the leader of the Syrian Communist Party.

But this group of Kurds had little to do with the large Kurdish population in northern and northeastern Syria (about two
million in the early years of the twenty-first century). Many of
these Kurds were the descendants of immigrants who had arrived from Turkey in the 1920s and were not given Syrian citizenship. Their nickname was *bidun* ("without," in Arabic). Successive Syrian Arab nationalist regimes treated the large Kurdish
population with malign neglect. No manifestations of distinct
Kurdish identity were allowed, and a policy of forced Arabiza-
tion was pursued. The section of the country dominated by the

Kurds—a potentially rich part of the country—was not allowed
to develop and prosper. A staunchly Arab nationalist regime, the
Ba'th would not integrate the Kurds into its political system and
remained suspicious of and hostile to an ethnic block residing
near two hostile borders—that is, close to the larger Kurdish
groups in Turkey and Iraq. The regime even tried to build an Arab
cordon sanitaire along the Turkish and Iraqi borders.

Kurdish exasperation with this status quo eventually led to
the Al Hasakah (sometimes called Qamishli) revolt (or large-
scale riots) in 2004. Harsh repression of the revolt by Maher
al-Asad, Bashar's brother, was followed by a more conciliatory
policy. Upon the outbreak of the Syrian rebellion the regime
sought to reinforce their neutrality by announcing that Syrian
citizenship would be granted to the Kurdish *biduns* and in 2012
withdrew forces from the Kurdish region in the northeast, preferring to employ them in other parts of the country. The vacuum thus created enabled the strongest Kurdish Syrian party,
the PYD (the Democratic Union Party), to expand its influence
in the Kurdish region. The PYD was founded in 2003 as the
Syrian affiliate of the radical Kurdish party in Turkey, the PKK.
This regime policy helps explain the Syrian Kurds' neutrality
when the Syrian rebellion broke out in 2011.

It was the rise of IS in 2013–14 that finally drew the Syrian
Kurds into the Syrian civil war—not as opponents of the regime but as defenders of their own territory. As it was building
its territorial state, IS focused its early effort in eastern and
northern Syria and began to attack and occupy Kurdish areas.
The Kurdish defensive effort was led by the PYD and its militia,
the YPG (People's Protection Units). The fiercest fighting between the parties took place in the city of Kobane on the Turkish border and ended in 2015 with a Kurdish victory. The battle
for Kobane marked also the escalation of US and international

military roles in the conflict. Turkey remained neutral during the struggle over Kobane but did allow several hundred Peshmerga fighters from Iraqi Kurdistan to cross its territory in order to reinforce the Syrian Kurds. Turkey had a good working relationship with the authorities of the autonomous Kurdish area in northern Iraq and was hoping that the Iraqi Kurds would exercise a restraining influence over their Syrian brethren.

The battle of Kobane was a turning point in Turkey's relationship with the Syrian Kurds. While Turkey reached a modus vivendi with the Iraqi Kurds predicated on the Kurdish decision not to cross the line from autonomy to independence, its relationship with the PYD was tense, and it became increasingly alarmed by the PYD's successes. In Turkish eyes, the PYD was simply a branch of the PKK, the radical wing of Turkey's Kurds headed by Abdallah Ocalan. Ocalan—who was in Turkish jail under death penalty after years of exile in Syria—was a Marxist who changed his party's doctrine in the aftermath of the Soviet Union's collapse. He adopted a doctrine of communalism derived from the writings of the fairly obscure American Jewish intellectual Murray Bookchin. Turkey was horrified by the prospect of an autonomous Kurdish area on their southern border and particularly by the prospect of continuity between the Syrian and Iraqi Kurds and of Kurdish expansion westward toward the Mediterranean, and Turkey's relationship with the Syrian Kurds was further poisoned by the collapse of Erdogan's relationship with the Kurdish Turks after the 2015 Turkish parliamentary elections. The partnership between the United States and the Syrian Kurds that began after the battle of Kobane reinforced Turkey's concern. From Washington's point of view on the other hand, the YPG was the single most effective local force in fighting IS. The Kurds provided "boots on the ground," so the United States could limit itself to using airpower and deploying a limited number of special forces. Turkish sensitivity aside, The United States was not willing to give up the collaboration with the YPG. From Erdogan's perspective, his NATO ally should not have allied itself with his domestic enemy. Turkey's anger at this further encouraged Erdogan to ally himself with Russia in the Syrian context.

Later, in October 2015 with US encouragement, the YPG formed a larger entity, the SDF (Syrian Democratic Forces). The SDF was another umbrella organization under whose wings other ethnic groups, namely Arabs, Armenians, and Assyrians, could take part in the fighting against IS. It was also a measure designed to reduce the tension created by Kurdish control of mixed areas in which the Kurds were actually a minority. At some point the Kurds—both directly and through the SDF—in fact controlled more than 25 percent of Syria's territory. The YPG and the SDF fought against IS and *not* against the regime (both in line with US policy and of their own choice). At no point did Kurds raise the prospect of secession or sovereignty; their more realistic goal was autonomy in the context of a Syrian federation. But while Russia advocated at different points the notion of a federation as part of a fundamental political solution to the Syrian crisis, this was never acceptable to the regime. As will be described below, President Trump's decision in December 2018 to withdraw his troops from Syria posed a question mark as to the future of Syria's Kurds.

Varieties of Local Reality: Life under the Opposition

At the height of the civil war, a large part of Syria's territory was governed by different opposition groups. This led to stark differences between different parts of the country, as the civilian population was governed and administered by radically different groups.

The IS-Controlled Area

Between 2014 and 2017, a large part of northeastern Syria was controlled and governed by IS. The organization tried to endow its territorial Caliphate with the properties of a state. The Islamic State established an alternative system of governance to that of the Asad regime, providing the population under its control with services and humanitarian aid that included food, water, clothing, fuel, electricity, medical services, and sanitation. In fact, one of IS's main projects was the provision of water and electricity to the population. The group managed the electric power stations in al-Raqqah and Aleppo in Syria and operated the al-Tabaqa Dam and the Lake Asad Dam on the Euphrates River, which supply electricity to the city of Aleppo. When the education system ceased functioning in Syria (especially in Aleppo and al-Raqqah), IS established elementary and high schools for the local populace.

The group worked to institute order and security through the use of policing and law enforcement apparatuses. The Islamic State established Islamic religious courts in a number of cities in northern Syria, which were designed—like other mechanisms of enforcement—to demonstrate the organization's power, to establish its status among the local population, and to prove its ability to effectively administer daily life in contrast to the ineffectiveness of the Asad regime. In Aleppo and al-Raqqah, they operated a morality police force (*al-hisba*). The Islamic State also issued an official passport of the Islamic Caliphate in July 2014. In a similar vein, in November 2014, it introduced its own currency and minted a series of coins in Syria. (These were never used and were issued primarily as a propaganda measure.) Another aspect of IS's introduced governance was the collection of taxes from the population. In fact, revenue from tax collection was one of the most important sources of income for this unusually wealthy terrorist organization.

The semblance of normalcy cultivated by IS could hardly mask the harsh reality of a population living in fear under terrorist rule.

Southern Syria

The region of southern Syria, also known as the Houran, with its capital in Dar'a, had both symbolic and a practical importance during the civil war. Dar'a was the cradle of the Syrian uprising, and the region also occupies a strategic position—close to the Jordanian border and to the Damascus countryside as well as to Israel. Between 2014 and 2018 the Houran and the Quneitra region were controlled by the armed opposition and the FSA, with the regime and the Islamic State trying to undermine it. In theory, the secular armed opposition was unified within the framework of the Southern Front, but in practice that front was a loose federation of almost fifty different local organizations (of the fifty, only twenty at most were large and cohesive enough to be counted as real organizations). Islamist groups, mainly Ahrar al-Sham and al-Nusra, challenged the dominance of the FSA in the region.[26]

The character of the armed opposition and the conduct of daily life during this period were influenced by the important roles still played by the three largest tribal groups in the region, the Zu'bis, the Hariris, and the Rifa'is. A sizable portion of the million or so inhabitants was made up of these sedentary tribes. Governance was provided by several actors: the armed groups, local councils, the main court known as Dar al-Adl (House of

Justice), and a Shura (consultative) Council. The main court dispensing justice in the province—Dar al-Adl, situated in Gharz, just east of the city of Dar'a—was staffed by professional judges and lawyers, and its work was respected by both the armed and the tribal groups. These different actors formed "some sort of hybrid, rebelocracy, that could potentially act as a semi-legitimate replacement for the Syrian government and is able to provide a level of normalcy and security to the population."[27] Security, such as it was, was provided by local forces, but the provision of services and commodities could not be implemented without external aid. Control of the provision of this aid was one of the most fiercely contested issues between the military and civilian actors on the ground.

Life under the Opposition: Idlib

The province of Idlib has played a particularly important role in the history of the Syrian civil war.[28] Lying at the country's northwestern corner, it shares a border with Turkey and is close to Aleppo, Hama, and the Alawi country. The first serious military response by the opposition to the regime took place in Jisr al-Shughur in the governorate of Idlib in June 2011. Contiguity with Turkey facilitated massive support to rebel groups from across the border. In the summer of 2012, the rebels took over the Bab al-Hawa border crossing; with Turkey, by 2014 rebel groups took over most of the province's larger territory, confining the regime to a few reinforced cities and towns and military bases. In March 2015, the newly announced Army of Conquest coalition captured the provincial capital. The opposition's military exploits in Idlib played a major role in Russia's decision to intervene militarily in Syria. At the time of the writing of this book (mid-2020), Idlib remains to this day the last rebel stronghold.

As the only province in Syria almost fully controlled by the opposition, Idlib became a significant arena for the opposition's building of an alternative to the regime, and for the opposition's challenge to the regime's claim to legitimacy through the continuity of state institutions. The opposition tried to provide basic services to a population of over three million through the construction of 144 local councils, and also by experimenting in a participatory government of sorts. But the Idlib provincial councils were only one set of the actors competing for influence in the province. The regime continued to pay salaries as well—to at least some of the government employees—as a way of preserving its status and influence. Powerful local families also exercised their influence in the province in civilian-built organizations, including the two most powerful armed groups, Ahrar al-Sham (who built the Service Administration Commission, or SAC) and Hay'at Tahrir al-Sham (who organized the Public Service Administration, or PSA and later the Salvation Government). Also active in Idlib from across the Turkish border was the Syrian Interim Government. All these groups and actors competed with one another over the provision of services and control of the local population. The result was inefficiency and a weakening of the opposition's claim to serve as a real, functioning alternative to the regime. A strict version of Islamic law was administered under the strong influence of the Islamist groups (though not as harshly as in the ISIL-dominated area), and minorities such as Druze and Shi'i were persecuted. In Jabal al-Soumak near the Turkish border in 2015, al-Nusra fanatics massacred part of the local Druze population and forced others to convert to mainstream Islam. The massacre reverberated across Syria, indicative of the FSA's decline in not just Idlib but Syria as a whole, as it began to position and influence in 2016.

After the end of the full-fledged civil war in Syria in December 2016, Idlib remained the last stronghold of the opposition. The conflict in and over Idlib in the years 2017–20 is described and analyzed below.

War by Other Means: The Intellectual and Cultural Arena

During the decades that preceded the outbreak of the civil war, the Ba'th regime's policy toward and relations with the intellectual, cultural, and artistic communities in Syria were not dissimilar from those of other dictatorial regimes. The regime had little patience for dissent and criticism and had no hesitation in throwing its critics in jail or encouraging their departure from the country. On the other hand, the regime attributed great importance to Syria's position as a major Arab cultural hub. So they also appreciated the prestige and legitimacy that the importance of Syrian theater, cinema, television shows, poetry, and other literature provided. The regime also realized that a *limited* degree of criticism was an important safety valve to release some of the pressure created by public dissatisfaction with the regime or its policies. It therefore allowed broad criticism as long as the legitimacy of the regime or the leader and his family were not criticized directly. The artistic and cultural community, for its part, knew these red lines and so directed its criticism at large issues such as corruption, inefficiency, or the ills of Arab society and politics in general. This was to some degree also a symbiotic relationship: most of the artistic and cultural community found its modus vivendi with the regime, studying in institutions paid for by the state, and producing films, plays, and television series that were funded by the government.

Many of these productions were distributed and shown around the Arab world; artists such as the playwright Sa'dallah Wanus[29] and the comic actor Durayd al-Lahham were household names in the region. Wanus was in fact openly critical of Arab politics and regimes and of the Syrian regime in particular, so much so that at some point his plays could not be produced in Syria. But in 2007, when Syria was chosen as the Arab Capital of Culture for 2008 (a UNESCO initiative), the production of a Wanus play was permitted. Furthermore, the play was directed by Na'ila al-Atrash, a critic of the regime who in 2000 had signed "the petition of the 99" and in 2001 had been fired from her post in the High Institute of Theater Arts in Damascus. It was a very good example of the delicate interplay between the regime's authoritarianism and its quest for legitimacy and prestige.[30] This delicate dance applied to the majority of the artistic and cultural community—but not to all. Some artists went further and participated in the Damascus Spring of 2001–2, criticizing the regime openly for the crackdown that ended the period of broader freedoms, and willing to pay the price for their principled position.

The three great men of Syrian letters, the poets Adonis and Nizar al-Qabbani, and the philosopher Sadiq al-Azm, were in a category by themselves owing to their prominence in Syria and the Arab world. Adonis, who was born in an Alawi village, spent his time outside Syria and settled in Paris. During the reign of Hafez al-Asad, Adonis returned for a few years to Damascus and published a regular column in the government newspaper *Al-Thawrah*—but his collaboration with its editor, Ali Suleiman, irritated the authorities because it was seen by them, in the words of Adonis, as "a garden of freedom"[31] and was terminated. Adonis moved to Paris, where he still lives. Qabbani had in fact served for a while as a Syrian diplomat but resigned in 1966 (without publicly criticizing the regime) and chose to live in Europe. His poetry was bitterly critical of the Arab condition and politics but was not directed specifically at the regime. Before he died in 1998, he asked to be buried in Syria. Finally, Sadiq al-Azm, a scion of a great Damascus family, was a Marxist philosopher and professor of philosophy. He taught in Lebanon and got in trouble when he published a critique of Islam. Al-Azm then spent time in European and American institutions, before returning in 1995 to Syria as chairman of the Department of Philosophy at the University of Damascus. He knew full well the limitations of functioning within the Syrian system and was willing to navigate within those familiar red lines in return for the ability to live in and make a contribution to his beloved community in Damascus. But in 1999, al-Azm had exhausted his ability to coexist with the regime and was pushed to leave. Al-Azm spoke openly about the dilemma of coexisting with the regime in one of his interviews:

> This reality constituted a type of inferiority complex (in me and in others) due to my impotence in the face of this military regime's overall power, as well as due to the impossibility of pronouncing a possible "no" against it (individually or collectively). I dealt with this inferiority complex by adapting slowly to this stressful tyrannical reality, and through the careful introspection of the rules and principles of interacting with it, with all that's required of hypocrisy and pretending to believe and accept, secrecy, word manipulation and circumvention of the regime's brute force. Otherwise, I wouldn't have been able to either continue with my normal life and do my routine work and daily errands, or preserve my mental and physical health.[32]

When the Syrian insurrection broke out in 2011, al-Azm became one of its most prominent intellectual supporters. At that point a controversy erupted between him and Adonis. Although Adonis did publish an open letter to Bashar al-Asad in 2011 that was critical of the regime, Adonis later moderated his criticism of the regime, arguing that the radical Muslim opposition was not preferable to the Asads. Sadiq al-Azm and others reprimanded Adonis for failing to criticize the regime and not supporting the revolution more forcefully; Adonis argued back that the Islamists were just as objectionable and harmful to Syria.[33]

The outbreak of the civil war changed the rules of the game for the larger community of Syrian artists and intellectuals. Some chose to openly support the opposition and the insurrection, while others chose (or were prompted) to defend the regime. The artists who remained in Syria and openly criticized the regime paid a steep price: the cartoonist Ali Farzat was attacked by Shabiha thugs, who broke his arms and hands. The singer Ibrahim Qashush, credited with the most popular anti-Bashar popular song, "Yalla Erhal Ya Bashar" (Go Away, Bashar), was found dead on July 2011, his throat cut and his vocal cords ripped out. The bulk of the community, however, remained passive, trying to continue with their life and work as best they could. It was difficult to maintain the pre–civil war routine even in Damascus, but some artistic productions continued. Like the urban bourgeoisie, as Islamists and Jihadists took over the opposition, that segment of the artistic and cultural community reluctantly came to prefer the regime over the prospect of Islamist or Jihadi control. Over time, though, more and more artists found the situation in Syria intolerable and left. By 2014, their ranks outside Syria had swelled. Realizing the cost of coming out publicly against the regime in Syria, they preferred to leave the country and find refuge in Turkey, Europe, and—more rarely—the United States. The Alawi actress Fadwa Suleiman, who demonstrated against the regime in

Homs, went into hiding and eventually left for Turkey and France. So did the actress May Scaff. Yaahya Hawwa, another popular singer and author of numerous protest songs, found herself on the Ministry of Interior's "wanted list" and escaped to Jordan. The theater director Na'ila al-Atrash left Syria for the United States. Other exiled and expatriate Syrian artists, including the well-known American Syrian singer Omar Offendum, continued to perform in Europe and in the United States. Curiously the novelist Khaled Khalifa, a critic of the regime, some of whose books were published in English during the civil war, remained in Syria, unharmed by the regime. In all likelihood his international reputation has protected him from regime persecution.

Anxious about the negative impact of the artistic and cultural community's perceived support of the opposition; in 2011 the regime organized a supportive petition signed by a hundred artists. The petition received a surprising endorsement by Syria's best-known comic actor, Durayd al-Lahham. Lahham had become famous in the Arab world for playing the role of "Ghawar" (a comic figure) in several movies and series. Over the years Lahham made critical comments about Arab politics and politicians and collaborated with the playwright Muhammad al-Maghut—who knew well how to play the game of attacking corruption, inefficiency, and national weakness in the Arab world without directly criticizing the Ba'th regime. Lahham spoke about his criticism and its limits in a number of press interviews over the years. He told the *New York Times* in August 2006: "Yeah, I felt disappointed. We had thought that artwork could shock and make change but no. Artwork at the end of the day even if it's critical is internment."[34]

So it was surprising that al-Lahham came out publicly in 2011 in support of the regime, and of the Iranian supreme leader,

Ali Khamenei, whom he praised for his Syrian policy. It may have been that, in the reality of the Syrian civil war when sectarian identity seemed to dominate, al-Lahham's Shi'i affiliation shaped his conduct. Al-Lahham was also joined in this support of the regime by the musician George Wasuf; the vaudeville actor Hamam Hutt began by supporting the regime but when the war reached his native Aleppo turned against it.

Another ardent supporter of the regime was the actor Zuhayr Ramadan, who was president of the Artists Syndicate. Ramadan became famous in Syria and the larger Arab world by playing the role of Abu Jawdat, the chief of a police station in the popular series *Bab al-Hara*. Ramadan was elected to his position in 2014 and proceeded to go after several artists who had criticized the regime and chosen to live in exile. He accused them of contributing to "shedding Syrian blood by supporting the opposition or by calling for military intervention in Syria."[35] Ramadan, in turn, was bitterly criticized by his victims: the opposition actor and a member of the Cairo Conference of the Syrian opposition Jamal Suleiman, for example, accused Ramadan of being a "fascist Shabih"[36] (a member of the Shabiha). It was easier for the regime to enlist the support of lesser artists— figures such as Najdat Anzur, a director who also served as deputy and interim speaker of the People's Assembly, who in 2012 produced *King of the Sands*, a film critical of the House of Saud.

The conflict between the regime's artistic supporters and opponents was also conducted on the larger Arab stage. In 2011, in film festivals held in Dubai and Cairo, Syrian opposition filmmakers objected to the presentation of films made by directors who received Syrian governmental support. The organizers responded by removing the regime-supported films from the list.[37]

Most of the artistic opposition to the regime took place on the web. It was impossible to stage theater productions or show films that were critical of the regime and supportive of the insurrection, but shorter videos could be broadcast easily through Facebook and other forms of social media. Sadiq al-Azm described this form of resistance in the following way: "Add to that the various innovative art, music, performances, plays, dances, balloons, prayers, satirical cartoons, sarcastic comments and critical graffiti that this revolutionary generation resorts to in resistance and you have what I would call the finest hour of Syrian civil society."[38]

These forms of protest and resistance produced a new crop of popular artists and performers, like the soccer player Abd al-Baset Sarut in Homs and the musical band Ahrar al-Sham (not to be confused with the rebel militia Ahrar al-Sham). Some of these had a huge following in the Arab world. Best known among them was the puppeteer group known as Masasit Mati. Their most popular show was called *Top Goon: Diaries of a Little Dictator*. Bashar was represented in the cast by a puppet known by the diminutive "Beeshu." This form of opposition was no match for the regime's airplanes and tanks, but it played an important role in mobilizing parts of the Syrian public as well as support for the insurrection in the Arab world.

By 2014—and in even greater numbers in subsequent years—a significant portion of Syria's artists and intellectuals had left the country. They created large, vibrant communities of expatriates but left a gaping void in Syria. It is an open question today as to whether and how soon the regime will be able to rebuild a Syria that can accommodate and draw home this exiled elite.[39]

CHAPTER 4

The Regional Arena

In 1965 the British Syria expert Patrick Seale published his now classic work *The Struggle for Syria*, in which he describes how regional and international actors fought over control of the weak Syrian state during the country's first thirteen years of independence. Control of Syria was seen at the time as a key to regional hegemony. The Syrians, buffeted by domestic conflict and external intervention, sought refuge in a political union with Egypt in 1958 that ultimately broke apart in 1961. Nine years later, after for Hafez al-Asad seized total power in a coup, the country's new strongman began building a powerful Syrian state that would gradually assume a leading role in Arab and Middle Eastern politics. The Syrian civil war of the years 2011–20 resurrected the previous struggle for Syria, as once again regional and international actors—acting both directly and through proxies—sought to shape and control a Syria that was both fractured and perceived as key to the region. While the international actors remained the same, the regional actors changed, with Iran, Turkey, and Israel playing major roles.[1]

Iranian Policy

Alongside Russia, whose policies toward Syria will be discussed in the next chapter, Iran has been Bashar al-Asad's most consistent supporter. As early as March 25, 2011, after the first wave of street protests against the regime in largely Sunni cities, the late Qasem Suleimani, then commander of the Quds Force, an elite fighting unit of Iran's Revolutionary Guards, was in Damascus to persuade the Syrian leadership to follow the Iranian example in 2009 and harshly suppress the opposition. By April, Teheran rallied to the side of its Syrian ally by offering logistics, instruction, and intelligence—assistance that has continued to this day. During this period Iran's policy went through several phases, and its straightforward support of a beleaguered ally evolved into a determined quest to use Tehran's new position in Syria to implement its own ambitious regional policy.[2]

When the Syrian rebellion broke out in 2011, Iran and Syria had been allies for more than thirty years. Hafez al-Asad and Iran's new leaders formed an alliance in the aftermath of the 1979 Iranian Revolution that built on a set of shared interests: common enmity to Iraq, the United States, and Israel; Syria's willingness to provide Iran with access to its Shi'i constituency in Lebanon; and Tehran's willingness to offer Syria's Alawi rulers Islamic legitimacy. Syria provided Iran with access to the core area of the Middle East and to Israel's borders, not just in Lebanon but also in the Palestinian arena, through support of Hamas and Islamic Jihad. The relationship, however, was not free of tension. Both countries competed for influence in Lebanon and its Shi'i community. While Damascus supported the majority Shi'a Amal movement, Tehran cultivated the Shi'a Islamist militant group and political party Hezbollah as the chief instrument of its Lebanese policy. There were also tensions

between the two countries arising from Asad's participation in
the US-led peace process, and by the prospect of Syrian-Israeli
peace and Syrian rapprochement with the United States. (The
eventual collapse of the peace process in 1996 and again in 2011
would relieve this Iranian concern.)

The relationship underwent a change when Bashar al-Asad
succeeded his father in 2000. What had been a genuine alliance
gradually acquired the character of a patron-client relationship.
Tehran was worried again by the improvement in Bashar's relationship with Washington after 2008, and by his indirect negotiations with Israel through Turkish mediation in 2008–9, and
through Washington in 2010–11. But when the rebellion against
Bashar broke out and acquired momentum in the spring of 2011,
Tehran did not hesitate to rally to his support. From its perspective, Syria was its most important Arab ally and a crucial link to
its most successful foreign policy investment—namely Lebanon and Hezbollah. The prospect of a threat to Hezbollah's position in Lebanon and an opposition victory—the fall of the
Asad regime, and a potential takeover by groups close to Saudi
Arabia and the West—were simply unacceptable to Iran.[3]

Iran's support of the Bashar al-Asad regime was initially
given primarily by several hundred members of the IRGC (Islamic Revolutionary Guard Corps) and its Quds Force and
consisted of military supplies, intelligence sharing, and training.
The Iranians who had acquired experience in neutralizing civilian resistance in 2009 offered the regime crucial help in sup-
pressing communication among the local coordination committees in the spring and summer of 2011. Likewise, Iranians
who had developed their own popular militia (Basij) helped the
regime transform its Alawi militias (the Shabiha) into a more
effective fighting force. By the end of 2011, Iran also began supporting the intervention of the Lebanese Hezbollah in the

fighting. Hezbollah's intervention became more substantial in 2013 and was particularly evident in the battle of al-Qusayr close to the Syrian-Lebanese border in May that year.[4] In time, more militias composed of Pakistani and Afghan Shi'is were trained in Iran and sent to Syria. By some estimates the number of the Shi'i militiamen in Syria grew to exceed twenty thousand.[5] Their members were paid by the Iranians and were promised residence and occasionally even citizenship in Iran. These Shi'i militias— and the support given by Turkey, Saudi Arabia, and Jordan to the military opposition—reinforced the sense and perception that the conflict in Syria was in fact a Shi'i-Sunni confrontation.

Iranian support for the Asad regime in its war with the op- position would not include direct participation in the fighting by Iranian forces until 2014. By then (and even more since Sep- tember 2015), as the regime encountered growing difficulties in dealing with military opposition, Iran abandoned its policy of indirect military intervention in Syria altogether and dispatched thousands of fighters to join the fighting in Syria from the Quds Force and the regular Iranian army. This change in policy was driven by the exacerbation of the opposition's challenge to the regime, as well as the emergence of IS, which Iran considered to be a significant threat to Iran itself.

By the middle of 2017, Iranian forces and its allied Shi'i mili- tias had lost, by some estimates, more than two thousand fight- ers in Syria[6] (this figure does not include the several thousand casualties sustained by Hezbollah), which began to provoke criticism in Iran. Iranian regime spokesmen felt compelled to defend the investment in Syria, and the spiritual leader himself, in January 2017, stated in an address to the families of Iranian commandos killed in Syria that "if the ill-wishers and sedition- ists, who are the puppets of the US and Zionism, had not been confronted [in Syria], we should have stood against them in

Tehran, Fars, Khorasan and Isfahan."[7] Other spokesmen provided a more graphic argument. Mehdi Taeb, a member of the spiritual leader's inner circle, stated in February 2013, "Syria is [Iran's] 35th province, and it is a strategic province for us. If the enemy attacks us and wants to take Syria or Khuzestan [an Iranian province], our top priority will be to preserve Syria. By preserving Syria, we will be able to retake Khuzestan—but if we lose Syria, we will not be able to preserve Tehran."[8]

The person most prominently associated with Iran's military intervention in Syria and its ambitious regional policies is the aforementioned, late Qasem Suleimani. Suleimani's influence and impact extended far beyond his official position as head of the elite Quds fighting force. As the chief Iranian advocate for an ambitious, activist policy in Syria, Suleimani seems to have acted on several occasions on his own without obtaining prior approval by higher authority. With Suleimani persuing his own line, there were indications of disagreements within the Iranian regime over the country's Syria policy.[9] And yet, curiously for someone so closely identified with Iran's relationship with the Asad regime and its investment in its preservation, Suleimani also occasionally spoke derisively about the regime's poor performance in the civil war. This may have reflected genuine exasperation with his partners—but perhaps also stemmed from the familiar sense of Persian superiority over the Arabs. The impact on Syria of Suleimani's killing by the Trump administration in January 2020 is yet to be determined.

It was this same Suleimani who, in July 2015, shortly after the signing of the agreement on the suspension of the Iranian nuclear program, flew to Moscow—almost certainly to persuade the Russians to intervene militarily in the Syrian civil war. The Russians would do so in September. Russia, too, was sensitive to potential losses in Syria and crafted a form of military collaboration with Iran according to which Russia provided the air support and Iran provided the "boots on the ground," largely through Shi'i militias but also through its own forces. This collaboration manifested itself most prominently in the offensive in Aleppo that ended in December 2016 with a victory for the regime and its Russian and Iranian supporters. This was a decisive turning point in the war between regime and opposition and led to a systematic mopping-up military campaign to defeat the remaining opposition strongholds.

The military successes achieved by the trilateral effort of the Asad regime, Russia, and Iran inflated Iran's self-confidence. Once the Syrian regime's victory in the conflict seemed secure, particularly after the capture of Aleppo in December 2016, the Iranian leadership sought to expand on its success and further its regional influence. Until 2011, Syria's value for Iran was primarily for its provision of access to Lebanon and Hezbollah. After its successful military intervention in Syria, Iran looked on Syria as an asset in its own right. It sought Syrian agreement to build a naval base on the Syrian coast, and to embed itself in Syria with a strategic infrastructure that would include long-range missiles and missile production facilities. The Iranian leadership became interested in transforming itself from a power in the eastern periphery of the Middle East to a power with naval and land presence in the Mediterranean and on its coast via "a land bridge" through Iraq and Syria to Lebanon. Iranian supplies to Lebanon had previously been provided by air, by sea, and only occasionally over land. The air route required Iraqi permission (not difficult to obtain, but not necessarily secure in the long range), and the sea route was lengthy and exposed to potential interception. In November 2016, the chief of staff of the Iranian army, General Mohammed Husein

Bakri, declared before an assembly of Iranian naval commanders that in the future, Iran might construct long-range naval bases on coasts, on islands, or as floating bases, and that it could possibly build bases on the coast of Yemen or Syria.

While clearly motivated in part as a deterrent to its enemies in Washington and Jerusalem, Iran's leadership has also been motivated by a quest for regional hegemony. This quest comes from two very different sources: a religious/ideological drive to export the (Shi'i) Islamic revolution, and the geopolitical ambitions of a powerful regional actor that still recalls its own glorious imperial past. This new Iranian mood was obvious by 2014, when IRGC commander Brigadier General Husein Salami stated that "Iran is more powerful that in any other time and our defense power against the enemies cannot be compared to the past. . . . Today we are able to hit all the vital interests of the enemies at any point in the region. . . . Today the regional Iran is turning into a global Iran. . . . While one day our nation was fighting the enemy at borders of Karkheh River (in southwestern Iran) now it has expanded its strategic borders . . . to the east of the Mediterranean and North Africa."[10]

The new swagger coming from Teheran and the Iranians' high mood exacerbated existing tensions between Tehran and Asad's regime. On July 13, 2018, Ali Akbar Velayati, international affairs adviser to Iran's supreme leader, gave a lecture to the Russian Valdai Club in which he boasted that the Asad regime would have fallen in weeks had it not been for the Iranian intervention in the Syrian war. The regime responded indirectly through the Syrian newspaper *Al-Watan* and Syrian journalist Firas Aziz al-Dib, who wrote,

This is an exaggeration, which we have become accustomed to hearing from numerous Iranian media outlets or political

commentators or from the lips of blatant Iran supporters. . . .
We have also become accustomed to hearing such exaggeration from figures representing Iran's official stream, from the
president to the ministers and down to the junior officials—
for example, the April 2016 [statement] by Iranian President
Hassan Rouhani at the Environment, Religion, and Culture
conference in the capital Tehran: "Without the Islamic Republic, Damascus and Baghdad would have fallen to IS." But
this may be one of the rare times we hear such statements from
figures directly representing [supreme] leader Khamenei.[11]

During 2017–18 Iran's investment in Syria deepened. Iran
shared with Russia a determination to help the regime to complete its victory; to perpetuate its presence and position in Syria
and consolidate its position; to launch a process of reconstruction; and to reap economic benefits from the economic reconstruction. But Iran was also now determined to build in Syria
that military infrastructure and presence that would create a
second line of confrontation with Israel, comparable to and
possibly superior to the assets it already has in Lebanon. To that
end it sought to build missile bases deep in Syria's territory, to
build facilities for the production of precision guided missiles,
to acquire air and naval facilities, and to station its Shi'i militias
in Syria.

The motivation for undertaking such a massive investment—
and the risks it entailed—was driven at its core by a deep,
powerful antagonism toward Israel and Zionism. As the leading
expert on Iranian policies and politics Karim Sadjapour wrote
in 2016,

> Distilled to its essence, Teheran's steadfast support for Asad
> is not driven by the geopolitical or financial interests of the
> Iranian nation, nor the religious convictions of the Islamic

Republic, but by a visceral and seemingly inextinguishable hatred of the state of Israel. Senior Iranian officials like Ali Akbar Velayati . . . have commonly said "The chain of resistance against Israel by Iran, Syria, Hezbollah, the new Iraqi government and Hamas passes through the Syrian highway. . . . Syria is the golden ring of the chain of resistance against Israel." Though Israel has virtually no direct impact on the daily lives of Iranians, opposition to the Jewish state has been the most enduring pillar of Iranian revolutionary ideology. Whether Khamenei is giving a speech about agriculture or education, he invariably returns to the evils of Zionism.[12]

But there was more to the anti-Israeli activism of 2018 than just hatred and ideology. Sunni Arabs were very angry at Iran's role in quashing and killing Sunni Syrians on behalf of the Asad regime. The Iranian leadership knew this full well and therefore had a clear interest in depicting the Syrian crisis as an Arab-Israeli issue, instead of as a war between Sunnis and Alawis.

In February 2018, Iran dispatched an armed drone into Israeli airspace from the Tiyas military air base, also known as the T-4 in central Syria. It is not clear what motivated Iran to this action, but whatever it was, it triggered a wave of Israeli attacks on Iranian targets in Syria that aimed to destroy or damage the military infrastructure Iran was trying to construct in Syria. For over six months, Israel enjoyed freedom of action in this regard. The Trump administration was supportive of Israel's actions, and Russia did not interfere—as long as Israel was attacking only Iranian (rather than Russian or regime) targets. On September 18, 2018, Syrian air defense finally ended this permissive state for Israel, when it mistakenly shot down a Russian plane, killing its crew of fifteen. Russia took advantage of this incident to suspend its tolerance of Israel's offensive against Iran's military buildup in Syria, thus enabling the Iranians to continue their campaign almost unhindered. This phase lasted for several months, but eventually the Israeli-Russian relationship was mended. Israel resumed its raids against the Iranian buildup in Syria so much so that in the spring of 2020 some reports suggested that because of these attacks or other pressures (the economic crisis and the challenge of the coronavirus pandemic) Iran either reduced its forces in Syria or redeployed some of them to the country's northern and eastern parts. Yet Iran's long-term quest to embed itself in Syria and to penetrate Syrian society, politics, and economy remains unchanged.

Turkish Policy

In some ways, Turkey is the perfect counterpart to Iran in the Syrian crisis.[13] Like Iran, it is a successor state to a former Middle Eastern empire, a country with a population of over eighty million with powerful military forces, a strong economy, and a sophisticated elite. Unlike Iran, however, it shares a long border with Syria, and its political system is therefore very sensitive to developments south of that border and particularly to the relationship between the Syrian Kurds and the radical Kurdish opposition in Turkey. Turkey is also a Sunni Muslim state and, since Erdogan's rise to power, has been dominated by an Islamist regime promoting politics and policies inspired by a version of Sunni Islamism close to that of the Muslim Brotherhood. As we have seen, in the late spring of 2011, Turkey became a critic and an opponent of Bashar al-Asad and a major supporter of the Syrian opposition. But unlike Iran's single-minded and consistent support of the regime, Turkish policy has undergone several major changes. Since 2014, Turkey's policy toward

Syria has been compounded by multiple and often contradictory considerations.

The long history of hostility between Syria and Turkey dates
back to the eve of World War II, thanks to Syria's persistent irredentist claims to the region of Alexandretta, which had been
annexed by Turkey just before the war, as well as to Syria's support of the radical wing of the Kurdish opposition in Turkey. At
the height of the Cold War, Turkey was a full NATO member
while Syria was a Soviet ally and client. Turkish-Syrian tensions
came to a head when Turkey threatened to go to war over Syria's
hosting of Abdallah Ocalan, the leader of the radical Marxist-
Kurdish opposition party PKK in 1998. Faced with this Turkish
threat, Hafez al-Asad backed down and expelled Ocalan, who
was captured by Turkey, imprisoned, and sentenced to death.

In the years before the outbreak of the Syrian insurrection,
the new Syrian regime under Bashar presided over a Turkish-
Syrian rapprochement. Turkey's rulers wished to enhance its
influence in the Arab world, while for Bashar the rapprochement was an opportunity to reduce tensions with a powerful
neighbor. Erdogan and Bashar al-Asad were able to put this
legacy of mutual hostility behind them and began to form a
close relationship. Erdogan served as a mentor to the younger
Asad, and Turkey made significant investments in Syria and
used its territory to transport goods to the Arabian Peninsula.
In 2008, Turkey even served as a mediator between Syria and
Israel in an effort to reach a peace settlement.

When the antiregime demonstrations broke out in Syria in
March 2011, Erdogan tried to persuade Bashar to calm the situation by offering meaningful concessions to his critics. His foreign minister, Ahmet Davutoglu, made several visits to Damascus, and Bashar promised to accommodate him. But Bashar's
promises to heed his mentor's good advice were never kept. A

disillusioned Davutoglu stated, "We wanted [Asad] to be the Gorbachev of Syria, but he chose to be a Milosevich; that is a problem."[14] A spurned Erdogan was even more hyperbolic, equating Asad with Mussolini and Hitler.[15] By May 2011, Turkey was calling for Bashar's resignation and beginning to extend support to the opposition.

Turkey would in fact become the most important military and political base of the Syrian opposition. The political opposition held its first meetings in Turkey, which was also the location of the Free Syrian Army's external headquarters. Alongside Saudi Arabia, Qatar, and Jordan, Turkey directly provided weapons and military support to the armed opposition. When Islamist elements began to play a dominant role in the opposition, Turkey—together with Qatar—promoted groups close to the Muslim Brotherhood. As the civil war intensified and Sunni Syrians began to escape, many of them crossed the border to Turkey; over time, Turkey came to host some 3.5 million Syrian refugees.

With the urging and active support of CIA director David Petraeus in 2012, Turkey was one of the states formally willing to participate in a program designed to train and equip several thousand Syrian fighters. The aim of this program was to form the nucleus of a moderate military force that would be a match to the Syrian armed forces and help bring about political change in Syria. Like its other partners to this plan, Turkey was disappointed by Obama's refusal to authorize the program. In 2013 Turkey was disappointed yet again, and probably more deeply, by Obama's failure to respect his own "red line." Yet despite this disappointment Turkey continued to support the political and military opposition together with Saudi Arabia and Qatar. In 2014, the Pentagon was authorized to lead a train-and-equip program for the Syrian opposition. It was in this framework that

Turkey created an operation room together with the United States north of the Syrian border (known as MOM).

But also in 2014, a series of developments began to unfold that would transform Turkey's policy from straightforward support of the Syrian opposition into conduct full of twists and turns.

One of these was the rise of IS, first in Iraq and then (since June 2014) in both Iraq and Syria. Turkey played a double game with the organization, taking exception to the organization's barbaric methods and—as a NATO member—officially opposing its agenda and terrorist activities. But Turkey also had an underlying sympathy for a Sunni movement fighting Shi'i domination in Iraq and a series of common enemies: first the Asad regime, and later the Kurds. In one of Turkey's early experiences with IS, Ankara was able to negotiate the release of the staff of its consulate in Mosul and thirty-five Turkish truck drivers that were taken hostage by the organization. These kinds of interactions led the Turkish regime to believe that it could selectively cooperate with IS, effectively "riding on the tiger's back."

Since 2013, Turkey was in fact the main gateway for Jihadi fighters from Europe and other parts of the world coming to join IS in Iraq and then in Syria. Islamic State fighters received medical treatment in Turkish hospitals; Turkish businessmen bought petrol from IS, helping to turn it into an unusually wealthy terrorist organization. The Islamic State relied on logistical support from across the Turkish border through Gaziantep and several other locations. There was even evidence of military supplies making their way to IS from Turkey's territory and this notwithstanding the Turkish government's insistence that it was not collaborating with IS.[16] But the relationship was not a simple one. The Islamic State could turn against Turkey at any time, and indeed in 2016–17 it threatened to launch terrorist activities against Turkey.

The pendulum began to swing back again when Turkey played an important role in the anti-IS coalition that the United States put together after September 2014. This role was solidified in 2015 after the terrorist attack in Suruc, and after the United States presented Turkey with evidence of the existence of several IS cells in Turkey.[17] But building the US-led coalition's cooperation with Turkey was not a simple task. It took General Allen, the US coordinator, ten visits to Erdogan in order to reach an eleven-point agreement in July 2015. The American warplanes that would play a major role in IS's defeat took off from three Turkish air bases, but Turkey insisted that it approve each and every sortie, and that other air forces would participate in the campaign as well, so as to make it look like a NATO rather than a US operation. Turkey did eventually claim credit in the West for its contribution, but the ambiguity over its relationship with IS lingered.

The complexity of Turkey's calculus and policy toward Syria was perfectly manifested in the battle of Kobane (September 2014 to March 2015). This mostly Kurdish town on the Turkish-Syrian border had been under the Kurdish PYD (Democratic Union Party) and YPG (People's Protection Units) control since 2012. In March 2014, the town was occupied by IS; for the rest of that year IS and the YPG fought over it. Throughout the months of vicious fighting the Turks refrained from offering Kurdish forces any help and, according to some reports, may have given some support to IS. But finally, by January 2015, the Kurds won control of the town. The costly victory in Kobane was a turning point in the PYD's ambitions and capabilities. Invigorated by their success, they now pressed forward in uniting the three Kurdish majority cantons along the

Turkish border into Rojava, the Kurdish federation. This dream was Turkey's nightmare—a nightmare exacerbated by the increased strength of mainstream Kurdish political parties inside Turkey itself. (In two successive elections in 2015 in Turkey, the mainstream Kurdish party for the first time obtained representation in parliament.) The last thing Turkey wanted to see was the creation of a second KRG (Iraqi Kurdistan) stretching along their border with Syria and possibly seeking access to the Mediterranean. Thwarting that ambition became a dominant element in Turkey's Syria policy by late 2015.

Then, in 2015, came Russia's military intervention in Syria. Turkey reacted sharply to this strategic change. It was hostile to Bashar al-Asad and was unhappy with a Russian military presence and air control infrastructure in its backyard. In November 2015 matters came to a head, when Turkey's air force shot down a Russian fighter jet. Putin responded with economic sanctions against Turkey, and Erdogan finally capitulated, apologizing and agreeing to a reconciliation meeting with Putin in August 2016. This was a major turning point in Turkish-Russian relations. Turkey adopted an entirely different tone regarding Russia's role in Syria, a mechanism for coordination between the two air forces was set up, and Turkey would eventually join the Russian-led peace process in Astana as well as other Russian initiatives.

This change of orientation reflected Turkey's coming to terms with Russia's military intervention and long-term involvement in the region. Turkey's response should be seen in the context of an American pivot away from this regional conflict and in the midst of significant irritants in the US-Turkish relationship, including Washington's harboring of Erdogan's arch enemy, Fethullah Gulen, a moderate Islamist leader considered the most serious challenger to Erdogan, who went into exile in Pennsylvania in 1999.

Tensions between the United States and Turkey over Syria were exacerbated further in 2015 by an American policy prioritizing above all the need to destroy the IS Caliphate, and the related decision to make the Syrian Kurds the main American allies in this endeavor. Washington remained determined not to become embroiled in fighting on the ground and found the Syrian Kurds to be the most effective anti-IS fighting force in the region. In October 2015 the United States created an anti-IS militia known as the SDF, the Syrian Democratic Forces, an essentially Kurdish entity that also included Arabs and other ethnic groups. Turkey bridled at this development, insisting that it empowered its arch enemy, the PKK, parent organization of the PYD.

By 2016, viewing the Kurdish PYD as the major threat to its interests in northern Syria, angry with US support for the Syrian Democratic Forces, and increasingly willing to work with Russia and Iran, Turkey decided to capture and occupy territory south of its border with Syria. To this end it launched two military campaigns. The first, code named "Euphrates Shield," was conducted between August 2016 and March 2017; using the label of the Free Syrian Army, Turkish and allied Syrian rebels occupied some two thousand square kilometers west of the Euphrates. Turkey claimed that the operation was aimed at both IS and the SDF, but the clear focus was in fact the SDF. Turkish conduct after the capture of this territory—notably its introduction into the region of the Turkish postal service, and the teaching of Turkish in the school system—reflected Ankara's intention to stay in the region. With this mission, Turkey's main goal of severing Kurdish contiguity along the Turkish Syrian border was accomplished. A second campaign, known as "Olive Branch," was launched by Turkey in January 2018. The target of this campaign was the city of Afrin. Although Turkey pretended once again to be targeting both IS and the Kurds, there was in fact no IS presence in Afrin. Russia and Iran meddled in the politics of the campaign as well. The city was taken in March 2018 after a ruthless campaign and massive flight of local residents. The one party not involved in the campaign, the United States, resigned itself to the idea that in order to preserve the Turkish alliance, the Kurds would have to give up their western possessions.

But Washington put its foot down when it came to Ankara's quest to also capture the town of Manbij. After a tense period in the American-Turkish relationship, Secretary of State Pompeo and Foreign Minister Caushoghlu were able to reach a compromise on joint Turkish-SDF patrols in charge of security in Manbij. And while Erdogan kept complaining about Washington's partnership with his Kurdish enemies and the asylum given to Gulen, Washington and Paris, too, were deeply disturbed by a NATO member's collaboration with Russia and particularly its decision to purchase the advanced Russian anticraft missiles known as S-400s (for subsequences developments in Turkey's Syria policy, see chapter 6 below).

Israeli Policy

One of the many ironies of the Syrian crisis was that during its first six years—from March 2011 to December 2016—of Syria's five neighbors, its nemesis, Israel, was the least involved in and least affected by the civil war raging north of its border. Israel's calculus and level of involvement underwent some changes but was not significantly transformed until the capture of Aleppo by the regime and its allies, signifying the regime's victory in the domestic civil war. This victory did not quite mean that the Syrian crisis was ending, or that a unified state controlling Syria was about to be reestablished. But it did mean that Israel had to assess the repercussions of a resuscitated Asad regime now controlling a large part of Syria under Russian and Iranian tutelage; an Iranian effort to construct an offensive military infrastructure in Syria; and the deployment of Syrian, Iranian, and Shiʿi militias in the Syrian Golan.

Israel's original response to the Syrian civil war was shaped by two decades of lingering hostility and sporadic diplomacy between the two countries. Since 1992 several Israeli prime ministers had negotiated seriously with Hafez and Bashar al-Asad in an effort to resolve the Israeli-Syrian conflict. Yitzhak Rabin, Shimon Peres, Benjamin Netanyahu, Ehud Barak, and Ehud Olmert all used different versions of a formula that included a willingness to withdraw from the Golan in return for a package of peace and security, modelled after the Israeli-Egyptian treaty of 1979. Time and again, however, the brink of peace was not crossed.[18] At the same time, the Asad regime continued to wage its conflict with Israel through its support for Hezbollah in Lebanon and Hamas in Gaza, and to bolster the regime's legitimacy by depicting it as the bastion of Arab resistance (*muqawama*) to the United States and Israel. The unsuccessful war in Lebanon in 2006 demonstrated to Israel the severity of the challenge posed by the Iranian-Hezbollah-Syrian axis. When the Obama administration launched a mediation effort between Israel and Syria in 2010, it was predicated not on the familiar "territories for peace" formula but instead on the notion of "territory for strategic realignment." In other words, in return for Israeli withdrawal from the Golan, Syria was to disengage from its alliance with Iran and Hezbollah, in addition to signing a peace agreement with Israel.

This mediation was terminated by the outbreak of the Syrian rebellion. Just before the outbreak of popular demonstrations in Syria in the spring of 2011, however, prospects for an Israeli-Syrian peace deal seemed real, as the American diplomat Fred Hof attested in a blog post published on July 20, 2018:

> For several months leading up to mid March 2011 I had been shuttling between Jerusalem and Damascus as a deputy to Special Envoy for Middle East Peace George Mitchell. I had in my briefcase a draft Israeli Syrian treaty of peace. A document I had composed with the help of a senior White House official [Dennis Ross]. My objective was formal Israeli Syrian peace. The phased gradual withdrawal of Israel from all territory taken from Syria in 1967 and Syria's complete geopolitical reorientation away from Iran. Hezbollah and Hamas toward the West. Syrian implementation of treaty terms would be matched by the step by step lifting of American sanctions.[19]

When the wave of antiregime demonstrations turned into a full-fledged rebellion and civil war in the spring and summer of 2011, Israel had to formulate its own policy. One possible Israeli stance would entail support for the uprisings against the Asad regime. Asad was a sworn enemy, an ally of Iran and Hezbollah, and leader who tried to develop a nuclear weapon. Israel, arguably, would benefit by his replacement. A new regime, ideally connected to the Sunni Arab states and to the United States, would tilt the regional balance in favor of the moderate, pro-Western states, weaken Iran, and weaken Hezbollah's position in Lebanon. As the war continued and the scale of the disaster in Syria transpired, a humanitarian argument could be added to the case for Israeli intervention.

But Israeli policy was instead shaped by a different line of thinking. Bashar was indeed an enemy, but Israel had taken his measure and had a long experience of dealing with him and his father. The likely alternative to him was not a moderate liberal democratic government but rather a radical Islamist regime on Israel's northern border. And were it to offer any support to the Syrian opposition, Israel would vindicate the claims of the regime that it was not facing a genuine revolt but a conspiracy hatched from the outside by the United States and Israel. These factors, combined with a pessimistic view held by Israel's political class (as a lesson on the 1982 failed war in Lebanon) that all efforts to shape the politics of Arab countries were doomed to fail, led the Israeli government to maintain a low profile in the Syrian crisis.

The policy adopted and announced by the Netanyahu government kept Israel on the sidelines of the Syrian conflict, with three important exceptions: Israel would be prepared to offer discreet humanitarian help; it would fire back in the event of firing or shelling into its territory; and it would interdict (without taking credit or responsibility) in order to prevent the transfer of sophisticated weapon systems to Hezbollah, or the fall of weapons of mass destruction (chemical or biological) into terrorist hands.

That profile began to change in late 2012 and early 2013 owing to several developments that changed Israel's calculus. One was the decision to intercept Iranian shipments of sophisticated weapons systems to Hezbollah through Syrian territory. The first Israeli air raid against such a shipment took place in early 2013. Israel kept silent, in order not to embarrass Asad's regime and prod it to respond. The regime, Iran, and Hezbollah, however, all chose to advertise the event and to denounce Israel—but still, all three refrained from retaliation since they were not interested in opening a new front with a powerful actor. In the coming years, this would become a pattern: Israel would mount similar raids against depots of weapons or against convoys carrying weapons or other shipments to Hezbollah.

At the very end of 2012, after a visit to the Golan in which he witnessed the plight of the civilian population on the Syrian side, another of Israel's "red lines" was crossed. Israel's chief of staff General Benny Gantz decided to launch an operation providing Syrians in the vicinity of the border with humanitarian aid. This operation was again not advertised, so as not to embarrass the aid recipients—but it assumed impressive proportions. The Israeli Defense Forces (IDF) named the project "Operation Good Neighbor," and aid was given in three ways: medical care, infrastructure, and food. Thousands of wounded Syrians were treated in Israeli hospitals.[20]

Not long after, in a decision motivated by a sense that the vacuum created in that part of Syria by the regime's decline was likely to be filled by hostile elements such as Iran, Hezbollah, and, with the rise of IS, Jihadism, Israel's operations in the Syrian Golan were expanded to include cooperation with local militias and residents in southern Syria. This activity was kept in strict secrecy until August 2018, when Israel helped evacuate more than a thousand members of the Syrian White Helmets organization (a humanitarian group identified with the Syrian opposition) on the eve of the region's occupation by the Syrian army. Some of the evacuees were Israel's former partners in the Syrian Golan. In September 2018 an Israeli researcher specializing in monitoring Syrian social media published some details of Israel's military aid to several local militias,[21] and the public indications of such Israeli activities began to grow.

In fact, as early as 2014–15, Israel had begun to deal with a recurrent, persistent effort by Iran and Hezbollah to establish a terrorist infrastructure in the Syrian Golan, and to launch terror attacks across the border. In January 2015, the IDF struck a vehicle in the Syrian Golan and killed Jihad Mughniyyah, his team, and an Iranian general. Jihad Mughniyyah was the son of Imad Mughniyyah, Hezbollah's chief of operations, who had been killed in Damascus in 2008. Mughniyyah had been tasked with building Hezbollah's infrastructure in the Golan. Hezbollah retaliated in northern Israel by killing two Israeli soldiers. Israel chose not to retaliate in kind.

This rise of IS further changed Israel's view of the Syrian arena and the challenges it presented and launched a debate within the Israeli national security establishment as to the severity of the threat. One school of thought was that the principal threat to Israel in and from Syria was the "resistance axis," namely Iran, Hezbollah, and Asad's regime; another school argued that this threat was dwarfed by the new Jihadi threat. But this was not a lengthy debate, and it ended when IS was first contained and then decimated by the international coalition and its other enemies.

Of greater importance from an Israeli perspective was Russia's military intervention in Syria in September 2015. The arrival of Russian warplanes and aerial control and defense systems threatened Israel's freedom of action in Syria's and Lebanon's airspace and raised concerns of a potential clash. Netanyahu personally invested a massive effort in building an understanding with Vladimir Putin, and mechanisms of coordination between the Russian forces in Syria and Israel were built through the two air forces that would function successfully in the coming years. But beyond the operational aspects of Russia's presence in Syria, Israel had to add Russia's hegemony in Syria to its calculus. After decades of close cooperation with the United States and enmity with the Soviet Union (replaced by a better but still uncomfortable relationship with

Russia), Israel now had to come to terms with a new reality of a diminishing US involvement, and Russian proximity and strong leadership.

After the capture of Aleppo by the Syrian regime and its Russian and Iranian supporters in December 2016, Israel realized that the scales in the Syrian crisis had been tipped. It anticipated a drive to capture the remaining rebel strongholds, including in the Golan, and that Russia and Iran would conduct themselves in a way that would perpetuate their respective influence in Syria. These developments materialized in 2018, and Israel accepted the restoration of Asad's regime in most of Syria as a fait accompli. It did not oppose the regime's return to the Syrian Golan and accepted the Russian proposal that the 1974 disengagement agreement be reapplied as the instrument governing its border relationship with Syria. This policy reflected an acceptance of the realities on the ground and was in fact consistent with Jerusalem's original policy of noninterference. With his record of the previous nine years, Asad was an even less desirable neighbor than he had been in 2011, but from the Israeli perspective he was the least bad option. At least there would nominally be one authority responsible for the territory north of Israel's border.

Iran's positions and policies in post–civil war Syria presented Israel with an entirely different challenge. Iran, seeking to build a land bridge to the Mediterranean and to build in Syria a sophisticated infrastructure of long-range missiles and production lines of such missiles, was clearly on a collision course with Israel. The collision was expedited by Iran's aforementioned decision to send an armed drone from an air base in Syria over Israeli airspace in February 2018. Israel responded by attacking the Iranian base and the Syrian defense system, which managed to shoot down an Israeli jet fighter. The following series of

Israeli raids against Iranian installations deep in Syria territory signaled to Iran that Israel would not tolerate the construction of a sophisticated Iranian infrastructure in Syria. The Israelis had erred once by allowing Iran to build Hezbollah's massive arsenal of missiles and rockets; they were determined not to allow the same development to repeat itself in Syria.

This Israeli policy was conducted with both the tacit understanding of Russia and the support of the Trump administration. The Trump administration's support was hardly surprising. The administration demonstrated support for the Netanyahu government across the board and was committed to confronting and restraining Iran. Russia's policy, on the other hand, was more complex. Although it was Iran's ally and partner in Syria, Russia was also committed to maintaining a good working relationship with Israel, and possibly interested in limiting Iran's influence in the new Syria (see chapter 6). The need to protect Israel's interests in Syria was one issue that Trump and Putin publicly agreed on during their summit in Helsinki on July 16, 2018.

This American-Russian understanding focused on the need to keep Iran and its proxies away from the Golan. But when the United States and Russia agreed on areas of deescalation in May 2017, the agreement regarding southern Syria was unsatisfactory from Israel's perspective—Iran's forces were to be kept just five kilometers north of the cease-fire line in the Golan. A year later, in the summer of 2018, Russia's special envoy to Syria, Alexander Lavrentiev, announced that Iranian forces had withdrawn their heavy weapons in Syria to a distance of eighty-five kilometers from the cease-fire line in the Golan. "The Iranians withdrew," he said; "and the Shi'i formations are not there," he added.[22] On the face of it, this sounded like a major improvement from Israel's vantage point, but in fact this would-be achievement of Russian diplomacy never materialized. The major issue for Israel was not the presence of Iranian or pro-Iranian forces close to the border but the threat of Iranian missiles, and Iran's overall influence in Syria. Iranian ballistic missiles, once deployed in Syria, can threaten Israel from the depth of Syria's territory. Russia was neither willing nor able to push the Iranian military completely out of Syria and, by the end of September 2018, began to limit Israel's freedom of action in Syria, thus facilitating Iran's efforts to develop a military infrastructure in the country.

The issue of Iranian ambitions and activities in Syria, its relationship with Moscow in that arena, and Washington's and Israel's responses to their policies continued to undergo changes well into 2020 (see chapter 6).

The Arab States

The Arab Spring, as the wave of popular protests and rebellions against authoritarian and dictatorial regimes in the Middle East and North Africa was optimistically named at the time, was in many ways the trigger for the Syrian rebellion that erupted in March 2011. In the early years of this conflict, Syria was a major preoccupation of Arab governments. The principal fault line dividing the Arab states was closely tied to the Sunni-Shi'i sectarian rivalries in the region. Iraq and Lebanon, dominated by domestic Shi'i forces and under Iranian influence, supported the Asad regime, while Saudi Arabia, the gulf states, and Jordan supported the opposition. Under Morsi and his short-lived Muslim Brotherhood–dominated government, Egypt supported the opposition, but the successor military regime under Abdel Fattah al-Sisi reversed Egypt's position because of its hostility to the idea of an Islamist takeover in Syria.

During the civil war's early years, the Sunni states had a clear majority in the Arab League and were able to impose an anti-Asad line. But the Arab League had no real influence on the course of the crisis. Later, as it transpired that the regime with Russian and Iranian support was winning the war, most of Asad's erstwhile Arab opponents reconciled themselves to that reality. Each of the major Arab actors pursued its own individual policy vis-à-vis Damascus.

Saudi Arabia

Alongside Turkey, Saudi Arabia was the Syrian opposition's main supporter during the height of the insurrection. Riyadh recognized the Syrian civil war as a crucial arena in its conflict with Iran and an opportunity to check Iranian expansionism and destroy that country's investment in both Syria and Lebanon. When the Obama administration refused to provide the Syrian military opposition with lethal military aid in 2012, the Saudis purchased weapons in Croatia and sent them to the rebels through Jordan. The Saudis were also partners in the CIA's 2012 plan to train and equip a moderate military force that would serve as the backbone of the armed opposition. Like others, they were ultimately frustrated by Barack Obama's refusal to approve the plan.

In 2013 the Saudi regime placed responsibility for its Syria policy into the hands of Prince Bandar Bin Sultan, the head of its intelligence service. Bandar is a seasoned diplomat who had an unusually long tenure as ambassador to the United States (1983–2005). His appointment was seen as an indication of the kingdom's decision to invest a greater and more effective effort in toppling Bashar al-Asad. But Bandar's Syrian mission ended in failure. Unexpectedly for a Washington veteran, he failed to develop a good working relationship with the Obama administration (his heyday was during the senior Bush's presidency). He was also reported to have taken part in a failed Saudi attempt to persuade Vladimir Putin to change his Syria policy. In 2014 Bandar was removed from his post.

The Saudis' views on which opposition groups to support also kept them from effectively coordinating their support of the Syrian opposition with Turkey and Qatar—who supported the Muslim Brotherhood and like-minded Islamist groups within the Syrian opposition. For the Saudis, these groups were an anathema. The main Syrian opposition group supported by the Saudis was Ahrar al-Sham, whose brand of Salafism was more to their liking. At Washington's urging the Saudis also provided logistical and financial support to the secularist Free Syrian Army.

In late 2015 Saudi Arabia launched a major initiative designed to consolidate the political opposition. It convened most of the opposition groups in Riyadh and pressured them to create the HNC (Higher Negotiations Committee) as a substitute to the practically defunct SNC, Coalition and Interim Government. The Riyadh meeting was an important stepping stone toward the passage of UN Security Council Resolution 2254, which addressed the prospect of a political diplomatic solution to the Syrian crisis (December 2015). But the Syrian regime's victory in Aleppo in December 2016, aided and abetted by Russia and Iran, undermined all efforts at a diplomatic resolution to the conflict. Unlike Turkey, a neighboring state with major interests in Syria, Saudi Arabia gradually came to accept the new reality, including the continued existence of a bolstered Asad regime, and shifted its full attention to the war in Yemen, much closer to home.[23]

The Gulf States

Of the gulf states, Qatar played the most prominent role in supporting the Syrian opposition. As we noted, Qatar tended to support groups affiliated with or close to the Muslim Brotherhood and also offered early support to the Salafist-Jihadist Al Qaeda affiliate Jabhat al-Nusrah. Former prime minister and minister of foreign affairs Hamad bin Jasem bin Jaber Al Thani shed unexpected light on Qatar's role in supporting the Syrian rebels in an unusually candid interview in October 2017. In a defense of his country against charges of supporting terrorism, Sheikh Hamad admitted that Qatar had supported Jabhat al-Nusrah and referred to this support as "a possible mistake":

> When the events first started in Syria I went to Saudi Arabia and met with King Abdallah. I did that on the instructions of his highness the prince, my father. He [Abdallah] said we are behind you. You go ahead with this plan and we will coordinate but you should be in charge. I won't get into details but we have full documents and anything that was sent [to Syria] would go to Turkey and was in coordination with the US forces and everything was distributed via the Turks and the US forces. And us and everyone else was involved, the military people. There may have been mistakes and support was given to the wrong faction. . . . Maybe there was a relationship with al-Nusrah, its possible but I myself don't know about this. . . . We were fighting over the prey [al-sayda] and now the prey is gone and we are still fighting . . . and now Bashar is still there. You [US and Saudi Arabia] were with us in the same trench. . . . I have no objection to one

changing if he finds that he was wrong, but at least inform
your partner . . . for example leave Bashar [al-Asad] or do
this or that, but the situation that has been created now will
never allow any progress in the GCC [Gulf Cooperation
Council], or any progress on anything if we continue to
openly fight.[24]

Since the early phases of gulf support for the Syrian opposition, it has been difficult to reconcile Qatar's preference for the
Muslim Brotherhood and Saudi Arabia's hostility to that movement and the organization affiliated with it. This difficulty was
exacerbated in 2017 when Saudi Arabia's conflict with Qatar
morphed into a boycott imposed on Doha by Riyad and its
allies.

Financial support by wealthy individuals was sometimes as
significant as state support. According to Thomas Pierret, a
French expert on religion and politics in Syria, Salafi networks
funded by wealthy individuals in Kuwait and other gulf princi-
palities played a major role in supporting Salafi and other Islamist groups in Syria in the years 2011–13.[25] He describes the
activity of two such Kuwaiti-based fundraisers: the Kuwaiti
preacher Hajjaj al-Ajami, and the exiled Syrian Salafi Surur
Zayn al-Abdin. Pierret distinguishes between two brands of
gulf Salafis: the more moderate "quietists" (favored by Saudi
Arabia), and the more militant "activists" (supported by Turkey
and Qatar). Gulf states raised money for Islamist groups like
Ahrar al-Sham and the Islamic Front, but also for the secular
Free Syrian Army under Saudi influence. The support peaked
in late 2013 and declined in 2014—owing to fatigue, the Egyptian crackdown on the Muslim Brotherhood, and US displea-
sure with gulf support of Jabhat al-Nusra.

Iraq

During the heyday of the Islamic State organization, the distinction between Iraqi and Syrian territory was blurred as the organization—which had originated in Iraq—used the Syrian rebellion to build its position, and then returned to Iraq, where it presented a severe challenge to the regime. The territorial Caliphate built by ISIL spanned the border between the two countries. Under Iranian influence, the Iraqi state as such was a consistent supporter of Bashar al-Asad's regime throughout the years of the civil war. Iraq's most important contribution to the regime's war effort was made by facilitating Iranian supply to the Syrian regime and Hezbollah of weapons systems, and by allowing Iran to make use of its territory and airspace for transporting troops and militias to and from Syria.

The Iraqi regime's support of Bashar al-Asad also reflects the deeply felt Shi'i identification with the Syrian Alawis. Iraq's policy in Syria was also influenced by its prime minister Nuri al-Maliki's strong connections to the Syrian regime, formed during his years of exile in Syria. Yet Al-Maliki's relationship with Bashar al-Asad was at times quite tense, but once the Syrian civil war broke out Al-Maliki was brought into line by Iran. Al-Maliki shared the concern commonly held in the region that that the victory of the Syrian rebels would mean the creation of a Sunni fundamentalist regime on Iraq's western border.[26]

Fouad Ajami described how al-Maliki and his circle of Shi'i Iraqi politicians spent years in exile during Saddam Hussein's years in power. Part of that exile was spent in Syria, where members of this group developed an antagonism toward the bastions of Sunni Islam in that country. In Ajami's own words:

Al-Maliki and the newly empowered Shia political class in Baghdad couldn't release themselves from history's grip. They were convinced that the Syrian rebellion, well intentioned at the beginning, had been hijacked by Salafists recruited and financed by Saudi Arabia.[27]

In the aftermath of the 2018 Iraqi elections a new administration came to power in Baghdad—one that is quite different from the strictly Shi'i regime of Nuri al-Maliki, whose overly partisan Shi'i policy antagonized the Sunni Arab minority and played into the hands of IS. But there are no indications that Iraq is distancing itself from Iran with regard to Syria. Iraq's territory and airspace continue to offer Iran access to Syria and are an essential part of the "land bridge" Iran aspires to build to the Mediterranean. It has yet to be seen how the massive opposition in Iraq and Lebanon manifested also by parts of the Shi'i population in both countries will affect the two countries.

Lebanon

Lebanon and Syria are connected by a powerful umbilical cord, and for decades political parties have operated across the Lebanese-Syrian border. After it became an independent country, successive Syrian governments claimed that all or parts of Lebanon belonged to Syria. Syria formally renounced its irredentist claims to Lebanese territory when formal diplomatic relations were established between the two countries in 2008. Syrian and Lebanese societies and politics remain intimately connected. The Sunnis of Tripoli are closely affiliated with Syria's Sunnis, particularly those of Homs. But Tripoli and its region also host close to 120,000 Syrian Alawis who now send elected representatives to the Lebanese parliament. Lebanon's Druze similarly maintain a relationship with the Syrian Druze, as does Syria's Christian population with Lebanese Christians. And for thirty years, from 1976 to 2005 Syria wielded massive influence in Lebanon by keeping an expeditionary force in its territory.

Given all that overlap and connection, it was hardly surprising that the outbreak of the Syrian civil war and its sectarianization generated sharp debates in Lebanon. Early in 2011, the patriarch of the Maronite Church and spiritual leader of the Lebanese Christian community Cardinal Nasrallah Sfeir resigned his position and was replaced by Bishara al-Rai. The new patriarch was less antagonistic toward the Asads, and when the Syrian civil war erupted, he expressed support for Bashar al-Asad and his regime. During a visit to Paris in early September 2011 he publicly defended Bashar, explaining that the Syrian regime was in the process of reform and needed time and space to bring about change. Were the opposition to Bashar to prevail, al-Rai said, the Sunnis of Syria would unite with their brothers in Lebanon and undo Lebanon's balance—by which he meant abrogating the nominal residual primacy of the Christian communities.[28] His statement provoked a storm of protest and denunciation. The Lebanese American columnist Michael Young eloquently wrote, "For believers, and even unbelievers, a church that sustains a butcher is a contradiction."[29]

By 2011 Lebanon's government and army were dominated by Hezbollah. The anti-Hezbollah political coalition of 2005—the so-called Cedar Revolution—had disintegrated, and Hezbollah's control remained unchallenged since. Despite an official Lebanese policy of "disassociation" from the Syrian civil war, the Lebanese state and Hezbollah supported Bashar and his regime at Iran's behest. The impact of Lebanon's support was most felt through the crucial role played by Hezbollah in the fighting as of 2013. And yet, on the other side of the equation, more than a million Syrian refugees crossed the border into Lebanon (the Lebanese government argues that the true number is closer to a million and a half). For a small, densely populated country, home to a fragmented society and to a significant population of Palestinian refugees, this has been a heavy burden. Lebanon's residency policy makes it difficult for Syrians to maintain legal status, heightening risks of exploitation and abuse and restricting refugees' access to work, education, and health care. Seventy-four percent of Syrians in Lebanon now lack legal residency and risk detention for unlawful presence in the country.

The other repercussions of the Syrian civil war for Lebanon unfolded in three stages: (1) During the war's initial stage in the summer of 2011 news of massive killing of Sunni demonstrators by Asad's regime raised tensions between Sunnis and Alawis in north Lebanon and prompted a significant number of Lebanese Sunnis to join the ranks of Islamist and later Jihadi rebels. (2) In 2012–13, when Hezbollah's role in the fighting in Syria became public, the Syrian opposition expanded the arena by attacking Hezbollah targets in Lebanon. The mountainous area of Qalamoun, on the Syrian-Lebanese border, became a focal point of such clashes. (3) In 2014 as Jihadi groups took the lead in the Syrian opposition, IS and HTS launched a sustained campaign to fight the regime and Hezbollah in Lebanese territory. The town of Irsal in the Qalamoun Mountains was the most prominent arena of a conflict that lasted into August 2017.[30]

Curiously, despite the criticism of Hezbollah's role and losses in Syria, Hezbollah performed well in Lebanon's parliamentary elections in 2018, winning 67 out of 128 seats in the parliament.

But the organization's hold over Lebanese politics was shaken by the massive demonstration in the fall of 2019. A large part of the Lebanese population, including many Shi'is were no longer willing to accept at the combined effect of corruption: inefficiency, absence of basic services, and more tacitly Hezbollah's role of exercising power without responsibility. The massive protests continued in 2020 despite the ban on large gatherings after the outbreak of the coronavirus pandemic.

Jordan

In 2012 Jordan was a partner to the scheme put together by the CIA to train and equip the FSA as an effective opposition force that could topple the Asad regime, but the plan was ultimately vetoed by President Obama. In a 2014, a MOC (Military Operation Center) was established in Jordan. It played an important role in supporting the Southern Front—an alliance consisting of more than fifty Syrian opposition factions affiliated with the FSA. The Southern Front was one of the most effective mainstream opposition group and in its heyday controlled a large part of Dar'a province.

Like Turkey, Jordan was a Sunni opponent of the Asad regime, shared a border with Syria, and offered the opposition and its major supporters access to Syria's territory. Like Turkey, Jordan took in a large number of Syrian refugees (close to a million) and hosted an operations center that tried to coordinate the opposition's war against the regime. But Jordan was more cautious in its opposition to the regime. For one thing, Jordan is a smaller, weaker country that tends to hedge its bets and minimize risks. The Jordanian state was also uncertain of the commitment and dependability of its larger partners in the anti-Asad coalition (owing primarily to the fluctuations of US policy). The country also had to take into account the real danger of a conflict spillover into its own territory. As a result, Jordan's role in directly supporting the Syrian uprising was not as significant as that of Turkey, Qatar, or Saudi Arabia.

Unlike Turkey, which remains heavily involved in northern Syria, Jordan has played down its hostility to the Asad regime since the end of the full fledging of the civil war. Jordan accepts the new status quo in Syria and does not seek to add an active conflict with Damascus to its own set of domestic challenges.

Egypt

The modest role played by Egypt in the Syrian civil war reflects the decline of Egypt's position overall in Arab politics in the wake of its recent domestic upheavals. For a brief period, when Mohammed Morsi and the Muslim Brotherhood held power in Egypt as part of the Arab Spring uprisings, Egypt did seek to play a more prominent role in Syria. President Morsi and his movement were very supportive particularly of the Islamist component of the Syrian opposition, and bitterly critical of what they saw as an Alawi regime's repression of a Sunni majority. In June 2013, Morsi threatened to send a military force composed of volunteers to Syria. He also announced his intention to hold a dialogue with Saudi Arabia, Iran, and Turkey in order to help him resolve the Syrian conflict. Neither the threat nor the promise were taken seriously by the regional and international communities. Morsi was removed from power shortly thereafter. Egypt hosts some 130,000 refugees, a relatively small number for a country of about a one hundred million.

Egypt's view of the Syrian civil war changed dramatically following the rise of Abd al-Fattah al-Sisi to power in 2014. Having chased the Egyptian Muslim Brotherhood out of power, Sisi viewed the Syrian Islamists with the same suspicion and quietly shifted Egypt's policy toward one of passive acceptance of Bashar al-Asad's regime. By the end of 2018 this Egyptian policy became part of and reinforced the all-Arab change of attitude toward Bashar and his regime.

CHAPTER 5

International Actors

Because of Syria's geopolitical importance in the core area of the Middle East and to the lingering expectations of humanitarian intervention and US support for democratic transition in that region, it was widely expected that the United States would play an important role in the Syrian crisis. Such a role was taken on late and was less significant than expected. Russia, for its part, lost no time in extending support to Bashar al-Asad and making a decisive military intervention to ensure his survival.

US Policy

Since the 1970s, ambivalence has been built into the very foundations of America's relationship with Syria. During the four decades that preceded the outbreak of the Syrian rebellion, Washington's Syria policy vacillated between two opposite poles. One line of policy, embraced by US administrations from Nixon to Clinton, recognized the regional importance of the powerful state built by Hafez al-Asad and sought to convert this state from adversary to partner. This policy was first crafted by Henry Kissinger, who tried to use the post-1973 Arab-Israeli peace process to lure Syria away from the Soviet orbit, where it had been since the mid-1950s. As noted in his memoirs, Kissinger was impressed by Hafez al-Asad, but the treatment he accorded to Egypt's Sadat did not work as well with the Syrian strongman, who neither wished to be a mere Soviet client nor wanted to cross over to the US side. But Kissinger did manage to build a community of American, Syrian, and Israeli interests that enabled Syria to intervene in 1976 in the Lebanese civil war and contain it (at least in the short run). Both the United States and Israel were willing to accept Hafez al-Asad's hegemony in Lebanon in order to contain the Lebanese crisis.

Later in the 1970s, Jimmy Carter would go much further in assigning an important role to the Syrian leader in the policy he formulated for resolving the Arab-Israeli conflict. Asad's participation in the peace process would have endowed it with Arab nationalist legitimacy. At the end of the day, however, Carter was disappointed by Asad, who obstructed his efforts to convene an Arab-Israeli peace conference. As Carter wrote in his memoirs, "This was the man who would soon sabotage the Geneva peace talks by refusing to attend under any reasonable circumstances and who would still later do everything possible to prevent the Camp David accords from being fulfilled."[1]

Fourteen years later, James Baker, secretary of state under President George H. W. Bush, persuaded Hafez al-Asad to join the US-led coalition in the First Gulf War. Baker's aim in doing so was to enhance the Arab legitimacy of this coalition at a time when Asad had to cope with the loss of his Soviet patron. One year after that war, with Baker having built a relationship of trust with Asad, the Syrian ruler was persuaded to join the Madrid conference and process. Baker viewed a prospective Syrian-Israeli peace agreement as the cornerstone of the Israeli-Arab peace settlement he was hoping to achieve.

The priority given to an Israeli-Syrian peace deal was inherited and continued in the 1990s by the Clinton administration. The administration (and Clinton personally) invested a massive effort at bridging the gaps between Damascus and Jerusalem. But the effort failed. Although two important Arab-Israeli agreements—the Oslo Accords and the Israeli-Jordanian peace treaty—were signed on Bill Clinton's watch, a Syrian-Israeli breakthrough eluded him (among other things owing to Asad's failing health and preoccupation with the succession). Still, the ongoing quest for an Israeli-Syrian peace produced in and of itself a viable working relationship between Washington and Damascus, despite the fact that Syria still figured prominently in the State Department's list of states engaged in terrorism.

George W. Bush and his administration, however, took the United States to another pole entirely with its policy on Syria. Far from continuing to treat the Asad regime as a viable partner, the new administration saw Bashar al-Asad's government as a brutal dictatorship, an enemy of the United States and its Middle Eastern allies, and a major sponsor of terrorism. By then Syria had collaborated with Saddam's Iraqi state and after 2003 was facilitating the traffic of Jihadi participants in the Sunni insurrection in Iraq. Another irritant from Washington's perspective was Syria's undermining of Lebanese sovereignty and democracy. For the second Bush administration, the existence of a viable democracy in Lebanon was proof that its invasion of Iraq in 2003 had led to the spread of democracy in the Arab world. The Bush administration sought to punish and isolate Bashar al-Asad's regime for these actions by imposing severe economic sanctions. Bashar was rattled by Washington's campaign, but by 2008 it was clear that he had survived the US onslaught. An invitation to Paris by President Sarkozy and the opening of a new negotiation with Israel (through a Turkish mediation with the Olmert government) were clear indications of the consolidation of Asad's legitimacy.

The tension and discrepancy between the two schools of thought in Washington with regard to Syria were demonstrated by the deliberations and report of the Iraq Study Group. This group was a bipartisan commission headed by the Republican former secretary of state James Baker, and the Democratic congressman and chairman Lee Hamilton. It was established in 2006 in order to seek a fundamental solution to the predicament produced by the 2003 American invasion of Iraq. In addition to recommending policy changes in Iraq itself, the group recommended that the United States adopt a new strategy in the Middle East. One major element in the new strategy would be to "engage Iran and Syria." The group argued that "given the ability of Iran and Syria to influence events in Iraq and their interests in avoiding chaos in Iraq, the US should try to engage them constructively. . . . Syria should control its borders with Iraq to stem the flow of funding, insurgency and terrorists in and out of Iraq." The other major element was a recommendation that the US launch a new initiative to resolve the Arab-Israeli conflict: "The US cannot achieve its goals in the Middle East unless it deals directly with the Arab-Israeli conflict and regional instability."[2]

It was hardly surprising that Condoleezza Rice, George W. Bush's national security adviser and representative of the anti-Syrian school of thought within the foreign policy establishment, was dismissive of the Iraq Study Group and its report. In her memoirs she wrote that the administration had already decided on its own to revive the Israeli-Palestinian peace process, "but as to Tehran and Damascus I made it clear that it was a non-starter. If they have any interest in a stable Iraq, they will do it anyway. My own view was that it was worth probing them—particularly Syria—but I was not going to petition these hostile regimes on bended knee to help us in Iraq." She proceeded to describe a meeting with Syrian foreign minister Walid al-Mu'allem in Sharm El-Sheikh, the Egyptian resort, where she raised the issues of Syrian interference in Lebanon and the transit of terrorists to Iraq. Receiving an evasive response from Mu'allem, Rice "decided then and there that cooperation with Damascus was a one way street. The Siren Song of engagement with Syria has attracted many US diplomats. I lost my appetite for any such effort that day in Sharm after talking to Mu'allem."[3]

But the Iraq Study Group had an entirely different impact on future president Barack Obama. When building his foreign policy team for his 2008 presidential campaign he recruited, among others, Ben Rhodes, a participant in the writing of the Iraq Study Group report. Obama adopted the term "engage with Iran and Syria" from the report's language, using it both in his campaign and in his policy statements after his election. In the speech he delivered to US Marines at Camp Lejeune, North Carolina, on February 27, 2009, the newly elected president outlined an Iraq and Middle East policy strategy reminiscent of the spirit and language of the Iraq Study Group report: "The United States will pursue principled and sustained engagement with all of the nations in the region, and that will include Iran and Syria."[4]

These priorities were soon converted into policy by Obama and his secretary of state, Hillary Clinton. Former US senator George Mitchell was appointed as emissary for the Arab-Israeli peace process. In 2009 Obama dispatched Senator John Kerry, chairman of the Senate Foreign Relations Committee, for a visit to Bashar al-Asad during which Bashar and his wife, Asma, charmed Kerry and his wife.[5]

Mitchell recruited the respected American Syria expert Fred Hof as a deputy, and Mitchell himself traveled to Damascus to meet with Bashar al-Asad. Hillary Clinton dispatched Assistant Secretary of State for Near Eastern Affairs Jeffrey Feltman and the National Security Council's Dan Shapiro to discuss bilateral issues with the Syrian government, who made two trips to Damascus in short order. In 2010 the administration made the decision to reappoint an American ambassador to Damascus, selecting Robert Ford, a seasoned and respected expert on Middle Eastern affairs. But disagreements over such issues as Syria's policy in Lebanon, its support of Hamas, and its meddling in Iraq made US-Syrian relations difficult despite this new thaw.

The Obama administration supplemented its bilateral dialogue with Syria with an effort to revive the Syrian-Israeli peace process. Fred Hof and Dennis Ross were the two principal US diplomats engaged in mediation between Asad and Netanyahu. That mediation lasted into March 2011, finally terminated by the persistence of the antiregime demonstrations in Syria. According to the two mediators, this was a serious exercise. Unlike in earlier Syrian-Israeli negotiations, the governing idea was not "territories for peace" but "territories for a strategic change"—in other words, a change in Syria's policy from the alliance with Iran and support for Hezbollah and Hamas to a different policy toward Israel.[6]

"A Wicked Problem"

"A Wicked Problem" is the title Hillary Clinton gave to the Syrian chapter of her memoirs as secretary of state.[7] The term refers to a dilemma that offers policy makers no satisfactory options: the United States did not want to intervene militarily in the conflict but could also not accept the human tragedy and strategic implications of the ongoing civil war. This sums up the stance taken by the Obama administration toward the Syrian civil war from the onset of the Obama years to their end.

It took a full year after the outbreak of the antiregime demonstrations before the Obama administration confronted the Syrian dilemma directly. The events in Syria were seen in the context of the Arab Spring. For the Obama administration, this meant associating the Syrian conflict with efforts to move the Arab world toward democracy. Administration officials were inclined to be sympathetic toward the demonstrators, to show themselves to be "on the right side of history."[8] But the realities of Middle Eastern politics were far more complex than the abstract, prodemocracy sentiments voiced by the president in his 2009 Cairo speech. In Egypt, the tension between the commitment to a long-standing ally and the need to preserve the stability of a major Arab state finally led Washington to support (if not encourage) Mubarak's departure. The United States chose to look the other way in Bahrain, when another US ally, Saudi Arabia, crushed the democratic opposition. In Libya, British and French pressure and Russia's abstention in the Security Council led the United States to play an active military role in toppling Qaddafi's regime. (This intervention failed to produce stability and created significant problems for the administration, which was severely criticized after the US ambassador was murdered in the course of a terrorist attack on the American consulate in Benghazi in September 2012.)

Syria, unlike Egypt, was not a US ally. Despite recent improvement in relations, the United States was not invested in the Asad regime's survival. But as the civil war grew in intensity Washington had to ponder the cost of action versus inaction. Obama's initial assessment was that Asad was likely to fall without American intervention. But by the summer of 2011 it was clear that the conflict had been militarized, that Islamists and Salafis were part of the opposition, that both the regime and the opposition were playing the sectarian card, and that the Syrian domestic conflict had also become a war by proxy between Iran and Saudi Arabia. This all meant that one could now expect a long, bloody conflict in the core area of the Middle East—a conflict that could easily destabilize Syria's neighbors, inflame chronic Arab-Israeli tensions, and ignite a regional war.

In May 2011 the Obama administration denounced the regime's brutality, supported the Syrian people's right to demonstrate peacefully, and imposed personal sanctions on several key members of the Asad regime. On July 8, US ambassador to Syria Robert Ford and his French counterpart traveled to Hama to meet with and show support for the antiregime demonstrators. Three days later Secretary of State Hillary Clinton told reporters, "We have absolutely nothing invested in [Asad's] remaining in power."[9] A month later President Obama went a step further and said, "For the sake of the Syrian people, time has come for President Asad to step down."[10] Obama's statement was in fact coordinated with his West European allies and with Turkey's leader, Erdogan, as part of Erdogan's strenuous efforts in persuading Bashar to seek a political accommodation with the opposition. But Obama saw no reason to reinforce his statement with military action. The president, who in his own words came into office to end two protracted wars in the Middle East (Afghanistan and Iraq), was instinctively opposed to the notion of military intervention in Syria and was content to accept the US intelligence estimates that Asad's days in power were numbered.

During the final months of 2011, two efforts to lay the foundations for international diplomatic action (through the Security Council and the Arab League) to resolve the crisis were made—but proved futile. Asad accepted the Arab League's initiative, but it soon became clear that he had no intention of living up to his commitment. An attempt to pass a mildly worded resolution in the Security Council was vetoed by Russia and China. Russia was unequivocal in its support of Bashar and, in the aftermath of the Western intervention in Libya, was determined to block even the vaguest and mildest resolution regarding Syria. Russia felt, not without some justification, that Western powers might take advantage of that resolution in order to launch a full-fledged military intervention as it felt had happened in the case of Libya.

Meanwhile, in Syria the fighting intensified, and the numbers of casualties and refugees began to mount. In early 2012, US senator John McCain and several of his colleagues demanded that the administration take military action, but Obama declined. Formally he relied on the position taken by the Pentagon, who argued that should the United States decide to impose a no-fly zone or take an equivalent measure, as many as seventy thousand troops and billions of dollars would be needed in order to deal with Syria's anti-aircraft defense system and with the aftermath of an American attack.[11] This was a classic example of a bureaucratic position designed to prevent the political leadership from taking action. The consensus view of the Washington security establishment was that it would be the first step in a slippery slope toward much-larger-scale operations, and possibly to a long and costly investment in another treacherous Middle Eastern arena. Even more important was the fact that the president shared this view. As Obama saw it, he was elected by the American people to end two costly (and essentially failed) wars in the Middle East, in Iraq and Afghanistan—not to start a third one. This led his administration to seek resolution of the dilemma by offering the opposition limited military assistance without fully admitting so publicly.[12]

Given the resistance in Washington to any form of US military involvement in the Syrian crisis and to military aid to the Syrian opposition, the focus of US policy in late 2011 and 2012 was on diplomatic activity led by Secretary of State Hillary Clinton. She collaborated with French president Sarkozy in building the Friends of Syria forum—which managed to attract a large number of participants, but had little effect on the course of events. She worked directly with her Russian counterpart, Sergei Lavrov, and joined Barack Obama when he met with Vladimir Putin, in an effort to move the Russians away from their solid support of Bashar al-Asad. But Putin and Lavrov were quite adept at creating a false impression during several discussions with their American counterparts that they were not necessarily fully invested in Bashar al-Asad. Clinton collaborated closely with Kofi Annan, the former UN secretary general and joint special representative for the UN and the Arab League for Syria, who put together a six-point plan for ending the conflict and then tried to implement it through the first Geneva conference. On the eve of the Geneva conference she met with Annan: "Kofi," she writes in her memoir, "had drafted an elegant solution"—the establishment of a national unity government exercising full executive power, which would be broadly inclusive but exclude "those whose continued presence and participation would undermine the credibility of the transition and jeopardize stability and reconciliation. That was code for excluding Asad."[13] Lavrov was not pleased with the formulation but eventually accepted a milder formula, one mandating mutual consent in the peopling of a transitional governing body, a formulation giving opposition and government alike veto power. Asad's participation in Syria's national unity government would therefore have been subject to the opposition consent. Clinton wanted to follow the compromise formula with a Security Council resolution that would turn the verbal agreement into a practical plan of action. But the Russians had no intention of going along with the Geneva formula. Having realized that the Obama administration had no intention to act militarily directly or by proxy, Moscow therefore felt no need to collaborate in deposing its Syrian client. The American secretary of state had no real leverage and had to console herself with the thought that "over time the opposition and civilians in Syria came to see the Geneva communique for what it was: a blueprint for Asad's departure."[14]

One of the interesting issues that comes to mind in studying Washington's policy toward the Syrian rebellion is the sharp contrast between the United States' persistent reluctance to intervene or offer military aid to the Syrian rebels and its enthusiasm for offering such assistance to opponents of Libyan dictator Muammar al-Qaddafi in 2011. The distinction made by Hillary Clinton in her memoirs between the Libyan and Syrian rebellions illustrates the Obama administration's perception of the costs of supporting Syrian opposition and of the opposition's weakness:

There were many voices, particularly among the Syrian opposition, crying out for us to support them as we had supported the Libyan rebels. But Syria was not Libya.

The Asad regime was much more entrenched than Qaddafi, with more support among key segments of the population, more allies in the region, a real army, and far more robust air defenses. Unlike in Libya, where the rebel Transitional National Council had controlled large swaths of territory in the east, including Benghazi, the country's second largest city, the opposition in Syria was disorganized and diffuse. It struggled to hold territory and to coalesce around a single command structure. And, of course, there was one other crucial difference: Russia was blocking any move at the UN on Syria, in large measure to prevent a replay of Libya.[15]

Because of Russia's persistent refusal to collaborate in seeking a diplomatic solution to the Syrian crisis, Hillary Clinton and several of her colleagues in Obama's national security team—General Petraeus, the director of the CIA; Leon Panetta, the secretary of defense; and General Dempsey—all came to the conclusion that in order to steer the Syrian conflict toward resolution, the United States had to collaborate with Western and Arab allies in training and equipping an opposition force that would be able to stand up to Asad's army and its Iranian and Hezbollah supporters. General Petraeus was the most active member of the group, discussing and planning the project with his European and Arab colleagues. But the idea met with stiff resistance inside the administration, particularly by the National Security Council. Multiple arguments were made against it: the opposition was weak, divided, and inchoate; there were too many radical Islamist elements in the opposition; weapons provided such as antitank and anti-aircraft missiles could end up in terrorist hands and be used against Western targets. Within Barack Obama's entourage it was the chief of staff, Denis McDonough, who led the opposition to any intervention in Syria, while Samantha Power, at the time member of the National Security Council and later UN ambassador, was a chief proponent of an interventionist American policy. Clinton led the pro-interventionist camp inside the administration. Significantly, most of the arguments raised during these debates focused on the potential negative consequences of US military intervention or aid to the opposition, and not on the potential damage of Washington's *failure* to take such action.

Clinton lost the debate. As a rule, she remained loyal to Obama, did not criticize his Syrian policy, and at crucial points, when he was criticized for it by others, offered him support. This remains true in the line and tone of her memoirs as secretary of state. But her frustration over the matter did come out in an August 2014 interview, when she admitted that "the failure to help build up a credible fighting force of the people who were the organizers of the protests against Asad . . . left a big vacuum which the Jihadis have now filled."[16] Members of Obama's circle such as Obama speechwriter Ben Rhodes reacted angrily to this public criticism, arguing that Clinton had not really fought for her position, and that the plan that she and Petraeus submitted was "half-baked."[17] Obama himself expressed his anger at the manner in which the 2012 policy debate was described, ridiculing the notion that arming the rebels would have made a difference as has "a fantasy."[18] As he elaborated: "this idea that we could provide some light arms or even more sophisticated arms to what was essentially an opposition made up of former doctors, farmers, pharmacists, and so forth, and that they were going to be able to battle not only a well-armed state but also a well-armed state backed by Russia, backed by Iran, a battle-hardened Hezbollah, that was never in the cards."[19]

In the early summer of 2012, intelligence reports began to accumulate about preparations by Asad's regime to use their chemical arsenal against rebel groups. Syria had a massive chemical arsenal that had been built as part of Hafez al-Asad's quest for strategic parity with Israel. The US administration issued private warnings to the Syrian government against the potential use of chemical weapons, and Obama publicly warned Asad that "the world was watching and that [Asad] would be held accountable by the international community should he use these weapons."[20] In August 2012, when Obama was asked by a journalist what would lead him to use military force in Syria, his response included the infamous "red line" statement that would haunt him thereafter: "We have been very clear to the Asad regime that a red line for us is we start seeing a whole bunch of chemical weapons moving around or being utilized. That would change my calculus."[21]

A president more experienced in foreign policy would probably not have used the term "red line," since when the said line is crossed, the person who draws it is required to take action or face massive embarrassment. That moment of truth came in 2013. First came a dress rehearsal in April of that year, when evidence that the Syrian regime was using chemical weapons against the opposition came to light. The chemical attack took place on March 19, 2013, in Khan al-Asl, north of Aleppo, and news of the event was revealed by the head of the research division in Israel's military intelligence, Brigadier General Itai Brun, in a lecture delivered at the Institute of National Security Studies at Tel Aviv University. Israel was more concerned with Asad's use of chemical weapons than was the Obama administration, whose analysts were still not ready to confirm that such use was made. The American intelligence community's handling of the Syrian chemical issue was clearly affected by the lingering impact of its wrong assessment of the Iraqi nuclear issue on the road to the 2003 invasion. And the Obama administration realized full well that an acknowledgment of Asad's use of chemical weapons would force the president to acknowledge his own red line.

The April 2013 episode embarrassed both the United States and Israel. The Obama administration did not want to admit that its "red line" had been crossed, while the Israeli government did not wish to embarrass Obama after having recently been at loggerheads over Iranian nuclear and Palestinian issues. The issue was taken up by the US press and several senators and congressmen, including Senators McCain and Levin. On April 25, the White House wrote a formal letter to Senators Carl Levin and John McCain responding to Levin's direct question, "Had the Asad regime—or Syrian elements associated with, or supported by, the Asad regime—used chemical weapons in Syria since the current conflict began in March 2011?"[22]

The administration's response letter fully illustrates the awkwardness with which it dealt with this issue. After explaining how difficult it was to establish with certainty that the regime had indeed used sarin gas against its enemies, it also stated, "Precisely because we take these issues so seriously, we have an obligation to fully investigate any and all evidence of chemical weapons use within Syria. . . . That is why we are currently pressing for a comprehensive UN investigation that can credibly evaluate any evidence and establish what took place."[23] On the very same day, the *New York Times* quoted another letter sent from the White House saying that "the nation's intelligence agencies assessed with varying degrees of confidence that the government of president Bashar al-Asad had used the chemical agent sarin on a small scale."[24]

In his memoirs, Ben Rhodes describes how difficult it was to make even a simple statement to that effect since every word and statement had to be checked with the White House lawyers (the latter were preoccupied with the limitations of military action in a sovereign country without international or congressional authorization).[25] A year later, Secretary of Defense Chuck Hagel became so exasperated with the cumbersome way in which such issues were dealt with in Obama's National Security Council that he wrote a critical memorandum on the administration's Syrian policy and as a result was pushed to resign. "They had these never-ending meetings which would never get to the real issues," and the president was "captive . . . to a very incompetent, inexperienced White House staff," Hagel wrote later.[26]

The dress rehearsal of April 2013 matured into a full play on August 21 of that year, when it became clear that the regime had used sarin gas on a massive scale against civilians in the rural suburbs of Damascus, killing at least a thousand people, including women and children. In White House consultations Obama's team, including Chairman of the Joint Chiefs of Staff Dempsey, argued that the United States needed to respond to the flagrant war crime and to the crossing of the president's own red line. President Obama then made a decision to punish Syria for its war crime. During the next few days, however, the president's decision met with several significant obstacles: the intelligence community's continuing reluctance to offer unequivocal opinion in such matters (given its failure on the eve of the Iraq war); opposition among some staff members within the administration, headed by Denis McDonough; demands by Republican members of Congress for the president to seek congressional approval before taking military action; the limitations imposed by White House lawyers and the president's particular sensitivity to legal constraints; timid support by Washington's European allies culminating in Prime Minister Cameron's parliamentary defeat over this issue; and, ultimately, Obama's own underlying reluctance. After a series of dramatic ups and downs, the president reversed his initial decision to act against Asad and announced on August 30 that he would seek congressional approval for military action. Obama then reached an agreement with Vladimir Putin (through Secretary Kerry) that Russia would "persuade"[27] Asad to destroy his chemical arsenal, and have the process verified by international supervision.

These events were some of the most significant turning points in the history of the Syrian civil war. Obama's decision to avoid military action despite the crossing of his red line had a devastating effect on the Syrian opposition and, as Hillary Clinton described, created a vacuum to be filled two years later by Vladimir Putin when he finally decided that he could afford to intervene militarily in the Syrian crisis. Obama's decision to seek congressional approval was also an important landmark for US political history, in the tug-of-war between the executive branch and Congress regarding the former's authority to launch military action that is short of full-fledged war. But it was not all for naught. The destruction of *most* of Syria's chemical arsenal was a welcome outcome of this episode (though, as subsequent events were to show, Asad kept some of his chemical weapons and continued to use them against civilian populations in subsequent years).

Barack Obama spent many hours explaining to numerous individuals his August 30 change of heart in a clear effort to defend his legacy. When asked to describe his thinking on that day,[28] Obama mentioned four major considerations:

1. The presence on the ground of UN inspectors: "We could not risk taking a shot while they were there."
2. "The failure of Cameron to obtain the consent of his parliament" (the British prime minister put the issue of British participation in punitive action against Asad to a parliamentary vote and lost it).
3. The most important factor, according to Obama: "our assessment that while we could inflict some damage on

Asad we could not through missile strikes eliminate the chemical weapons themselves, and what I would then face was the prospect of Asad having survived the strike and claiming that he had successfully defied the US, that the US had acted unlawfully in the absence of UN mandate and that would have potentially strengthened his hand rather than weakened it."

4. And finally, the question of executive power: "This fall[s] in the category of something that I had been brooding on for some time. . . . I have come into office with the strong belief that the scope of executive power in national security issues is very broad but not limitless."[29]

But there was more. In defending his decision Obama told journalist Jeffrey Goldberg of the *Atlantic* that he felt "liberated" on August 30—liberated from the pressure of the Pentagon trying to "jam" him into taking a decision he did not want to take, and liberated from the "Washington playbook" of the conglomerate of the administration's and Washington's national security experts, and the external think tanks who dictated the country's conventional wisdom on foreign policy and national security affairs.[30]

A more controversial issue concerns the degree to which Obama's determination to reach an agreement with Iran affected his Syrian policy. Ambassador Fred Hof's mediation efforts between Asad and Netanyahu to revive the Israeli-Syrian negotiations ended after the outbreak of the Syrian rebellion. He then collaborated with Ambassador Ford as the administration's chief desk officer for the Syrian crisis. Both became increasingly critical of the administration's Syria policy; both resigned and became public critics of that policy. Hof relied on Obama's *Atlantic* interview with Jeffrey Goldberg and Ben Rhodes's profile in the *New York Times Magazine*[31] (and naturally on his insider's knowledge) to argue that at the core of Obama's Middle Eastern policy was the desire to reach an agreement on the nuclear issue with Teheran. An agreement like that would enable Washington to eliminate the "structural tension" with Iran in order to "create the space for America to disengage itself from the established system of alliances with countries like Saudi Arabia, Egypt, Israel, and Turkey. The idea was that with one bold move the administration would effectively begin the process of large-scale disengagement from the Middle East."[32] The Obama administration's policy in Syria, Hof argued, derived from this larger policy. Hof argued:

> In its single-minded pursuit of a nuclear agreement with Iran, the Obama Administration adopted a Syria policy rich in rhetoric and empty of substantive action. Until June 2014 when the Islamic State used its bases in Syria to overrun much of Iraq, the administration could use the indifference of the US and European publics to Syria's agony to duck the fact that Asad had continuously undermined the White House's credibility. . . . Getting a legacy boosting nuclear deal with Iran was everything for the Obama Administration. Nothing should be done in Syria that would offend Iran's supreme leader, Ayatollah Ali Khamenei, or the Islamic Revolutionary Guards Corps' support for Asad's mass murder strategy. Offending them—or so the theory went— might cause Iran to walk away from the nuclear talks.[33]

Hof's explanation of his decision to resign his position is quite telling:

> I had concluded in the late summer of 2012 that President Barack Obama's words of a year earlier about Assad stepping

aside were empty and that my efforts in government to bring words to life were futile. Instead of implementing what had sounded like the commander in chief's directive, the State Department was saddled in August 2012 by the White House with a make-work, labor-intensive project cataloguing the countless things that would have to be in place for a post-Asad Syria to function. But how to get to post-Asad? The White House had shut down the sole interagency group examining options for achieving that end.[34]

Hof's argument is supported as well by Michel Duclos, France's former ambassador to Syria, who wrote in his study of the Syrian civil war that Obama's reluctance to use force in Syria should be attributed "perhaps more importantly, as John Kerry later admitted, to Barack Obama's will not to compromise the prospect of an agreement on nuclear power by risking to confront Iran on a regional level."[35]

For his part, Ambassador Ford also resigned from the State Department in 2014. Since then, Ford, true to his public service ethos, has refrained from personal criticism of the president, but he publicly declared that "he could no longer defend US policy"—strong words for a career diplomat. Still more resonant was the memorandum signed by fifty-one State Department diplomats in June 2016 through the department's "dissent channel" that criticized US policy in Syria, calling for tougher US military action in Syria, arguing that talks with Russia over a political transition had all but collapsed, that the cease-fire continued to disintegrate, and that US policy in Syria was going nowhere. When asked by the *New Yorker* in 2016 to comment on his colleagues' dissent, Ford explained:

Frustration at the State Department has come to a boil. People don't write in the Dissent Channel every day. The cessation of hostilities in Syria has broken down completely. The bombings of hospitals in Aleppo and Idlib are a violation of every human norm and that's not including the barrel bombs and the chemical weapons. The effort to get a political deal is going nowhere. The Asad government has refused to make any serious concessions. It won't let in food aid, in violation of U.N. resolutions. And the Americans are watching it all happen. So the Dissent Channel message is a reflection of frustration by the people who are responsible for conducting policy on the ground. I felt that way when I left—and that was after Geneva II, in January–February, 2014.

The existing policy is failing and will continue to fail. Why? I don't sense, in the message, dissent from the strategic objective, which is a negotiated settlement of the Syrian civil war, but I sense a sharp disagreement with the tactics the Administration is or is not using. The dissent message says that, without greater pressure on the Asad government, it will be impossible to secure the compromises necessary to win a political agreement and end the war. The message says that the Administration needs to reconsider tactics to generate that pressure.[36]

Obama's War on IS

The Obama administration did eventually come to exert pressure on the regime. They did so by launching a limited, covert program to support vetted military opposition groups, primarily by providing them with TOW antitank missiles, which were very effective in their clashes with the regime's forces.

The rise of IS in Syria and Iraq led to a major change in Washington's view of, and conduct in, the Syrian crisis. The threat of a major terrorist wave directed at the United States and its allies and the televised atrocities perpetrated by the organization prompted the United States to take action against IS. Unlike its reluctance to act against the Asad regime, the administration took decisive action. Its main effort was invested in fighting the organization by building a large international coalition and by mobilizing local forces, most significantly the Kurdish YPG militia. The Obama administration provided overt support to groups fighting IS—in particular the anti-IS coalition in Iraq and Syria, which was given air cover from US air force bases in Turkey. It also sent a limited number of US troops to help and advise local forces, and it provided some of these groups with arms and training. Always mindful of the legal dimension, the administration relied in these operations on the Iraqi government's invitation to fight against IS.

At the same time the administration, primarily through Secretary of State Kerry, continued the effort to seek a comprehensive solution to the Syrian crisis and, failing that, more limited arrangements that would at least reduce the level of violence. These diplomatic efforts met with limited success, particularly after Russia's military intervention in Syria in September 2015. Moscow was now in the driver's seat, and Moscow was not interested in any diplomatic solution that could not guarantee the perpetuation of the Asad regime. Kerry met with Lavrov several times during this period (it sometimes seemed that he was chasing after him, in a manner that seemed humiliating for the more powerful of the two powers). But Russia on the whole was uninterested in agreements.

Starting in late 2013, the Obama administration began a limited covert program to provide military support to a select group of Syrian opposition militias, primarily by supplying them with antitank missiles. It was still unwilling, however, to make a real commitment to or investment in Syria through a robust military presence in the country. It was therefore relegated to the sidelines.[37]

The Trump Administration

On January 17, 2018, Donald Trump's secretary of state, Rex Tillerson, presented the first coherent comprehensive description of the new administration's policy in Syria. In a speech delivered at Stanford University, Tillerson set five "key end states" for the United States in Syria: first, to ascertain that IS and Al Qaeda do not resurface in Syria; second, to ensure that the "underlying conflict between the Syrian people and the Asad regime is resolved through a UN-led political process prescribed in UN Security Council Resolution 2254, and a stable, unified, independent Syria, under post-Asad leadership, is functioning as a state"; third, to ensure that "Iranian influence in Syria is diminished, their dreams of a northern arch are denied, and Syria's neighbors are secure from all threats emanating from Syria"; fourth, to ensure that "conditions are created so that the refugees and IDPs can begin to safely and voluntarily return to Syria"; and fifth, to ensure that "Syria is free of weapons of mass destruction."[38]

The secretary of state explained that these policy goals would be pursued primarily through diplomacy, but that the United States would also maintain a military presence in Syria in order to ensure that IS could not reemerge. Tillerson further argued that a continued US military presence was vital for an acceptable political settlement, that such a settlement required Asad's departure, and that a US military disengagement from Syria would provide Iran with the opportunity to further strengthen its position in that country.

There were three problems with Tillerson's speech. For one thing, most of the goals he set were unattainable without the allocation of massive US resources and a commitment to pursue them over time. Second was the president's own position articulated in the campaign that the United State should disengage from Syria and end its military presence there. Furthermore, the secretary's own position within the administration was eroding. Two months later he was fired by the president and replaced by then CIA director Mike Pompeo. A month after that, President Trump stated that he wanted the US troops still stationed in Syria to be evacuated as soon as possible—but he was persuaded by his own national security bureaucracy and by French president Macron to suspend that decision.

As a rule, Trump has been critical and dismissive of his predecessor. This attitude was manifested in the Middle East, when Trump reversed Obama's policies with regard to Iran and the Israeli-Palestinian conflict. But with regard to Syria and specifically to the campaign to insure IS's "enduring defeat," Trump adopted Obama's approach and took it in substance and style further afield.

The discrepancy between Trump's persistent desire to disengage from Syria and the national security bureaucracy's quest to retain US military presence in order to maintain the struggle against IS, but also in order to limit Russian and Iranian involvement, has remained an important dimension of US conduct in Syria under the Trump administration.

The new administration entered into office after the Syrian regime and its allies' capture of Aleppo had left Russia in the driver's seat on the ground and in the Syrian diplomatic arena, and had left the mainstream internal political and diplomatic opposition in disarray. It was Trump's common practice to complain about the legacy of his predecessor, Barack Obama, and he did so also with regard to Syria, perhaps more justifiably than in other cases. Donald Trump was clearly not interested in making a major investment in Syria nor in confronting Russia and Iran in that arena, and his foreign policy was conducted in a haphazard fashion with presidential tweets undermining senior officials. Before Tillerson's announced strategy, the Trump administration clearly lacked a comprehensive, integrated policy.

As reluctant and uninterested as the president and most of his administration were with regard to the Syrian crisis, they had to make decisions with regard to several issues: the fighting on the ground continued to intensify, and in April 2017 the regime once again used chemical weapons against civilian population in the area of Khan Shaykhoun in the province of Idlib. A second such attack was launched in April 2018 in Duma and in a Damascus suburb, both of which drew US military retaliation. The Islamic State had lost its territorial "Caliphate," but the campaign against IS and other Jihadis had to be completed by fully eradicating its presence in Syria and Iraq, and an effort had to be invested in making sure that it did not rebound. Washington continued to rely in this campaign on the Kurdish militia, YPG, and the larger SDF militia, while Turkey was incensed by Washington's collaboration with what it regarded as a hostile force. Iran continued to consolidate and expand its position in eastern Syria and other parts of the country, and the president, who had presented Iran's containment as a high priority, had to deal with Iran's activities in the most important arena of its regional policy. And the Trump administration as a whole had to concern itself with all this while attempting to understand the president's own complex—and secretive—relationship with Russian leadership.

The original agreement between the Trump administration, Russia, Turkey, and (with regard to southern Syria) Jordan on the establishment of four deescalation zones in Syria was reached in Astana in May 2017. The goal was to reduce violence and tension, to facilitate the return of refugees, and to lay the ground for more ambitious, comprehensive arrangements in the future. In July 2017, when Trump and Putin met at a G20 summit, they came to a specific agreement on one of the four areas of deescalation, in the southwestern part of the country. Jordan was a partner to this agreement, and Israel was informally consulted and expressed dissatisfaction with an arrangement that would keep Iranian and pro-Iranian forces just five kilometers away from the Golan.

These deescalation agreements were indeed implemented, with partial initial success. But when the Syrian regime—with Russian and Iranian support—pursued its military campaign to extend its control over rebel-held areas and captured all deconfliction areas, Russia again played an enabling role in the fighting, through indiscriminate bombing of Syrian opposition forces.

The Trump administration barely responded to Syrian and Russian infringement of the deescalation agreement as the regime and its supporters took over territory near Damascus and in southwestern Syria (preferring to complete their operation in these regions prior to dealing with the massive challenge in the Idlib area). Other than denouncing the regime's and Russia's excesses during the military campaign, and the use of chemical weapons by the regime near Damascus on April 9, the United States, together with Great Britain and France, responded with a limited missile attack.

In the spring of 2018 Trump completed the overhaul of his national security team by appointing John Bolton as national security adviser in April. These changes did not spell an immediate modification of the administration's Syria policy, which remained focused on the need to respond to the military campaigns conducted by the regime and its allies, to resolve the tension with Turkey over the Kurdish issue in northern Syria, and to deal with the Iranian-Israeli conflict in Syria.

With regard to eastern and northeastern Syria, the Trump administration decided for the time being to keep its two thousand troops in place despite repeated statements to the contrary by the president (in fact the number was quietly increased to about four thousand). Keeping US troops in Syria was explained by the (real) need to prevent an IS recrudescence, but advocates of this policy were also motivated by a sense of commitment to the Kurdish allies as well as by a determination to limit Iran's control of the border crossings between Iraq and Syria. The United States did not prevent Iran's proxies from taking over the Abu Kemal crossing point, but US troops held onto their position in Al-Tanf further south.

Washington under the Trump administration has never fully resolved the tension with Ankara over its collaboration with and support of the Kurdish YPG. Turkey, which had captured sizeable territory on the Syrian side of the Turkish-Syrian border, launched a campaign in the area of Idlib in January 2018 and ended up capturing the town of Afrin in March. Its next target was the larger city of Manbij. The US-Turkish relationship had been tense for some time over a variety of issues; the capture of the city of Manbij, and Turkey's quest to drive the YPG further east, created yet another, particularly acute, source of tension. The United States was willing to accept the Turkish capture of Afrin, a more remote city and district, quite removed from the war with IS. But when it came to Manbij, Washington felt that a red line had to be drawn in regard to Ankara's feud with the Kurds. After an unsuccessful effort by Secretary of State Tillerson and his Turkish counterpart to resolve the issue of Manbij in March 2018, Tillerson's successor, Pompeo, and Minister

Cavusoglu were able to reach an agreement on April 27, 2018. According to that agreement, the YPG military forces were to evacuate the city, and the United States and Turkey, through local Arab actors, were to manage its affairs.

As Bashar al-Asad's victory in the domestic Syrian civil war was turning into an established fact, and as his army and its Russian and Iranian supporters were moving southward, the tension between Israel and Iran became more acute. Israel was willing to accept the regime's return to the south of the country but was prepared to accept neither the presence there of Iranian or pro-Iranian forces, nor the Iranian quest to establish deeper in Syria sophisticated military infrastructure and production facilities.

The Trump administration gave Israel open support in its effort to deal with Iran's quest to embed itself militarily in Syria. Not only was the Trump administration very supportive of Israel, but the Israeli drive suited the administration's overall policy toward Iran.

Washington and Moscow were in agreement regarding the need to keep Iran away from the Golan, but not with regard to Iran's position in Syria. While the United States was supportive of Israel's demand (and its gulf allies' more tacit demand) that Iranian forces leave Syria, Russia showed no willingness to seek that result. In July 2018 Trump and Putin had a summer meeting in Helsinki that was eventually criticized for Trump's willingness in it to give Putin greater credibility than he gave to his own intelligence services. The Iranian-Israeli conflict in Syria was reportedly discussed by the two leaders in privet meetings that were described as both substantive and meaningful.[39]

In the summer of 2018, the Trump administration finally formulated a coherent Syria policy. Driven by Secretary of State Pompeo and Secretary of Defense Mattis, this policy sought to keep pressure on the regime and its two main supporters, Iran and Russia. The regime's and its allies' dependence on US resources and goodwill for Syria's reconstruction was an important dimension of this new policy. To this end, they recruited from retirement Ambassador James Jeffrey and appointed him as the secretary's special representative for Syria engagement. Retired colonel Joel Rayburn was also appointed as special envoy for Syria. The authors of the new policy were fully aware that it was being put together after years of neglect and equivocation, and that the Syrian regime and its allies had effectively won the domestic civil war. But they felt that with a commitment to keep US troops in eastern Syria and with the hope for the cooperation of such US allies as Turkey, Israel, and Jordan, the United States could keep the regime under pressure and considered internationally illegitimate, and to seek Iran's military departure from Syria. The first step in this new direction was taken when the United States conveyed to Russia its opposition to the anticipated offensive against the last rebel stronghold in Idlib. On the face of it, the United States threatened to respond should the regime use chemical weapons against its opponents—but tacitly the United States told Russia that it objected to the very idea of such an offensive.[40]

This policy line pursued by the United States during the latter half of 2018 was thrown into disarray by Donald Trump's decision in late December of that year to withdraw his troops from Syria. The decision and its aftermath are discussed in detail in chapter 6.

Russian Policy

When the Syrian civil war erupted in 2011, Russia saw a threat to its last remaining ally in the Middle East and to its naval base in the northern Syrian port city of Tartus. This base became particularly important in 2010, when Russia decided to establish a permanent flotilla in the Mediterranean—the primary turnover space for Russia's five navies, with logistical support from Syria and the Black Sea. American and western European denunciation of Asad and his regime, the support given to the Syrian rebels by America's Sunni allies in the Middle East, and the Western assault on Qaddafi's Libya in 2011—which seemed to the Russians to presage similar treatment of Asad—all reinforced Russia's determination to protect its Syrian ally.

In sharp contrast to its American rival, whose policy in Syria was constrained by ambivalence and legal limitations, Russia has seen the Syrian uprising as a crucial issue from the start. It has formulated a coherent policy and executed it in a single-minded and often brutal fashion. Asad's regime has been an important asset for Moscow, and an ally whose fall would be a major blow to its interests. During the civil war's first four years Putin's government gave Bashar military aid and sweeping diplomatic support that protected him from Security Council resolutions and their implications. In 2015 Russia decided to intervene militarily in the Syrian crisis in collaboration with Iran and did so in September of that year when the opposition's military pressure threatened to topple the regime. Russia's military intervention tipped the scales in Syria's domestic civil war and led to the regime's survival and victory. Since that turning point, Russia has been the dominant actor in the Syrian arena, helping the regime consolidate its victory and perpetuate its own position. Russia has also sought to cap its achievement with a political solution to the Syrian crisis. Putin's resolve and the effectiveness of his support and intervention has served to improve Russia's position in the Middle East and in the global arena.[41]

The decision taken in 2015 to intervene militarily was neither an easy nor a simple one. Putin was fully aware of the risks involved in sending his armed forces to Syria. Such an enterprise would be unlike his military interventions in Georgia, Crimea, and eastern Ukraine, which took place close to Russia's borders. Russia's last major military intervention in a distant arena—the Soviet Union's invasion of Afghanistan in the 1970s—ended disastrously. The decision to transform Russia's support of Asad into a military intervention was motivated by a complex calculus. There were three primary considerations: first, the need to save Asad's regime from collapsing under the pressure of successful rebel attacks in northwestern Syria and close to Damascus; and second, Moscow's preoccupation with the threat presented by the Jihadis who had joined the Islamic State from Russia and the Caucasus. Western analysts tend to underestimate the latter consideration, which has in fact played a major role in Russia's calculus.[42] Since 2014, thousands of volunteers from Russia itself, from the Caucasus and central Asia, have joined the fighting in Syria and Iraq. Calls have been made to launch a Jihad in Russia itself that have resonated against the background of religious radicalization among Russia's twenty million Muslims (one-sixth of the population). The Russians estimate that between two and five thousand such volunteers have joined IS and other Jihadi groups.[43] So the Kremlin views the Sunni Jihadis as an immediate and large-scale threat—in their view, easier to destroy in Syria and Iraq rather than after some of them return home. Third, the military intervention in Syria was an important part of a policy design to restore Russia to a position close to, if not equivalent to, the Soviet Union's international position during the Cold War. The Middle East has been an important arena for implementing this policy, and Syria became its focal point. This foreign policy had an important domestic dimension in enabling Putin to portray himself as restoring Russia's greatness.

These considerations were reinforced by the view of the Syrian insurrection as yet another episode in what the Russians see as a "Western hybrid war" against its interests. Just as in the West policy makers and analysts speak of Putin's adoption of a hybrid of innovative methods of conducting covert warfare against the West (e.g., cyber war, meddling in elections), the Russians viewed Western intervention in Libya as a form of warfare designed to deprive Russia of its last assets in the Middle East.

All this was taking place during a time in which the Putin regime was struggling to counter international isolation and the sanction regime imposed by the West after the Russian capture of Crimea and its intervention in eastern Ukraine. Moscow seized the opportunity to become the broker in the Syrian crisis and to use that position to improve its overall position in the Middle East. The Syrian arena, so the thinking in the Kremlin went, could become an asset in a new form of give-and-take, the basis for a potential grand bargain, and a way of demonstrating Russia's robust military capacity and showcasing the effectiveness of Russian weapons systems for potential buyers.[44] Launching ballistic missiles from the Caspian Sea into Syria was a demonstration exercise of this sort.

In order to minimize the risks of military intervention, Putin applied a principle of old Soviet military doctrine known as "reasonable sufficiency." In practice this means limiting Russia's direct military intervention to the deployment of airplanes and air defense systems. In coordinating its intervention with Iran, Moscow made sure that Iran committed troops through its Shiʻi militias while Russia focused on formulating the overall strategy and conduct of the campaign, providing aerial support, sophisticated weapons systems, strategic and operative intelligence, and logistics. In addition to all this, Russia also sent thousands of officers and technical experts (special forces, electronic warfare, air defense, etc.), who were integrated at all levels of the Syrian army. Russia's naval base in Tartus was supplemented in 2015 by exclusive access to a new air base in Khmeimim, near Latakia. In March 2016 Putin announced that Russia would be withdrawing its troops from Syria—probably in order to allay domestic concern and criticism—but in practice, its military presence and activity remained unchanged.

Russia's achievements went well beyond salvaging its Syrian client. Its own activism against the backdrop of Washington's near exclusive focus on the war on IS turned Putin into the arbiter of the Syrian arena. This enhanced his larger position in the Middle East, as traditional US allies like Saudi Arabia and Egypt opened new channels to Moscow. The impact on Syria's neighbors was greater. Israel, concerned with Russia's new military proximity and its own freedom of action in Syria's and Lebanon's airspace, was quick to establish coordination mechanisms with Russia; Netanyahu became a frequent visitor to Moscow and Sochi for meetings with Putin. Russia's relationship with Turkey proceeded less smoothly. When Turkish warplanes shot down a Russian fighter jet on November 24, 2015, Putin responded immediately by imposing economic sanctions on Turkey. Several months later Erdogan swallowed his pride, apologized for the incident, and in August 2016 traveled to St. Petersburg for a meeting with Putin. Collaboration was restored and expanded. In December 2016 Turkey joined the Astana process (the Russian-led alternative to the Geneva Syria peace process). Putin reciprocated with a visit to Ankara, and meetings between the two leaders became a routine. In September 2017 Turkey crossed another Rubicon when it announced that it was going to buy the Russian-made S-400 advanced air defense system—an unusual step for a NATO member.

Moscow's Syria policy during the final year of the Obama administration and for most of the Trump administration has been consistent: it has provided steadfast military support for the Asad regime and has run its own peace process in Astana and Sochi—thus marginalizing the US role. In Moscow's view, military victory had to be followed by a political solution, but there was no urgency to finalizing that solution prior to the completion of the military campaign. In the course of 2017 and 2018 the leaders of Russia, Iran, and Turkey met several times to discuss both the larger Syrian picture and a variety of other more limited issues: mediating between Turkey and the regime in anticipation of the major offensive in Idlib; trying to lay the foundations for a political solution.

Moscow has been accommodating on paper in its dealings with Washington regarding Syria, often going through the motions but unwilling to take up and contribute to the implementation of Washington's policy suggestions. When Secretary of State Kerry wanted to make arrangements to reduce violence and promote a political settlement, Russia went along. It agreed in the fall of 2016 to set up a joint operations center but nonetheless played a major, brutal role in Aleppo a few weeks later. In 2017 Putin and Trump discussed Syria twice in person and agreed among other things on the creation of four deescalation areas, but less than a year later, Russia and Iran participated in the regime's conquest of most of the territory covered by that arrangement.

During 2018 Russia continued to dominate the Syrian diplomatic arena. The Astana forum continued to meet; a Russian, Iranian, Turkish summit involving the leaders of these countries was held in Tehran; and Putin and Erdogan met twice in order to deal with the issue of Idlib on the basis of the May 2017 deescalation zones agreement, in which Russia promised not to launch a military offensive against Idlib and to establish a buffer zone of fifteen to twenty kilometers between the Syrian regime's forces and the local rebels. These new arrangements, it was decided, would be supervised by the Turkish army and Russian military police. On October 27, 2018, another forum was convened in Istanbul when Erdogan hosted Putin, Merkel, and Macron. Not much was accomplished, but Russia has emerged from these high-level encounters as the key player in the Syrian arena. The United States, by contrast, has been glaringly absent.

One major challenge facing Russia during this period concerned Iran's presence and ambitions in Syria. The Trump administration continued to argue that Iran must withdraw its forces from Syria, while Israel continued to attack Iran's efforts at building a long-term military infrastructure in Syria. The Russians did not interfere with Israel's aerial raids until September 2018, when Moscow used the shooting down of a Russian plane by Syrian air defense as a pretext for changing its policy. The Russians accused Israel of the incident, began to limit its aerial activity in Syria's airspace, and announced a decision to supply Syria with an advanced version of its S-300 air defense system.

As we look back on Russia's decision to intervene militarily in Syria, a mixed picture is revealed. Russia's incursion yielded dividends, but nearly four years later the prospect of consolidating the situation in Syria and ending its military intervention seems remote.

The Western Europeans

In contrast to the Libyan crisis, where Great Britain and France took the lead while the United States famously chose "to lead from behind,"[45] the role of the larger countries of western

Europe in the Syrian crisis remained limited. Only France and Great Britain have played an active role in the conflict, with Germany choosing to keep its role marginal. This German stance is striking given how profound the Syrian crisis has affected domestic German politics.

By the same token the EU also played a marginal role in the Syrian civil war and crisis, limiting itself to issuing statements. The one issue that prompted an active EU role has been the prospect of a large wave of Syrian refugees. In order to cope with this threat, the Europeans have paid Turkey, Jordan, and Lebanon to keep some five million refugees in their territories.

In 2012 Great Britain was willing to join the CIA-led effort to equip and train a moderate opposition military force, but Prime Minister David Cameron's failure in 2013 to win parliamentary approval for participating in that military action had an impact on Barack Obama and clearly precipitated his change of mind. In 2018, a new British government under Prime Minister Theresa May joined the Trump administration in penalizing the Asad regime for yet another use of chemical weapons in the Damascus region, but this stance and the overall British engagement with Syria has had a marginal impact on the region.

France's role in the Syrian crisis has been more substantial owing to its historic role in the Levant and the special interest the French have always had in Syrian and Lebanese affairs. The French ambassador, Eric Chevallier, joined US ambassador Robert Ford in a significant visit to Hama in July 2011. France has been a steady ally of the United States during the Syrian crisis but has also been repeatedly reminded of the limits of its influence in an arena where two major powers, the United States and Russia, were the principal actors. A previous French ambassador to Syria, Michel Duclos, offered in 2018 the following observations about how a middling power contends with larger, more powerful countries in the international arena. His words are worth citing at length:

> The Syrian tragedy highlighted the limits of what countries like France can do in this type of situation. Once it was clear that Asad's regime would abide by no political settlement and that the protests would turn into an uprising, France, alongside its American, British and regional allies, contributed to support rebel armed groups. However, such support remained limited as many feared the sophisticated weapons might end up in the hands of jihadists. Meanwhile, French authorities continuously supported the opposition in its quest for a representative political structure. They also sided with the United Nations in its attempts to mediate the conflict, de facto agreeing to engage negotiations with Asad. . . . These several paths ended up in a stalemate, mostly because the regime, as the French initially predicted, never even considered the possibility of negotiations. . . .
>
> The bottom of the problem for France in the Syrian crisis has not been the positions adopted by its leaders but rather the absence of adequate means to act. Yet, the Macron administration is precisely working on acquiring such tools: Paris avoids the temptation of funding Syria's reconstruction for as long as Asad will be in charge, which would amount to turning down a potential leverage. Meanwhile, the French sustain their military presence, along with the US and others, in the area liberated from the Islamic State in North-East Syria, thus securing a token for the future.
>
> Seven years after the start of Syria's revolution, the scale of the disaster, of human losses, of sufferings and destructions profoundly upsets ordinary French people. . . . The Syrian issue is still touching a raw nerve.[46]

CHAPTER 6

Syria 2019–20

After nine years of war, the weakening of its army and security services, the decline and in some cases disappearance of the state apparatus, the rise of new local and national actors, and the enhanced presence and role in the country played by Russia, Iran, and Turkey, Syria has been transformed almost beyond recognition.

The outcome of the Syrian civil war was essentially decided in December 2016 with the conquest of Aleppo, and the conflict has been waning ever since. In 2017 and 2018 the regime (with Russian and Iranian help) captured all but one of the areas still held by the armed opposition. Still, as of this writing the regime controls only 60 percent of Syria's territory. Idlib continues to be held by rebel forces under a Turkish umbrella; the SDF controls (with US support) a large part of northern (nearly 30 percent of the national territory prior to the Turkish invasion in October) and a small part of southeastern Syria; and Turkey has captured significant territory along its border with Syria. And while the level of violence in Syria has declined dramatically, the conflict continues to contribute to the heightening of regional and international tensions.

The regime currently continues to expand the area under its control and to reinforce, to the best of its ability, Syria's position as a sovereign state. It seeks to consolidate its hold over the areas under its sway, to regain control of the areas held by others, and to normalize Syria's diplomatic and international position. Having defeated the main opposition, the regime is facing new challenges such as the need to cope with Russia's and Iran's enhanced ambitions in Syria, Turkey's occupation of a large strip along the Turkish-Syrian border, and the presence of autonomous Shi'i militias. Asad's regime seeks to accomplish these goals without having undertaken meaningful political reform and without having proposed a political diplomatic solution acceptable to at least part of the international community and the Syrian opposition and, finally, without addressing the issue of five million Syrian refugees in Turkey, Jordan, and Lebanon. This poses a major obstacle to reconstruction and economic recovery. The one area where rapid progress has been achieved has been the reconstruction of the armed forces.

The Domestic Scene

Bashar al-Asad remains unconvinced that significant reform is needed to reestablish the legitimacy and stability of his government. On the contrary, in his eyes, he has confronted and defeated an illegitimate revolt hatched from outside. His victory is proof that he was right all along. Here his Russian patrons disagree. They believe that Asad's military victory should be completed by a political diplomatic solution, at least of a cosmetic variety. Putin's regime has expressed an interest in seeing new elections in Syria and a new Syrian constitution, to project the image of political resolution. But Asad resists even the mildest political reforms.

The essence and structure of the Asad regime has remained unchanged, with a set of formal structures wrapped over a core of family, clan, and close personal confidants of the ruler. Several confidants have risen to prominence, and others have been eclipsed, reflecting the reality of a "transactional state" in which war profiteers, warlords, and individuals within the military and security service take advantage of the war and its chaotic outcome to build and control checkpoints, operate local power stations, sell petrol, and appropriate other state functions or economic activities.[1] The most important development in this context was the open conflict that broke out between Bashar and his wife, Asma, and his cousin Rami Makhluf. Uncharacteristically, the conflict became public when Makhluf used the social networks to complain about his cousin. On YouTube he asked rhetorically, "Who would have believed that intelligence agents will arrive in Rami Makhluf's companies and arrest our workers while I am the greatest supporter of these intelligence agencies?"[2] It seems that underlying tensions between the presidential couple and their cousin were exacerbated by a dispute over the division of spoils. It also seems that this particular dispute was eventually settled, at least for the time being.

On December 28, 2018, Asad announced the appointment of ten new leaders to the army's most important divisions, including the Republican Guard. According to some commentators, these new commanders—all relatively new faces—are close to Russia and devoid of Iranian connections. Thus, Major-General Malek Alia was appointed commander of the Republican Guard. His predecessor, Talal Makhluf, Bashar's cousin, was appointed commander of the Second Corps; Major General Murad Khair Bek was appointed commander of the Fifth Corps, an entity created under Russian pressure and supervision. It is Russia's policy to push for normalization and institutionalization as essential elements of the reconstruction process. In April 2019 Lieutenant General Salim Kharba was appointed as the new chief of staff of the armed forces, a further concession to Russia and a blow to Iran. During the summer of 2019 several significant personnel changes were made in the top echelon of Syria's national security establishment, giving rise to a wave of speculation that such moves reflected Russian pressure to promote supporters of Moscow and to demote supporters of Iran.[3]

Over time the regime undoubtedly will seek to normalize conditions in the country, reassert itself, and reimpose central control. Given the damage the regime has sustained, this process is likely to unfold slowly. Asad is now rebuilding the central government, the army, and the security apparatus as the first step in this lengthy process. At the cabinet level, several ministers have been replaced, most notably the minister of defense and the minister of the interior. Several proregime militias have been disbanded; some members have been discharged, while others joined regular army units. The Desert Hawks Brigade—one of the two most important militias of the war years—was merged into the Maghawir al-Bahr militia and became part of the Russian-backed Fifth Corps. The Desert Hawks were funded by the Jaber brothers (Muhammad and Ayman), who, unlike most other regime-related tycoons, were seen by Bashar as a thorn in his side.

The policy of integrating the militias reflects the regime's effort to rebuild, expand, and strengthen the Syrian army, whose ranks were decimated during the civil war. Presidential Decree Number 8 was issued on June 4, 2018, in order to bestow significant benefits to active and retired military: housing, educational opportunities, and a salary raise of 25 percent. While the regime has so far refrained from seeking genuine reconciliation with the opposition (an attitude matched by a lingering hostility by most of the political opposition), it also published Presidential Decree Number 18, in October 2018, which granted a general amnesty for military deserters inside and outside the country. This decree had a dual purpose: it was part of Asad's efforts to normalize life in the country, and it was part of his effort to facilitate the rebuilding of the Syrian army. While this move allowed for the integration of some former opposition fighters into regular army units, it was not a genuine effort at a domestic reconciliation. Syrians who live in areas liberated by the regime such as the southwest who remain in touch on social media with Western observers testify to persecution of individuals suspected of disloyalty. As one of these observers noted: "The terror exercised by the Syrian state that was open and well documented during the war has now returned to the torture basements. Instead of disfigured bodies, destroyed homes and children fluttering in the aftermath of chemical attacks, Syria is returning to clear cut, familiar patterns of violence: arrests, disappearances and obituaries."[4] Other reports indicate that large numbers of political prisoners, some old, some new, are being executed by the regime.[5]

The integration of loyalist militias into the regular armed forces has proved to be a challenging task. Such local militias have resisted the efforts to disband them, some owing to their size and power and others to their patronage (one notable example is the militia financed by Rami Makhluf). These have continued to operate, oftentimes embarrassing the regime by acts of extortion. It has been easier for the regime to deal with smaller groups normally by assigning individual members to regular units.[6]

One important lesson learned by Bashar from the uprising was the realization that the weakening of the Ba'th Party during the first decade of the century had significantly weakened the regime's hold over the country. In an authoritarian regime, a major function of the ruling party is to penetrate the society and create a two-way flow between the regime and the population. The consequences of the regime's downgrading of the party were manifested by its failure to realize the extent of popular discontent and to deal with it early on. During the years of fighting between regime and opposition, the regime's policies were formulated at the highest level, mostly by military and security leaders, without due consideration of input by party loyalists on the local level. As the regime in 2017 and 2018 began recapturing areas that had been under opposition rule, it has been using the Ba'th Party as a major instrument for reestablishing its control. It has also been recruiting large number of mostly young persons into the party's ranks. In Hama, for example, fully under regime control, party membership is a prerequisite for employment in state institutions. In Afrin, when it was controlled by the Kurdish YPG militia, the party was used in a limited way in order to maintain at least an element of regime authority.[7] At the extreme end of this spectrum is southern Syria, where the regime is still hard put to impose its control and restore at least a semblance of normalcy.

A detailed report from the province of Dar'a (retaken by the regime in the summer of 2018) describes a confused reality. The crucial dividing line is between communities that negotiated capitulation agreements with the regime or with the Russian military police, and those that were captured by force. In the case of towns that made a deal, such as Busra al-Sham, Jasem, and Tafas, local actors—many of them former rebels—continue to operate and have the capacity to negotiate the provision of basic services with the regime and with the Russians. These locations enjoy seminormal services and are free of governmental terror. Other locations taken by force, such as Inkhil, have no services and are terrorized by the army. Residents who complain of nightly abductions and arrests complain also of Shi'ization (by which they mean the empowerment of the Shi'i population).[8] These complaints need not be taken literally. At least a quarter of Busra's residents were Shi'a who were forced out when the rebels captured the town in 2015; they have yet to return. Complaints of Shi'ization may well refer to their efforts to return as well as to the role played by Hezbollah in the region. In December 2018 reports circulated of graffiti and antiregime demonstrations in different parts of the province where the Syrian revolt had broken out in March 2011. These were manifestation of local discontent as well as of the fragility of the regime's authority in parts of Syria.

The discrepancy between the regime's nominal control and the reality on the ground has been most acute in the governorate of Dar'a, where the 2011 revolt began. The rebel forces in Dar'a were forced to surrender to the regime in July 2018 and sign "reconciliation agreements," as part of which they surrendered their weapons, after the United States informed them that it would no longer protect them against the attacks of the regime's army and the Russian forces. But the July agreement failed to provide peace and quiet. The residents of the governorate are furious at the regime, which, they say, continues to arrest locals and to send former rebels to fight in the north of the country in violation of the reconciliation agreements.

The statue of Hafez Al-Asad in the city's Tishreen Square, which had been pulled down in 2011, was reerected. The protests in Dar'a were exacerbated by that. Since March 2019 Dar'a has been witnessing several waves of protests, with resident demanding the fall of the regime, and more concretely with the removal of Iranian militias from the area, and the release of prisoners. The chants voiced by the demonstrators included

"Freedom forever, in spite of you Asad" and "We don't want your Shabiha checkpoints."[9]

A report from central Syria in mid-September 2018 described the grim reality in the area north of Homs and south of Hama in a similar vein. Capitulation agreements ("settlement and reconciliation" was the term used to refer to the agreements made between the regime and the rebels during the reconquest of rebel held areas) were not honored, and dozens of former opposition fighters were arrested. Residents complained of "thefts, looting and stealing by the regime forces and militiamen loyal to them, where they looted jewelry and money with no party to hold them accountable."[10] Displaced persons who returned hoping to regain their employment encountered a regime policy of assigning governmental positions to family members of proregime soldiers and fighters who had been killed or wounded during the civil war.

In 2017 the eastern part of Aleppo was still in ruins. Like in parts of Syria retaken by the regime, government presence was hardly felt; war profiteers appropriated such services as electricity and water supply, and the population was subject to checkpoints, extortion, looting, even murder, all perpetrated mostly by the Tiger Forces, the brutal Alawi militia. Pro-Iranian militias operating under the umbrella of LDF (Local Defense Forces) were also busy embedding themselves across the province, also offering the services that the state was not providing at the time. But as of 2018 the regime is making a visible and, to some extent effective, effort at reconstruction and normalization. Curiously, Russian military police plays a role in providing security, and Russian welfare organizations are providing humanitarian aid. In areas that are fully under the regime's control such as Damascus and Aleppo the overall situation is better, and the reconstruction process is more evident than in other parts of the country, but there too the transition from war to a normal way of life is very slow.

The regime's improved relationship with several Arab states has been a key part of its quest for returned normalization and legitimacy. Although only two Arab states (the United Arab Emirates and Bahrain) had renewed diplomatic relations with Syria by the end of 2018 and Syria has yet to be readmitted into the Arab League, its relations with a number of Arab states has improved significantly. Sisi's Egypt had never been particularly hostile to Asad, given its hostility to the Muslim Brotherhood and, by extension, to the Islamist and Jihadist components of the Syrian opposition. Other Arab states have now adopted a pragmatic approach. As they see it, Asad won the civil war and is here to stay; Syria is too important an Arab country to be ignored or shunned. One early significant step was the signing in November 2017 of a memorandum of understanding between Syria and Oman to cooperate in the energy sphere, presented at the time as a step in the reconstruction of Syria's damaged oil facilities.

Jordan, a major supporter of the military opposition, agreed with the regime to reopen the border crossing at al-Nassib as a first step in restarting economic cooperation. In November 2018, a Jordanian parliamentary delegation visited Damascus and met with Asad. Ignoring the real history of the past few years and overcome by his own rhetoric, the head of the Jordanian delegation stated, "The Jordanian people in its entirety supported Asad during the years of fighting since Syria's victory is the victory of the Arab world over Western elements prompted by Israel who wish to undermine stability and the Arab pact."[11] Invoking the Israeli dimension in this context was yet another indication of the return to pre-2011 rhetoric after several years of almost total preoccupation with domestic Arab politics. In December 2018, Omar Bashir, Sudan's controversial president at the time, became the first Arab head of state to visit Syria since the start of the civil war—flown to Syria in a Soviet plane.

These developments led David Lesch, author of *Syria: The Fall of The House of Assad*, to publish a paper written with Kamal Alam on December 7 entitled "The Road to Damascus: The Arabs March Back to Befriend Asad."[12] The paper described these improved relations with other Arab states and argued (with some exaggeration) that the Saudis, the Emiratis, and the Egyptians are all now courting Asad in an effort to contain the Iranians, the Turks, and the Qataris—and as a result, Asad can thus return to the familiar and more comfortable game of inter-Arab and regional politics as an actor rather than as an object.

On December 27, 2018, Tunisia announced the resumption of commercial flights to and from Syria (its decision was followed two days later by a similar Italian decision). In an interview Asad granted to the Kuwaiti newspaper *Al-Shahed* in October 2018, he acknowledged this more optimistic outlook on his position in the Arab world: "Soon the curtain will fall on this terrorist war, the game will change and Syria will return to its pivotal role in support of the causes of the Arab nation."[13] On October 24 Husam Zaki, assistant secretary general of the Arab League, told reporters in Cairo that there has been no consensus on ending the suspension of Syria's membership in the League. For a country whose capital, Damascus, was known as "Arabism's pulsating heart," suspension from the Arab League was a major humiliation, and readmission into its ranks would be a major symbol of a return to normalcy.

Political Settlement, Reconstruction, and Return of Refugees

The issues of reconstruction, political settlement, and reconciliation in postwar Syria are closely connected. Huge sums of money will be required to rebuild a country devastated by more than nine years of war. The more modest estimates are in the range of $250 to $300 billion dollars; US diplomat and head of the administration's professional task force on Syria Ambassador James Jeffrey stated in December 2018 that "according to the UN, $400 billion dollars will be required."[14] Such large sums of money can come only from the United States and Europe, from international agencies funded by them, or from Arab Gulf countries (Russia and Iran, both under sanctions, do not have that kind of money and in any event are not keen to spend money on Syria's reconstruction except on projects that benefit Russian and Iranian corporations). Long-standing US policy, unchanged under the Trump administration, is that the United States would not participate in Syria's reconstruction unless three conditions are met: political reform; the return of refugees; and the emergence of a legitimate regime in Syria. Given Asad's opposition to any real political reform and his reluctance to admit back most of the refugees, these conditions will be impossible to meet.

As we have seen, efforts to reach a political settlement in Syria during the last few years have been conducted on two separate tracks: the Astana process, led by Russia, Iran, and Turkey; and the UN process, led by the UN envoy Staffan de Mistura, based on Security Council Resolution 2254, and supported by the United States and its western European allies. Since both tracks are stalemated, the focus has turned to an effort that began in October 2018, to convene a constitutional committee to draft a new Syrian constitution. The regime and the opposition are each to appoint fifty delegates; fifty more will have to be mutually agreed on. As might be expected, this has proved to be a stumbling block as the parties cannot agree on such a common list. Furthermore, the Syrian HNC (High Negotiations Committee) suspended its participation in the process as long as the regime's campaign in Idlib is being pursued. Even if this issue is resolved and the joint committee begins its deliberations, coming to an agreement on the most fundamental issues of governance in Syria through this committee will prove to be a herculean effort. De Mistura himself ended his term on January 1, 2019, and was replaced by the Norwegian diplomat Geir Pedersen, who began his work with visits to Damascus and Moscow. In May 2019, he insisted that "US-Russia cooperation is a key to pushing ahead a peace deal for Syria, but the Damascus government must agree to [make the necessary] steps. . . . Without that, we risk what I call a 'no war, no peace' scenario where things will continue to be complicated and we will not see a Syria that is a normal part of international society in the future."[15]

During the final month of 2019 some apparent progress was made when an agreement was reached on the composition of 150 members of the constitutional committee made up of fifty representatives of the regime, fifty representatives of the opposition, and fifty representatives chosen by UN members of civil society. In a move conducted on both the Astana and the UN tracks, the committee was convened twice by Pedersen. But the meeting failed to produce any concrete progress and by the end of the year was stalled by the inability to convene a third meeting.[16]

A second highly complex issue is the future of the approximately twelve million refugees and IDPs (internally displaced persons) produced by the Syrian civil war. Officially the regime expresses support for the return of all refugees, but the reality is more complex. It is estimated that some five million refugees live close to Syria's borders: 3.25 million in Turkey, close to a million in Lebanon, and close to seven hundred thousand in Jordan. It is estimated that the million or so refugees who managed to get to Europe (and in smaller numbers, to the United States and Canada) are unlikely to return. Another seven million or so are displaced within Syria, having left their homes to seek shelter in more secure areas. Foreign Minister Mu'allem stated in October 2018 during the UN General Assembly that "there was no longer any reason for refugees to stay outside of Syria. The doors are open for all Syrians abroad to return voluntarily and safely,"[17] but others, including members of the regime's inner circle, have spoken differently, making clear that they would rather have the refugees remain outside Syria. In their eyes those refugees are a disloyal, potentially rebellious element that choose not to support the regime. Asad loyalists have suggested that a smaller Syrian population with a higher percentage of Alawis would be preferable to an attempted reintegration of this diaspora. For example, Jamil Hasan, head of Air Force Intelligence, said in public that "a Syria with ten million trustworthy people obedient to the leadership is better than a Syria with thirty million vandals."[18] Bashar al-Asad himself articulated the same view in a more subtle fashion when he said: "I would like us to understand that what we are experiencing is not an isolated stage, but linked to those that have preceded it for several decades. We have lost the best of our young people and an infrastructure that has cost us a lot of money and sweat over several generations. But in return, we have gained a healthier and more harmonious society."[19]

In 2010, Syria's population was estimated at twenty-one million, while in 2019 it was estimated to be about seventeen million, with more than six million living outside Syria. Of the seventeen million living in Syria, close to seven million are estimated to be IDPs, and among the seventeen million, the proportion of Alawis is estimated to have gone up to 17 percent.[20]

Uncharacteristically, Russia's position as the regime's patron is similar to that of the West. In Moscow's view, the refugees would be an essential work force in a revived economy and a catalyst for international aid and investment, and the return of the refugees would expedite the reconstruction process, help revive the Syrian economy, and bring the country closer to normalization. Russia would be happy to see Western participation in a repatriation process that would legitimate the regime and bolster Russia's standing.

While these issues remain unresolved, the regime, as part of the transition to a new, post-Aleppo-victory phase, launched a program of reconstruction. During 2018 the regime realized that in order to upgrade the process it had to shift the focus from the tactical level to strategic planning and management. The government decided to abandon the policy of allocating funds to different cities, and to focus its efforts instead on the national level. A new authority, the Syrian Planning and International Cooperation Commission (ICC) headed by Imad Sabuni, was to deal with five issues: institutions, services, economy, society, and policy. It is still unclear what real effect the committee's work has had so far. In 2020 the need to deal with the coronavirus pandemic was added to the regime's challenges. Syria imposed a lockdown and reported a strikingly low number of infected and dead. Given the regime's low credibility, these figures are not taken seriously at home or abroad. In the long run Syria is most likely to be affected by the reluctance or inability of potential regional and international donors and participants in reconstruction efforts.

In Bashar's Syria, the formal structures dealing with reconstruction often serve to conceal the oversized role assigned to members of the country's corrupt business elite who form the core support group for the regime. Thus Rami Makhluf launched a new corporation in September 2018 whose activities in a variety of fields were described as part of the reconstruction effort. A relatively new face, Samer al-Foz, is in charge of reconstruction projects in Homs. Foz is a newcomer to Bashar's circle, having made the bulk of his fortune during and from the war. A man with a shady past, Foz had been wealthy prior to the civil war but dramatically increased his fortune during and after the war. In 2017 his company, Aman Holding, was transformed in collaboration with the regime into the larger Aman Damascus Group. In June 2019 the US Treasury Department announced that Foz and some of his companies were blacklisted for their financial support of Bashar al-Asad.

Despite the failure to attract major international investment, the regime was able to allocate several projects to Syrian businessmen affiliated with the regime (one notable example is Marota City, a residential construction project in Damascus assigned to Rami Makhluf). This particular project is emblematic of the politics and reality of postwar Syria, as original poor residents were forced out in order to create space for a project designed to benefit supporters and assigned to Asad's family banker. The government's current policy can rely on initial investments made by such businessmen with a view to making future profits.

In the absence of Western investment in the country, most of the initial funding for reconstruction efforts (rehabilitation of infrastructures and of the armed forces) has come from Russia and Iran and, to a lesser extent, from China. The not-so-subtle competition between Russia and Iran is manifested in the reconstruction efforts as well. Both countries are interested in Syria's oil industry; it was Russia that secured long-term concessions for developing and extracting Syrian oil. In August 2018, Iran's minister of defense visited Syria in order to secure a role in the reconstruction of Syria's military as well as defense industries. The Iranians were compensated by being awarded contracts for the reconstruction of Syria's electric grid and were accorded a role in the telecommunication market. Iranian companies affiliated with the (Iranian) Revolutionary Guards were also given control of mining facilities and the extraction of phosphates, only to find out later that Russian companies were subsequently given precedence in this domain.[21]

The United States' Role and Policy

The crucial American decisions with regard to the Syrian rebellion were made by President Obama in 2012 and 2013, when he overruled the plan formulated by his own national security team to arm and train the FSA, and when he decided to ignore his own red line and refrain from penalizing Asad for massive use of chemical weapons against his own civilian population. Until the end of his term Obama continued to resist massive US involvement in the Syrian civil war. He did authorize logistical support and training to parts of the Syrian military opposition but objected to any US participation in the fighting. Since the appearance of the IS challenge, the United States has played the leading role in building and managing the international coalition designed to defeat and destroy the organization. But the

United States refrained from any military action that could be seen as directed against Asad's regime.

This mode and approach, surprisingly, were adopted, perpetuated, and taken further by Obama's successor, Donald Trump, in his position on Syria. On December 14, 2018, President Trump conducted a telephone conversation with Turkey's president, Recep Tayyip Erdogan, to follow up their conversation two weeks earlier during the Group of Twenty meeting in Argentina. As he did in Argentina and on numerous other occasions, Erdogan complained of Washington's support of and cooperation with the Kurdish PYD. For Erdogan the PYD was an extension of the PKK, a terrorist group and a threat to Turkish national security. As he saw it, the original purpose of this collaboration—the defeat of IS—had essentially been accomplished. The residual challenge by IS, Erdogan argued, could be dealt with by the Turkish military. Surprisingly Trump responded by saying to his Turkish counterpart, "You know what? It is yours. We are leaving."[22] A week later, on December 19, Trump made a public announcement of his decision when he tweeted, "We have defeated ISIS in Syria, [my] only reason for being there during the Trump presidency."[23] Later that day, speaking outside the White House, Trump stated again: "We have been fighting for a long time in Syria. I have been president for almost two years and we have really stepped it up and we have won against ISIS. We have beaten them badly. We have taken back the land and now it's time for our troops to come back home."[24]

Trump's decision generated much criticism and debate in the United States. On December 20, Trump tweeted three times at greater length, saying: "Getting out of Syria was no surprise. I have been campaigning on it for years, and six months ago when I very publicly wanted to do it, I agreed to stay longer." In a subsequent tweet Trump asked rhetorically, "Does the US want to be the policeman of the Middle East, getting nothing but spending precious lives and trillions of dollars protecting others who, in almost all cases, do not appreciate what we are doing. Do we want to be there forever, time for others to finally fight?"[25]

It is true that six months earlier Trump had wanted to pull America's two thousand troops from eastern and northeastern Syria and had said so in public. But at the time he was persuaded by his national security team and by French president Macron to keep the troops in place in order to continue the unfinished campaign against IS. His decision in December (and the fashion in which it was made and announced) surprised and embarrassed his own team and several of his allies. Ambassador James Jeffrey had spoken in December 17 at the Atlantic Council in Washington and presented a very different perspective on US policy in Syria. Implying a US commitment to a long-term presence and effort, Jeffrey again described the three goals of the United States in Syria: (1) enduring defeat of IS; (2) "changed regime" (importantly, not "regime change," i.e., getting rid of Asad); and (3) eliminating Iranian ground troops and long-range missile capabilities from Syria.[26]

By "enduring defeat" of IS Jeffrey meant that the struggle against IS will not end with their final defeat in Syria, rather that the United States and its allies will have to monitor the organization's efforts at a comeback. With regard to Asad, Jeffrey expressed the view that Asad's continued rule in Syria would be a destabilizing force, and he suggested that a leadership change was needed. By saying "changed regime" not "regime change," Jeffrey intended to signal that the United States was not conducting a campaign to topple Asad, but rather was seeking political reform and change in Syria that will produce "a regime that does not produce the kind of horrors that we have seen . . .

a different kind of regime that rejected sponsorship of terrorism, use of chemical weapons and violence against its own citizens."[27] In theory a reformed Asad regime could meet this definition, but Jeffrey knew very well that in reality such transformation of Asad's regime was unfeasible.

Partners of the United States such as the Syrian Kurds, France, and to a lesser extent Israel were alarmed by the repercussions of Trump's decision. Other US allies such as Saudi Arabia were further alarmed by the sense that the United States was expediting the pivot away from the Middle East begun by Obama, as well as by the message that the United States was not a reliable partner or patron.

One of the most significant responses to Trump's decision was the resignation of Secretary of Defense James Mattis. Mattis's letter of resignation, published on December 20, 2019, was poignant. Mattis wrote:

> One core belief I have always held is that our strength as a nation is inextricably linked to the strength of our unique and comprehensive system of alliances and partnerships. While the US remains the indispensable nation in the free world, we cannot protect our interests or serve that role effectively without maintaining strong alliances and showing respect to those allies. Like you, I have said from the beginning that the armed forces of the United States should not be the policeman of the world. Instead, we must use all tools of American power to provide for the common defense, including providing effective leadership to our alliances. NATO's 29 democracies demonstrated that strength in their commitment to fighting alongside us following the 9–11 attack on America. The Defeat-IS coalition of 74 nations is further proof.

My views on treating allies with respect and also being clear-eyed about both malign actors and strategic competitors are strongly held and informed by over four decades of immersion in these issues. We must do everything possible to advance an international order that is most conducive to our security, prosperity and values, and we are strengthened in this effort by the solidarity of our alliances.

Because you have the right to have a Secretary of Defense whose views are better aligned with yours on these and other subjects, I believe it is right for me to step down from my position.[28]

Trump was particularly hurt by Mattis's resignation and the tone and language of his announcement. Mattis was the last of the three internationally esteemed generals (the others were McMaster and Kelly) who had joined the administration out of a strong sense of duty. Trump reacted by firing him immediately, undermining the secretary's original decision to stay in office until February 2019.

On December 23, Brett McGurk, the US special presidential envoy for the global coalition to defeat IS, also tendered his resignation. In his letter of resignation, McGurk directly contested Trump's attempt to justify his decision by arguing that IS had been defeated. The US envoy argued that "IS militants in Syria were on the run but not yet defeated. . . . Withdrawing US forces from Syria would create the conditions that gave rise to IS."[29] On January 18, 2019, McGurk expanded his criticism of Trump's decision and the fashion in which it was made and communicated it in an angry op-ed he published in the *Washington Post*.[30]

In February 2019 General Joseph Votel, who as the commander of CENTCOM had been in charge of the anti-IS campaign came out with his own criticism of Trump's policy.[31]

In a United States buffeted by bitter debates between Trump's supporters and critics, the decision to withdraw from Syria and the fashion in which it was made brought the public discourse to a new level of acrimony. Trump's defenders endorsed his refusal to invest resources and risk lives in an arena most Americans do not know or understand, while his critics argued that the future of Syria and IS are important to America's national security, that the United States was accomplishing much with a small investment, and that commitments to allies and partners must be honored. Under the weight of the vocal criticism, Trump tried to cushion the impact of his decision. His visit to US troops in Iraq on December 26 was likely motivated in part by the desire to send a message of determination to pursue Washington's interests and commitments in the Middle East. During the visit, Trump also stated that the United States could use its presence in Iraq should it decide or need to act again in Syria. Later, after a conversation with Republican senator Lindsey Graham (who had criticized Trump's decision), and with Israel's prime minister Netanyahu, the US president agreed to implement the withdrawal from Syria in a gradual manner over four months rather than in thirty days.

The concerns of and the complaints by the president's own national security team, American critics, and European and Middle Eastern allies had an impact. While it is not President Trump's habit to admit mistakes, during the next few weeks several actions and statements by the Trump administration were taken in order to mitigate the impact of the president's decision. Among them were a tour of several Sunni states in the Middle East by Secretary of State Pompeo; a visit to Israel by the national security adviser, John Bolton; and a number of statements in January from Pompeo and Bolton about stretching the withdrawal from Syria over time and keeping US troops in the strategic border crossing between Iraq and Syria in Al-Tanf. Pompeo's and Bolton's statements in fact directly contradicted Trump's original statement and tweet. The license Trump gave to his aides to try to reduce the damage with these conflicting statements resulted in confusion (and in the case of Erdogan, anger) without effectively mitigating the effects of the president's action. The subsequent announcement on January 11 by the president that the evacuation of US troops (or equipment) from Syria had begun served only to compound this confusion.

Other than the damages described above, the net effect of Trump's decision was minimal. Without admitting it, the administration did not implement the withdrawal announcement, and in the summer of 2019 the same two thousand American soldiers remained in Syria. Furthermore in March 2019, the SDF, backed by the international coalition, completed the campaign against IS by capturing the town of al-Ba'ruz al-Fawqani in the eastern part of the Euphrates.

On March 25, 2019, the Trump administration added yet another twist to its Syrian policy when Trump published a presidential decree recognizing Israel's annexation of the Golan. This was a rather peculiar step given that in fact Israel had not annexed the Golan. In December 1981, Prime Minister Begin chose to extend Israeli law to the Golan rather than annex it. Other than seeking to penalize the Asad regime, the only plausible explanation was Trump's sustained effort to help Benjamin Netanyahu in the March elections in Israel. In yet another unusual step, Secretary of State Pompeo and US ambassador to Israel David Friedman joined forces in publishing an op-ed in the *Wall Street Journal* on May 14, 2019, trying to justify the president's decree. Among other things they argued that "Damascus has for fifty two years rejected the negotiating framework of Resolution 242."[32] It was a peculiar and hollow statement given that since 1991 Syria had negotiated on the basis of that resolution with six Israeli prime ministers including Benjamin Netanyahu.

The December 2018 episode was repeated in a starker fashion in October 2019 in another phone conversation with the Turkish president Erdogan, when Trump succumbed to the latter's persistent pressure and agreed to Turkish invasion into the area held by America's Kurdish allies in northeastern Syria. Trump's decision launched a rapid chain of events.

On October 9 the Turkish air force launched aerial and land attacks on the SDF's positions in northeastern Syria, focusing on the border towns including Ayn Issa.

Turkey's own military units were joined by the Syrian National Army (SNA), the name given to the remnants of the Free Syrian Army (FSA), which had become fully subordinated to Turkish control. Ironically, an operation named by Turkey "Operation Peace Spring" resulted in more than a hundred casualties and the uprooting of some three hundred residents (for further elaboration, see below).

These developments—the abandonment of Washington's Kurdish allies in the fight against IS, the haphazard fashion in which Trump made crucial foreign policy decisions, his unexplainable softness vis-à-vis Erdogan, and the new opportunities presented to Russia and Iran in Syria, as well as the prospect of an IS resurgence produced a wave of criticism more powerful than the one produced in December 2018. The US president contributed to an exacerbation of the controversy by vilifying American Kurdish allies, charging among other things that the Kurds had not contributed to the allies' landing in Normandy.

Under these circumstances, Trump once again reversed the bulk of his decision. While some US troops were pulled out of the area captured by Turkey, most of the US contingent in Syria was kept in place under the pretext that their mission was to protect Syria's oil fields. For a president who seeks an economic rationale for foreign involvement, the notion of keeping troops in Syria in order to control its oil fields was more attractive than other justifications. Throughout this episode, the discrepancy between the substance and style of a volatile president and his bureaucracy's efforts to conduct a rational national security policy was particular stark.

At the end of 2019, according to American officials, at least six hundred troops remained in Syria, two hundred near Al-Tanf near the border in the southeast and the rest in the north. And while the president continues to justify their presence by arguing that they protect the oil fields, his team is in fact pursuing a different agenda: keeping the cooperation of the Syrian Kurds, preserving the achievements of the anti-IS campaign, and trying to limit Iranian and Russian expansion. In this context it should be mentioned that in October, thirty US navy seals successfully killed Abu Baker al-Baghdadi. President Trump took credit for this success choosing to ignore the fact that it would not have been possible without America's presence and partners in the region.

In December 2019, the US Congress initiated and passed the Syria Civilian Protection Act (known as the Caesar Act), imposing fresh sanctions on the Syrian regime, including the president, for war crimes against the Syrian population. The bill itself was not passed into law, but parts of it were incorporated in the National Defense Authorization Act for fiscal year 2020.

Russia, Iran, Turkey

Even with a small US force remaining in Syria, Russia, Iran, and Turkey are the three principal external actors present in the country. Of the three, Russia is the predominant actor. Russian air force and naval units occupy the bases in Khmeimim and Tartus, and Russian military police play a role in enforcing agreements to deescalate the conflict and maintain law and order in parts of the country.

Russian policy in Syria is pursuing multiple aims. Moscow is interested in stabilizing the country by limiting—if not eliminating—all violence; promoting a political settlement and normalization of public life; encouraging the process of reconstruction; rebuilding and strengthening the Syrian army; reducing its own investment and expenditure; and recouping past expenses by benefiting from the reconstruction process and the country's natural resources. In 2020 a series of articles in the Russian press critical of Bashar al-Asad, and depicting him as corrupt and devoid of public support, were either a reflection of exasperation with Asad's refusal to move on with reconciliation and political reform or a means of pressuring him to grant Russian companies a larger share of Syria's economic pie. Russia's interests in Syria go well beyond the country itself. Moscow wants to be (and to be perceived as) an arbiter in the Middle East, and it views its achievement and position in Syria as an asset in its global give-and-take with the United States.

The degree of Russia's influence in Syria was once again demonstrated by the role it played after Turkey's incursion in October 2019. One of the by-products of the invasion was an agreement between the SDF and the Syrian regime. Given the Turkish threat, the Syrian Kurds saw partnership with the regime as a lesser evil and invited the return of Syrian military units to the territory controlled by them. This raised the prospect of a military confrontation between the regime and Turkey. It was in order to eliminate this risk as well as to demonstrate its role as the final arbiter in Syria that Moscow interceded. On October 22 in Sochi, Putin and Erdogan reached a ten-point agreement that limited the scope of the Turkish operations, put an end to the fighting, and established a mechanism of joint patrol in the new security zone created by the Turkish invasion.

From Moscow's perspective, Iran in Syria is a partner whose interests overlap but are not identical with its own. Once Moscow felt that Asad had won the civil war, its reliance on Iran's "boots on the ground" declined. Moscow became increasingly uneasy with Iran's aggressive campaign to embed itself militarily in Syria in 2017 and 2018. This campaign mitigated Russia's effort to obtain stability in Syria and provoked Israeli countermeasures. Russia tolerated Israel's military campaign against the construction of an Iranian military infrastructure in Syria but grew increasingly uneasy with it as well. It exploited the shooting down of its plane in September 2018 to limit Israel's freedom of action in Syria's and Lebanon's airspace. Russia also continues to make a large investment in Syrian air defense, whose importance goes beyond the Syrian arena. Air defense systems are an important component of Russian defense export. The performance of its systems in Syria—one of the few arenas of active aerial combat—is a matter of both prestige and revenue (given the Russian drive to sell weapon systems around the globe).

The Iranians, for their part, began after 2016 to develop their own military infrastructure in Syria, seeking to end their almost exclusive dependence on Hezbollah's arsenal of missiles and rockets in Lebanon. The Iranian strategy seeks to develop an arsenal of sophisticated missiles and rockets in Syria, and to deploy the nine thousand or so Shi'i militiamen in different parts of the country, including in the Syrian Golan. Israel's attacks on their emerging infrastructure demonstrated their inferiority in the Syrian arena. One of their responses to this reality has been a further shift of some of their efforts to Iraq, close enough to threaten Israel and less exposed to Israeli attacks. In this context the announced US withdrawal from eastern Syria, and in particular from the crucial area of Al-Tanf, could play into Teheran's hands.

The killing of Qasem Suleimani, the chief architect of Iran's policy in Syria (and in the region), raises a question mark as to Teheran's ability to maintain the same level of efficacy. The speculations concerning this issue were enhanced by Vladimir Putin's decision to pay a visit to Syria in the immediate aftermath of Suleimani's killing. Putin's visit to Syria held two years after his first visit to that country in 2017 led commentators to argue that Moscow was trying to take advantage of the anticipated decline in Iran's influence in order to increase its own.[33] Increasing economic pressures and the impact of the coronavirus pandemic seem to have induced Iran in the spring of 2020 to reduce and redeploy some of its forces to Syria's eastern and northern parts.

Turkey, for its part, is consolidating and expanding its presence and position in Syria, and limiting if not eliminating Kurdish autonomy in the area. Another Turkish concern is the prevention of yet another wave of Syrian refugees, particularly from Idlib. Over time the Turkish government became concerned with the long-term impact of close to four million Syrian refugees on the country. The government refuses to accept the refugees as permanent residents that will have to be integrated into Turkish society, and its official position is that they will have to go back to Syria.

At the same time Turkey uses the presence of the Syrian refugees on its soil as means of pressuring Europe. For one thing Turkey received from Europe some three billion Euros a year in order to keep Syrian refugees in place, and when criticized for his brutality during his invasion of Syria, Erdogan threatened to undermine Europe by sending another wave of Syrian refugees. Erdogan's desire to rid Turkey of at least some of its Syrian refugees was manifested in October 2019. Turkey's original plan was to capture a large swath of territory along the Turkish Syrian border and to use it both as a means of separating the Syrian from the Turkish Kurds and as a means of settling in it a large number of refugees residing in Turkey. This grandiose plan had to be abandoned and replaced by a more modest scheme.

Erdogan relishes his role as one of the three partners to the Astana process, and he scored a major achievement when Donald Trump communicated to him and announced his decision to withdraw from Syria and to end his partnership with the Syrian Kurds. The Syrian Kurds are seeking regime support against the Turks and are likely to get some but not full support from Damascus. Turkey will likely stay in the border areas that it had occupied and increase that area by taking over some of the territory that had been held by the Kurds.

The Turks also use the pro-Turkish Syrian forces that had originally been the FSA as an instrument for exercising control and influence in northern Syria. Initially pleased by Trump's decision to withdraw, on January 7, 2019, President Erdogan signed an op-ed published in the *New York Times*: "President Trump made the right call to withdraw from Syria," Erdogan wrote. But then came a qualification: "The US decision, however, must be planned carefully and performed in coordination with the right partner."[34] That partner, needless to say, was

Turkey. Turkey considered itself to have fought the Islamic State effectively and without inflicting collateral damage, and to be amply qualified to bring stability and good governance to northern and northeastern Syria (it is important to note that Turkish influence on local governance in northern Syria is not projected from Ankara but rather from such localities as Gaziantep). Turkey was also the only country other than Israel that could work with both the United States and Russia in the Syrian context. The op-ed continued with the presentation of a thinly disguised plan to create local councils that would scrap the powers acquired by the Kurdish PYD and YPG, which made no secret of Turkey's intention to embed itself in that part of Syria.

But just as Erdogan's piece was being published, National Security Adviser John Bolton poured cold water on Turkey's plan by announcing in Jerusalem that the United States objected to further Turkish military action in Syria that was not "fully coordinated" with Washington. The United States, he said, "will condition its Syria pullout on Turkish assurance to safeguard its Kurdish allies."[35] Erdogan responded to this furiously. He said that Bolton's statement was "a serious mistake"[36] and refused to meet with him during his visit to Ankara. The US-Turkish feud was further escalated by Donald Trump when on January 13 he threatened to destroy Turkey's economy should it attack the Syrian Kurds.

But this episode was followed by yet another twist in US policy when President Trump agreed to host Erdogan in the White House in November 2019 and showered him with praised. During the visit, the *New York Times* reported that the US-Turkey relationship was in fact conducted through an informal channel made up of Trump's son-in-law and Erdogan's son-in-law, a Turkish magnate with business connections to the Trump's family.[37]

In contradistinction to Trump's inconsistent attitude toward Turkey's president, Emmanuel Macron emerged as the most stridently opposed to the liberty taken by Turkey as a NATO member, purchasing a Russian-made weapon system and undermining the campaign against IS by its attack on the SDF. Macron spoke on anticipation of a NATO summit in London, and Erdogan responded to him by denouncing France and its president in an unusually sharp language.

The twists and turns of US policy, the rapprochement between the Syrian Kurds and the Asad's regime, and Russia's intervention with the view of preventing a Turkish-Syrian military collision led to the suspension of Operation Peace Spring. Turkey had to temporarily abandon the operation's ambitious goals, but it threatens to resume its offensive, claiming the Kurds do not live up to the understandings reached between Erdogan and Putin.

Alongside the United States, Turkey played at the end of 2018 an important role in preventing a regime offensive in the province of Idlib, the last stronghold of the opposition. In 2017–18 Jihadists from different parts of Syria migrated to Idlib, where they now form a powerful presence.

The arrangement that was reached in order to prevent a regime offensive with Russian and Iranian aid was predicated on a Turkish commitment to rein in the Jihadists. To Moscow's chagrin, Turkey did not quite live up to that commitment.

Yet another twist in Turkey's Syria policy occurred when Turkey decided to send some fifteen hundred soldiers, remnants of the FSA now purely under Turkish control, to fight as de facto mercenaries in the Libyan civil war on the side of Turkey's ally the Libyan president.

In May 2019, when the Salafi Jihadi organization Hay'at Tahrir al-Sham (HTS) launched an attack against the Russian air base Khmeimim, it seems for a while that Russia might opt out of the arrangement and launch an all-out offensive. Moscow was openly critical of what it saw as a Turkish failure to live up to Ankara's commitments. In the event, the Russians and the regime launched what was defined as a limited offensive, but which caused massive damage to innocent civilians. The regime's and Moscow's efforts to depict the offensive that began in May as "limited" needs to be taken with a grain of salt. The regime, supported by its allies, is determined to eliminate the opposition in Idlib and to bring the city and the province under their full control.[38]

Russia and the regime continued their persistent military pressure in Idlib, which occasionally developed into massive air and land campaigns, including indiscriminate bombing of civilian populations and targets; a particularly ferocious campaign in December 2019 resulted in a large wave of IDPs estimated at 230,000.

Owing to Turkey's strict policy of the cordoning of the border, only a small number of refugees manged to cross into Turkey.

Idlib remains one of the most significant powder kegs in the Syrian arena. This was demonstrated in February 2020 when Turkish-Syrian tensions in the province escalated into full-fledged fighting between units of the Turkish and Syrian armies.

Israeli Policy

Israel views recent developments in Syria with concern. While the US troops had no direct bearing on Israel's security, their very presence and the message of US involvement and commitment to a satisfactory outcome in Syria were seen as essential by Israel. In Israel's view, the Syrian arena was abandoned by

Washington, in a step bound to serve the policies of Russia, Iran, and Turkey. On December 25, 2018, the Israeli Air Force conducted a large-scale raid against Iranian and Hezbollah targets near Damascus. It was the first such large-scale operation since the change in Russian policy in September, and it was clearly meant to signal Israel's resolve to expand its campaign against Iran in Syria in the wake of the US decision.

Israel realizes that the Asad regime and the Syrian armed forces are back as players and need to be taken into account as hostile forces. Russian policy changed in September 2018, and, as we saw, it acted for several months to limit Israel's freedom of action in Syria and Lebanon. Israelis also noted with concern the anti-Semitic dimension of some of the Russian criticism of Israel's aerial activity in Syria. Thus, senior-level members at the Russian Ministry of Defense are reported to complain that Putin was subjected to excessive Jewish influence.[39] This phase ended as evidenced by Russia's willingness to turn a blind eye to the escalation of Israeli attacks on Iranian and Syrian targets in 2020. This escalation derives from Israel's determination to thwart Iran's entrenchment in Syria and its effort to deploy and to provide Hezbollah with precision guided missiles.

On June 24, 2019, another twist was added to Russia's policy in Syria when Russia's national security adviser joined his US and Israeli colleagues in a one-day meeting in Jerusalem. Little is known about the contents of their discussions, but while Israel tried to depict the event as a diplomatic coup—expressing Russian willingness to discuss the future of Iran's military presence in Syria—Russia's statement gave no indication of the future direction of Moscow's policy.

Iran's campaign to embed itself militarily in Syria has been moderated but not abandoned. And Israel is worried by the repercussions of Donald Trump's erratic decisions. Trump's flippant statements about giving Turkey freedom of action in Syria ("It is all yours") and his indifference to Iran's freedom of action in Syria raised concerns in Israel that the visit by National Security Adviser John Bolton on January 6, 2019, designed to reassure Jerusalem, will not necessarily allay concerns. The significance of Trump's decision goes well beyond the Syrian arena. Trump continues and intensifies Obama's policy of pivoting away from the Middle East. For Israel, a Middle East with a lesser American presence and commitment and greater Russian influence is a more dangerous place. Statements by the US president and other officials about continued support for and commitment to Israel's security therefore sound increasingly hollow to the state of Israel.

Trump's decision to kill the architect of the Iranian policy in Syria, Qasem Suleimani, was taken in a larger regional context and was a response to a repeated provocations and challenges to the United States. It is yet to be seen whether this was an isolated act or part of a larger coherent and sustained strategy.

CONCLUSION

From the Syrian Civil War to the

Lingering Syrian Crisis

The year 1965 saw the publication of British writer Patrick
Seale's classic book *The Struggle for Syria: A Study in Post-war
Arab Politics, 1945–1958*. In it Seale described how the weak Syr-
ian state that had won independence at the end of World War II
was the main arena of regional and international rivalries. Four
Arab states (Egypt, Saudi Arabia, and the Iraqi and Jordanian
Hashemite monarchies) and four foreign powers (Britain,
France, the United States, and the Soviet Union) exploited the
weakness and divisiveness of Syria in order to influence and seek
control over political opposition forces across the Middle East.[1]

Syria's weakness and instability culminated in 1958, when
the country's rulers sought refuge in a union with Egypt. Another twelve years of unstable politics ensued until Hafez al-
Asad, who took power in November 1970, managed to turn
Syria into a comparatively stable and powerful state. At last,
Syria became an effective actor in regional—and, to some extent, in international—politics.

Hafez al-Asad's achievement was destroyed by the Syrian
civil war of the years 2011–20. Hafez al-Asad's son Bashar was

able to prevent neither the outbreak of domestic revolt in the context of the larger Arab Spring nor its evolution into a full-fledged civil war. Bashar survived the civil war primarily owing to the military intervention of Russia and Iran. But the regime's victory has been far from complete, and a domestic, regional, and international conflict continues to unfold in Syria in 2020. And these conflicts are unlikely to end any time soon.

Bashar al-Asad's Survival

At the height of the civil war, numerous parties and observers predicted Asad's and the regime's fall. Yet he and his regime survived, and the opposition was defeated. This outcome can be explained by the following distinct but interrelated factors: (1) Asad's resilience and ruthlessness; (2) the weakness and divisiveness of the opposition, and the early prominence of Islamist and then Jihadi groups; (3) the emergence of IS, which created a parallel war that overshadowed the original Syrian crisis; (4) Russia's and Iran's effective support; (5) the ineffectiveness of the opposition's regional and international supporters; more specifically, (6) the reluctance of two successive US presidents, Obama and Trump, to be drawn into the Syrian crisis, thus denying the Syrian opposition the only external support that could have balanced Russia's and Iran's role; and (7) the failure of the international community to respond to the Syrian crisis with a humanitarian intervention similar to that which helped put an end to the crisis in the former Yugoslavia.

Bashar al-Asad clearly matured in office over the course of his first eleven years in power. The young heir, who was unsure of himself and not fully accepted by his father's inner circle, who vacillated between conflicting responses to the so-called Damascus Spring, who set a collision course with the George W.

Bush administration and became embroiled in Rafik al-Hariri's assassination, finally began asserting himself in 2005–6. During the next five years, Asad introduced massive changes in the regime's policies and in its traditional sources of support in Syria. These changes—combined with a severe drought and the impact of the Arab Spring—led to the outbreak of massive political protests in March 2011. During the Syrian revolt's early weeks and months, Asad acted under the contradictory advice of those who urged a ruthless crackdown on demonstrators, and others who argued that real concessions could calm the country. He finally chose the former strategy and proceeded to galvanize sectarian tensions by mobilizing the Alawi community against a mostly Sunni revolt, and to radicalize the revolt by releasing Islamist and Jihadi prisoners. During the next five years, Asad's most notable success was his ability to stay the course until his external supporters (and the brutal proregime militias) defeated his enemies. His willingness to use barrel bombs and chemical weapons against his own population and to destroy large parts of his own country, together with his Russian and Iranian supporters, gave him victory. But the long-term impact of these decisions has yet to be seen.

The overarching weakness of the opposition proved to be ultimately insurmountable. During the rebellion's early months, it seemed that a mainstream opposition was taking shape. But this trend evaporated in 2012 and 2013. The Free Syrian Army failed to become a coherent structured entity. It and other secular military groups were overshadowed by Islamist and Jihadi groups, and the political leadership was torn by intrigue and factionalism. It failed to act as a united front and to maintain a durable connection with the Syrian people. The prominence of Islamist groups (in part as a result of the regime's release of Islamist prisoners) played an important role in driving the Sunnis of Damascus and minority communities away from Bashar al-Asad's political opponents. Perhaps most critically, the political opposition failed to produce a leader that would be perceived by Syrians, Arabs, and the international community as a superior alternative to Bashar al-Asad.

The limited, uncoordinated, and halfhearted support offered to Syria's opposition by regional Sunni-majority states, the European Union, and the United States also contributed to the failure of the rebellion. Among the opposition's regional Sunni supporters, the most important dividing line was the one separating Turkey and Qatar from Saudi Arabia. The first two have been supporters of the Muslim Brotherhood and have tended to support Muslim Brotherhood–affiliated Islamist groups. For the Saudis, such groups were an anathema. Consequently, the opposition was torn between different supporters. Many local opposition military groups attached themselves to the varying sources of financial support and weapons. The result was a confusing and shifting patchwork of local alignments. The problem was exacerbated by the arrival on the scene of the Islamic State, which offered better pay and more coherent leadership, resulting in a siphoning off of significant numbers of opposition fighters from other groups. By contrast, the support extended to the Syrian regime by Russia and Iran was consistent and coordinated.

Common enmity to IS created a limited community of interests between the United States, Russia, and Iran. They remained on opposite sides of the Syrian civil war but shared the aim of defeating IS. The strategic decision made by the Islamic State's leadership in Iraq to take advantage of the Syrian civil war—to intervene, capture territory, and launch a major campaign in Iraq—resulted ultimately in the derailment of the Syrian rebellion. The Obama administration made a clear choice to fight the Islamic State while avoiding direct attacks on Bashar al-Asad's forces. The terrorist threat presented by IS in the global arena and to the Iraqi and Jordanian states led the United States to build and lead an international coalition that was ultimately able to destroy IS's territorial base, though not fully root it out in Syria and Iraq. The campaign against IS also provided Russia and Turkey with useful covers for entering Syria. Turkey announced that it was entering Syria in order to fight IS but, in fact, targeted the Syrian Kurds. Russia, while announcing it was sending its air force to fight IS, in fact used it to pummel Asad's Syrian rivals. The Islamic State did participate in the Syrian civil war and operated in parts of Syria beyond its territorial base in the east and northeast, but the organization and Asad's regime also collaborated (among other things by the regime's purchase of oil from IS). In this regard IS was very different from the other Al Qaeda–related organization, Jabhat al-Nusrah, that became a crucial part of the military opposition. For the United States, al-Nusrah remained first and foremost an Al Qaeda–related group, part of global Jihad, and therefore a target of US bombing campaigns.

The Enduring Crisis

In the coming years, Bashar al-Asad's regime is likely to continue its current drive to restore its pre–March 2011 position and status. By early 2020 the regime had reestablished control of approximately 60 percent of Syria's territory. Donald Trump's decision to withdraw US troops from Syria led the Kurds to seek a rapprochement with the regime, a policy that is likely to lead to Kurdish territorial concessions to Asad—already manifested by the Kurds' willingness to give up Manbij. The Turkish invasion of the Kurdish areas in October 2019 opened the door further to a gradual return of the Syrian regime to that part of the country. In the years ahead the regime will have to compete with Turkey over control of the territory given up by the Kurds. Getting Turkey to evacuate the territory it has already captured will be a difficult task. By the same token, the regime's quest to take over Idlib, the opposition's last remaining stronghold, is being constrained by Turkey's vested interests in that part of Syria.

In the winter of 2020, the regime's main military effort to expand the territory under its control was invested in Idlib, reinforced by indiscriminate Russian bombing. This campaign has resulted in civilian loss of life, massive destruction, and the flight of nearly a million civilians in the direction of the Turkish border.

Turkey, hosting close to 3.5 million Syrian refugees, is determined to prevent a fresh wave of immigrants. In addition to closing its border, it has resisted the Russian-Syrian military campaign to the point of risking its good relationship with Russia and colliding for the first time since 2011 directly with the Syrian army.

Given the complexity of the issues involved in the problem of Idlib (including the presence of close to thirty thousand Jihadists), that part of Syria is likely to remain a festering wound as well as a continuing humanitarian tragedy.

Russia and Iran, the regime's saviors and supporters, are ironically likely to become major obstacles to the reinstatement of full Syrian sovereignty when the fighting ends and the regime no longer has to rely on them for survival. Russia has secured long-term naval and air bases in Syria, exercises its influence over the regime's armed forces, and seeks to recover at least part of its investment throughout the war by being given a role in the reconstruction of Syria and by exploiting its natural resources. Iran's ambitions are more far reaching. It seeks not only to expand and deepen its military presence in the region, but also to penetrate Syrian society and its economy. In the years ahead Asad will likely continue to maneuver between these two allies. At present he seems inclined to tilt in Russia's direction—by, for example, acting to limit the role of pro-Iranian militias, deflecting Iran's requests for a naval base in Syria, and offering advantages to Russian companies over Iranian ones.

The road to full normalization for the Syrian state seems insurmountable, considering the daunting list of obstacles the Syrian state faces. These include the continuing refusal of significant parts of Syrian society to accept Bashar as a legitimate ruler, the challenge of overcoming the trauma of the disastrous civil war, the enormous difficulties to be faced in reconstruction, and the lingering issue of the refugees. The sharp divisions that tore Syrian society apart on the eve of the civil war have only been exacerbated, and Asad is not (and is certainly not perceived to be) a healer. The Islamic State also retains some presence in eastern Syria. It and other Jihadi groups are likely to continue to exploit Sunni resentment of Alawi control and Shi'i influence in order to recruit new adherents, and to challenge the regime with terrorist attacks.

These challenges facing Bashar al-Asad call to mind the contradiction inherent in his father's basic strategy: seeking to build a strong unified state through a regime predicated on the fervent loyalty of a minority community.

The Syrian Crisis and the Arab Spring

"The Arab Spring" is the term used to designate the series of challenges to authoritarian Arab regimes that began in Tunisia in December 2010. It stemmed from a popular refusal to comply further with the combined effects of political repression and socioeconomic stagnation. The events of the Arab Spring provided the spark that ignited the Syrian tinderbox in March 2011.

While the Syrian rebellion was a product of the Arab Spring, it has also been a symptom of its crises. Tunisia is the only country that emerged from the Arab Spring with democratic politics intact and enhanced. Other countries in the region have not been so fortunate. They have seen ancien régimes successfully contain popular agitation, defeat it completely, or plunge the country into a protracted phase of civil war and violence. Syria, as we have seen, belongs in the third category. And yet it may be too early to announce the ultimate failure of the Arab Spring. Political developments in different parts of the Arab world, including recent mass anticorruption demonstrations in Lebanon and Iraq, indicate that the effervescence that had fed the Arab Spring has not fully dissipated.[2]

The term "Arab Turmoil" has been often used in Middle Eastern public discourse and in the academic literature to describe the years that followed the decline of the short-lived first phase of the Arab Spring. It referred both to the domestic upheaval in several Arab states and to the collapse of the old regional order. The Syrian civil war and crisis played a major role in that turmoil—the brutal fighting in a major Arab state, the challenge presented by IS, the abrogation of the border between Syria and Iraq, and the massive intervention by regional and international actors. By 2019 the prospect of a transformation of the state system produced by World War I in the core area of the Middle East had vanished, but domestic and regional stability were not restored. In Iraq, Syria, and Lebanon weak states are not in full control of their territory. Regional politics are shaped by the new roles of Iran and Turkey, and by America's withdrawal and Russia's resurgence. Syria in its current domestic state and as a major arena of the new regional and international actors is emblematic of the current phase of Arab and Middle Eastern politics.

NOTES

Preface

1. Yassin-Kassab and Al-Shami 2016; Pearlman 2017; Zeid 2018.

2. Van Dam 2017; Lesch 2012.

3. Yazbek 2016.

4. al-Haj Saleh 2017.

5. *The Political Science of Syria's War*, POMEPS (Project on Middle East Political Science), Briefings, no. 22 (December 2013).

6. Dagher 2019.

7. Ajami 2012.

8. Kershaw 2011, 14–15.

Chapter 1. The Ba'th in Power, 1963–2011

1. Andrew and Kanya-Forstner 1981.

2. Neep 2012.

3. Khoury 1987; Batatu 1999.

4. The issue of sectarianism is discussed in greater detail in chapters 2 and 3.

5. There have been numerous studies of the Ba'th regime's history and transformations, among them Hinnebusch 2004; Zisser 2001; Rabinovich 1972; Rabinovich 2008; Heydemann 1999.

6. For an excellent analysis, see Malcolm Kerr 1965.

7. On the Ba'th regime's relationship with the Sunni religious establishment in Syria, see Pierret 2013.

8. For books on Bashar al-Asad and his reign, see Zisser 2006; Lesch 2005; Tabler 2011.

9. Interview with US diplomat Rob Denin, who attended the meeting.

10. Dagher 2019, 120–21.

11. "Damascus Declaration in English," *Syria Comment*, November 1, 2005, http://joshualandis.oucreate.com//syriablog/2005/11/damascus-declaration-in-english.htm.

12. Iraq Study Group Report, James A. Baker and Lee H. Hamilton cochairs, December 2006, p. 36, https://www.iraqsolidaridad.org/2006/docs/gei-1.pdf.

13. The phrase in the subheading is from Hinnebusch and Schmidt 2009.

14. International Crisis Group (ICG) 2004, p. 22, http://www.mafhoum.com /press6/181P81.pdf. For a more benign view of Bashar's policies at the time, see Perthes 2004.

15. Quoted in George 2015, 172–73.

16. Quoted in George 2015, 175.

17. Pierret 2018.

18. Lesch 2012, 31. Several years after publishing his *The New Lion of Damascus* (2005), Lesch published a book, *Syria: The Fall of the House of Assad* (2012, 31), on the outbreak of the Syrian revolt that offered a more critical view of Bashar al-Asad.

19. Duclos 2017, 22–23.

20. Dagher 2019, 84–86.

21. Olmert 2018, 229.

22. US Damascus Embassy, November 26, 2008, https://wikileaks.org/plusd /cables/08DAMASCUS847_a.html.

23. In 2015, Andrew Tabler published a "regime chart" on the Washington Institute's website that showed Bashar's relationship with a several dozen persons who made up his immediate circle. See https://www.washingtoninstitute.org/uploads /Documents/infographics/SyriaRegimeChart20150526v2.pdf. In 2019, Sam Dagher published *Assad or We Burn the Country*, in which he included numerous details concerning Bashar's circle.

24. Quoted in "Notification of Treasury Designation of Muhammad Hamshu," WikiLeaks, January 7, 2009. Available at: https://wikileaks.org/plusd/cables /09STATE1467_a.html.

25. US Department of the Treasury, "Treasury Designates Director of Syrian Military Intelligence," https://www.treasury.gov/press-center/press-releases/Pages /js3080.aspx.

26. Lund 2018. Manf Tlas was one of Sam Dagher's main sources for the book mentioned above (2019), and the story of the relationship between the Asads and the Tlases is a major theme in that book.

Chapter 2. The Syrian Civil War and Crisis, 2011–18

1. Interview with Syrian President Bashar al-Asad, *Wall Street Journal*, January 31, 2011, https://www.wsj.com/articles/SB10001424052748703833204576114712441122894.

2. Joan Juliet Buck, "A Rose in the Desert," *Vogue*, February 25, 2011, http://www .fouadhamdan.org/cms/upload/pdf/Asma_Assad_2articles_voguemeeting_with _aid_workers_2011.pdf.

3. See the introductory chapter in Michael Kerr and Larkin 2013.

4. See Yazbek 2012.

5. Samar Yazbek's (2016) memoir the crossing provides a vivid account by a young activist from the town of Kafr Nabel of how resistance to the regime began spontaneously in that location.

6. Lesch 2012, 116.

7. Lister 2016a.

8. O'Bagy 2012.

9. Lister 2016b.

10. Richard Spencer, "Muslim Brotherhood Cleric Calls for Sunni Jihad in Syria," *Telegraph*, June 2, 2013, https://www.telegraph.co.uk/news/worldnews/middleeast/syria/10094590/Muslim-Brotherhood-cleric-calls-for-Sunni-jihad-in-Syria.html.

11. Chapters 5 and 6 will address these questions in some detail.

12. The White House, August 18, 2011, https://obamawhitehouse.archives.gov/blog/2011/08/18/president-obama-future-syria-must-be-determined-its-people-president-bashar-al-assad.

13. One such effort was Hashemi and Postel 2013.

14. Ignatieff 2013, 49–50.

15. The White House, August 20, 2012, https://obamawhitehouse.archives.gov/the-press-office/2012/08/20/remarks-president-white-house-press-corps.

16. "Kofi Annan's Six-Points Plan for Syria," Al Jazeera, March 27, 2012, https://www.aljazeera.com/news/middleeast/2012/03/2012327153111767387.html.

17. Lister 2016a.

18. Sergei Loiko and Paul Richter, "U.S. Russia Agree to Convene talk on Syria," *Daily Press*, May 7, 2013, https://www.dailypress.com/la-fg-wn-us-russia-syria-talks-20130507-story.html.

19. Laila Bassam and Tom Perry, "How Iranian General Plotted Out Syrian Assault in Moscow," Reuters, October 6, 2015, https://www.reuters.com/article/us-mideast-crisis-syria-soleimani-insigh/how-iranian-general-plotted-out-syrian-assault-in-moscow-idUSKCN0S02BV20151006.

20. "Al-Nusra Leader Jolani Announces Split from al-Qaeda," Al Jazeera, July 29, 2016, https://www.aljazeera.com/news/2016/07/al-nusra-leader-jolani-announces-split-al-qaeda-160728163725624.html.

21. He called it "turning point" (not point of transition). "U.S., Russia Reach Agreement on Syria," Arkansas Online, September 10, 2016, https://www.arkansasonline.com/news/2016/sep/10/u-s-russia-reach-agreement-on-syria-201/?page=1.

22. Quoted in Orion and Dekel 2016. The reality and appearance of Washington's diplomatic weakness vis-à-vis Moscow in the Syrian arena are well reflected in John Kerry's (2018) memoir, esp. 548, 555.

23. "Memorandum on the Creation of De-escalation Areas in the Syrian Arab Republic," Ministry of Foreign Affairs of the Russian Federation, May 6, 2017, https://www.mid.ru/en/foreign_policy/news/-/asset_publisher/cKNonkJEo2Bw/content/id/2746041.

Chapter 3. The Domestic Scene

1. QuotesDin Michel Duclos 2017, 22–23.

2. The two most prominent military defectors were General Ali Habib, who was deposed by Bashar from his position as minister of defense in August 2011, and Brigadier General Manaf Talas.

3. Duclos 2017.

4. Balanche 2018.

5. Michael Kerr and Larkin 2013, 159–79.

6. On the role of artists and intellectuals in the ranks of the opposition, see the last section of the present chapter.

7. See Wieland 2015.

8. Lund 2013.

9. Al-Haj Saleh 2017, 45–64.

10. Quoted in Lund, 2013, 219.

11. Lucas Winter, "Suheil al-Hassan and the Syrian Army's Tiger Forces," *Small Wars Journal*, https://smallwarsjournal.com/jrnl/art/suheil-al-hassan-and-the-syrian-army%E2%80%99s-tiger-forces#_ednref6.

12. Rabinovich 1979.

13. Ajami 2012.

14. "How a Victorious Bashar al-Assad Is Changing Syria," *Economist*, June 28, 2018, https://www.economist.com/middle-east-and-africa/2018/06/28/how-a-victorious-bashar-al-assad-is-changing-syria.

15. Dukhan 2014.

16. James Bowker and Andrew J. Tabler, "Beyond Islamists and Autocrats," Washington Institute, 2017, https://www.washingtoninstitute.org/uploads/Documents/pubs/BeyondIslamists-Tabler.pdf.

17. Andrew Quinn, "Clinton Calls for Overhaul of Syrian Opposition," Reuters, October 31, 2012, https://www.reuters.com/article/us-syria-usa/clinton-calls-for-overhaul-of-syrian-opposition-idUSBRE89U1AY20121031.

18. Cafarella and Casagrande 2016.

19. Charles Lister, "The Free Syrian Army: A Decentralized Insurgent Brand," Brookings, Analysis Paper No. 26, November 2016, p. 5, https://www.brookings.edu/wp-content/uploads/2016/11/iwr_20161123_free_syrian_army.pdf.

20. See Lister 2016a; Lund 2015b.

21. Hamid and McCants 2017.

22. Lund 2013.

23. Lister 2016b.

24. Lister 2015.

25. Gunter 2014; Bengio 2014.

26. Sosnowski 2018; Heras 2014.

27. See the first pages in Haddad 2011; Sosnowski 2018, 314.

28. Sam Heller, "Keeping the Lights On in Rebel Idlib," Century Foundation, November 29, 2016, https://tcf.org/content/report/keeping-lights-rebel-idlib/?agreed=1.

29. Myers and Saab 2019.

30. See Ziter 2015.

31. Authors' interview with a member of Adonis family, December 2018.

32. Quoted in Rabinovich 2017, http://www.itamarrabinovich.tau.ac.il/publications/147-in-memoriam-sadiq-jalal-al-azm-19342016.html.

33. Adonis defended his position in a number of interviews; see, for instance, his interview with Jonathan Guyer in the *New York Review of Books*, April 16, 2016, https://www.nybooks.com/daily/2016/04/16/syria-now-writing-starts-interview-adonis/.

34. Michael Slackman, "An Arab Artist Says All the World Really Isn't a Stage," *New York Times*, August 19, 2006, https://www.nytimes.com/2006/08/19/world/middleeast/19lahhman.html.

35. "'Abu Jawdat' Is Lost between the Artists Syndicate and the Position of Police Chief," *Enabbaladi*, June 18, 2017, https://english.enabbaladi.net/archives/2017/06/abu-jawdat-lost-artists-syndicate-position-police-chief/.

36. Ibid.

37. Ben Hubbard, "Division among Syrian Artists Reflects Societal Splits of Civil War," Associated Press, December 12, 2012, https://www.timescolonist.com/entertainment/division-among-syrian-artists-reflects-societal-splits-of-civil-war-1.26020.

38. Sadiq Al-Azm, "Syria in Revolt—Understanding the Unthinkable War," *Boston Review*, August 18, 2014, http://bostonreview.net/world/sadik-al-azm-syria-in-revolt.

39. Eliza Griswold, "Mapping the Journeys of Syria's Artists," *New Yorker*, January 28, 2018, https://www.newyorker.com/culture/culture-desk/mapping-the-journeys-of-syrias-artists.

Chapter 4. The Regional Arena

1. Hinnebusch and Sauli 2020.

2. Fulton, Holliday, and Wyer 2013; Kagan et al. 2012; Kam 2018, 19–30; Von Maltzahn 2015.

3. Ahmadian and Mohseni 2019.

4. Adham 2020.

5. Phillip Smyth, "Iran Is Outpacing Assad for Control of Syria's Shia Militias," Washington Institute, April 12, 2018, https://www.washingtoninstitute.org/policy -analysis/view/iran-is-outpacing-assad-for-control-of-syrias-shia-militias.

6. Memei Reports, Twitter, March 13, 2013, https://twitter.com/MEMRIReports /status/1105696984265097217; Borzou Daragahi, "Iran Wants to Stay in Syria Forever," *Foreign Policy*, June 1, 2018, https://foreignpolicy.com/2018/06/01/iran-wants-to-stay -in-syria-forever/; "2,000 Afghan Soldiers Killed in Syria," *ANF News*, January 7, 2018, https://anfenglish.com/news/2-000-afghans-in-iranian-army-killed-in-syria-24069.

7. "Iran's Justifications for Its Syrian Intervention Have a Hollow Ring," *National*, January 8, 2017, https://www.thenational.ae/opinion/iran-s-justifications-for-its -syrian-intervention-have-a-hollow-ring-1.32352.

8. Memeri website, March 11, 2013, https://www.memri.org/reports/iranian -official-loss-syria-will-lead-loss-tehran-itself-syria-iranian-province-iran-has.

9. Kagan et al. 2012.

10. "The Most Memorable Quotes from New IRGC Chief Commander Hossein Salami," *Al Arabiya*, April 22, 2019, https://english.alarabiya.net/en/features/2019 /04/22/The-most-memorable-quotes-by-newly-appointed-IRGC-chief -commander-Hossein-Salami.html.

11. Firas Aziz al-Dib, "Sorry Ali Akbar Velayati, the World Could Fall but Syria Wouldn't" (in Arabic), *Al-Watan*, July 15, 2018, alwatan.sy/archives/158590.

12. Karim Sadjapour, "Iran's Real Enemy in Syria," *Atlantic*, April 16, 2018, https:// www.theatlantic.com/international/archive/2018/04/iran-syria-israel/558080/.

13. Joost Hiltermann, "Turkey Made a Bet against Assad—and Lost," *Atlantic*, August 27, 2018, https://www.theatlantic.com/international/archive/2018/08 /turkey-syria-war-assad-erdogan-isis-kurds-pkk/568561/.

14. "We Wanted al-Assad to Be Gorbachev, He Turned into Milosevice," *Hürriyet*, February 10, 2012, http://www.hurriyetdailynews.com/we-wanted-al-assad-to-be -gorbachev-he-turned-into-milosevic-davutoglu---13467.

15. Mark Memmott, "Compering Assad to Hitler, Turkey's Prime Minister Calls on Him to Resign," NPR, November 22, 2011, https://www.npr.org/sections/thetwo -way/2011/11/22/142653413/comparing-assad-to-hitler-turkeys-prime-minister-calls -on-him-to-resign.

16. Lister 2015.

17. Interview with a former US diplomat.

18. For an account for Israel-Syria peace negotiations, see Rabinovich 1998.

19. Frederic C. Hof, "The Golan Heights: Avoiding an Unforced Error," Atlantic Council, July 20, 2018, https://atlanticcouncil.org/blogs/syriasource/the-golan -heights-avoiding-an-unforced-error/.

20. IDF website, July 19, 2017, https://www.idf.il/en/minisites/operation-good-neighbor/operation-good-neighbor-inside-the-idf-s-effort-to-provide-aid-to-syria/.

21. Elizabeth Tsurkov, "How Israel Won Over the Syrian People," *Forward*, April 19, 2018, https://forward.com/opinion/399181/how-israel-won-over-the-syrian-people/.

22. Polina Nikolskaya and Dan Williams, "Russia Says Iranian Forces Pulled Back from Golan in Syria; Israel Unsatisfied," Reuters, August 1, 2018, https://www.reuters.com/article/us-mideast-crisis-syria-golan/russia-says-iranian-forces-pulled-back-from-golan-in-syria-israel-unsatisfied-idUSKBN1KM4GS.

23. Darwich 2020.

24. Tyler Durden, "In Shocking, Viral Interview, Qatar Confesses Secrets behind Syrian War," *Zero Hedge*, October 29, 2017, https://www.zerohedge.com/news/2017-10-28/shocking-viral-interview-qatar-confesses-secrets-behind-syrian-war.

25. Pierret 2018.

26. Ajami 2012.

27. Ibid., 110.

28. Ibid.

29. "Lebanon's Troublesome Political Priest," Michael Young's blog, September 15, 2011, http://michaelyoungscolumns.blogspot.com/2011/09/lebanons-troublesome-political-priest.html?m=0.

30. Larkin and Minha 2015.

Chapter 5. International Actors

1. Carter 1995, 293. See also Carter 2007.

2. Iraq Study Group Report, 6–7, https://www.bakerinstitute.org/media/files/Research/88085bb4/iraqstudygroup_findings.pdf.

3. Rice 2011, 561.

4. Ross Colvin and Jeff Mason, "Obama Sets Iraq Deadline, Unvails New Strategy," Reuters, February 28, 2009, https://www.reuters.com/article/us-obama-iraq/obama-sets-iraq-deadline-unveils-new-strategy-idUSTRE51P0AY20090228.

5. Dagher 2019, 149–52.

6. Interviews with Ambassadors Ross and Hof.

7. Clinton 2014.

8. To be "on the right side of history" is a favorite Obama idiom.

9. "Syria: Assad No Longer Legitimate, Says Clinton," BBC, July 12, 2011, https://www.bbc.com/news/world-middle-east-14115762.

10. Chris McGreal and Martin Chulov, "Syria: Assad Must Resign, Says Obama," *Guardian*, August 19, 2011, https://www.theguardian.com/world/2011/aug/18/syria-assad-must-resign-obama.

11. *Guardian*, July 22, 2013, https://www.theguardian.com/world/2013/jul/22/us-military-intervention-syria; *Hill*, July 22, 2013, https://thehill.com/policy/defense/312675-gen-dempsey-syria-no-fly-zone-could-cost-1b-per-month; *USNEWS*, April 30, 2013, https://www.usnews.com/news/articles/2013/04/30/dempsey-syrian-no-fly-zone-wouldnt-work.

12. For the disagreements within the US national security establishment on this issue, see the memoirs of former secretary of defense Leon Panetta, *Worthy Fights: A Memoir of Leadership in War and Peace* (2015). This choice was severely criticized by the Dutch diplomat Nikolaos Van Dam in his book *Destroying a Nation: The Civil War in Syria* (2017).

13. Clinton 2014, 385.

14. Ibid., 388.

15. Ibid., 388–89.

16. Jeffrey Goldberg, "Hillary Clinton: 'Failure' to Help Syrian Rebels Led to the Rise of ISIS," *Atlantic*, August 10, 2014, https://www.theatlantic.com/international/archive/2014/08/hillary-clinton-failure-to-help-syrian-rebels-led-to-the-rise-of-isis/375832/.

17. Greg Jaffe, "Washington's Foreign Policy Elite Breaks qith Obama over Syrian Bloodshed," *Washington Post*, October 26, 2016, https://www.washingtonpost.com/politics/washington-foreign-policy-elites-not-sorry-to-see-obama-go/2016/10/20/bd2334a2-9228-11e6-9c52-0b10449e33c4_story.html.

18. Thomas L. Friedman, "Obama on the World," *New York Times*, August 8, 2014, https://www.nytimes.com/2014/08/09/opinion/president-obama-thomas-l-friedman-iraq-and-world-affairs.html?_r=0.

19. Ibid.

20. Ben Rhodes, "Inside the White House during the Syrian 'Red Line' Crisis," *Atlantic*, June 3, 2018, https://www.theatlantic.com/international/archive/2018/06/inside-the-white-house-during-the-syrian-red-line-crisis/561887/.

21. Ibid.

22. *Haaretz*, April 25, 2013, https://www.haaretz.co.il/st/inter/Hheb/images/WhiteHouse.pdf.

23. "Background Conference Call by White House Official on Syria," White House, April 25, 2013, https://obamawhitehouse.archives.gov/the-press-office/2013/04/25/background-conference-call-white-house-official-syria.

24. Mark Landler and Eric Schmitt, "White House Says It Believes Syria Has Used Chemical Arms," *New York Times*, April 25, 2013, https://www.nytimes.com/2013/04/26/world/middleeast/us-says-it-suspects-assad-used-chemical-weapons.html.

25. Rhodes 2018.

26. Landler 2016, 226.

27. David E. Sanger and Anne Barnard, "Russia and the United States Reach New Agreement on Syria Conflict," *New York Times*, September 9, 2016, https://www.nytimes.com/2016/09/10/world/middleeast/syria-john-kerry-ceasefire-deal-russia.html.

28. Jeffrey Goldberg, "The Obama Doctrine," *Atlantic*, April 2016, https://www.theatlantic.com/magazine/archive/2016/04/the-obama-doctrine/471525/.

29. Ibid.

30. Ibid.

31. David Samuels, "The Aspiring Novelist Who Became Obama's Foreign Policy Guru," *New York Times Magazine*, May 5, 2016, https://www.nytimes.com/2016/05/08/magazine/the-aspiring-novelist-who-became-obamas-foreign-policy-guru.html?_r=0.

32. Ibid.

33. Frederic C. Hof, "America's Self-Inflicted Wound in Syria," *Foreign Policy*, August 21, 2015, https://foreignpolicy.com/2015/08/21/americas-self-inflicted-wound-in-syria/.

34. Frederic C. Hof, "Leaving," Atlantic Council, March 28, 2018, https://www.atlanticcouncil.org/blogs/syriasource/leaving/.

35. Duclos 2017, 17.

36. Robin Wright, "Former Ambassador Robert Ford on the State Department Mutiny on Syria," *New Yorker*, June 17, 2016, https://www.newyorker.com/news/news-desk/former-ambassador-robert-ford-on-the-state-department-mutiny-on-syria.

37. Kerry 2018, esp. 389–93. Kerry's memoir reflects the weakness of Washington's hand in its dealings with Russia regarding Syria in the aftermath.

38. "Secretary of State Rex Tillerson on the Way Forward for the United States regarding Syria," US Department of State, January 17, 2018, https://translations.state.gov/2018/01/17/secretary-of-state-rex-tillerson-on-the-way-forward-for-the-united-states-regarding-syria/.

39. See, for instance, Patrick Wintour, "Helsinki Summit: What Did Trump and Putin Agree?," *Guardian*, July 17, 2018, https://www.theguardian.com/world/2018/jul/17/helsinki-summit-what-did-trump-and-putin-agree.

40. Zvi Barel, "Syria's Idlib: The Hot Potato the U.S., Russia and Turkey Are Fighting Over," *Haaretz*, August 5, 2019, https://www.haaretz.com/middle-east-news/syria/.premium-syria-s-idlib-the-hot-potato-the-u-s-russia-and-turkey-are-fighting-over-1.7620282.

41. Adamsky 2016. And see also Jennifer Cafarella with Jason Zhou, "Russia's Dead-End Diplomacy in Syria," Institute for the Study of War (ISW), November 2019, http://www.understandingwar.org/sites/default/files/ISW%20Report%20-%20Russia%E2%80%99s%20Dead-End%20Diplomacy%20in%20Syria%20-%20November%202019.pdf. We are also grateful to Ambassador Zvi Magen for his insights.

42. Adamsky 2016.

43. Shaun Walker, "Russian-Speaking Jihadis in Syria 'Could Threaten Moscow in Future,'" *Guardian*, March 16, 2016, https://www.theguardian.com/world/2016/mar/16/russian-speaking-jihadis-syria-pose-threat-moscow-report.

44. "Coping with the Russian Challenge in the Middle East: U.S.-Israeli Perspectives and Opportunities for Cooperation," Kennan Institute, June 3, 2019, https://www.wilsoncenter.org/article/coping-the-russian-challenge-the-middle-east-us-israeli-perspectives-and-opportunities-for.

45. Michael Boyle, "Obama 'Leading from Behind' in Libya," *Guardian*, August 27, 2011, https://www.theguardian.com/commentisfree/cifamerica/2011/aug/27/obama-libya-leadership-nato.

46. Michel Duclos, "Syria Seven Years Later—Lessons Learnt by France," Institute Montaigne, March 22, 2018, https://www.institutmontaigne.org/en/blog/syria-seven-years-later-lessons-learnt-france.

Chapter 6. Syria 2019–20

1. Lina Khatib and Lina Sinjab, "Syria's Transactional State—How the Conflict Changed the Syrian State's Exercise of Power," Chatham House, October 2018, https://www.chathamhouse.org/publication/syrias-transactional-state-how-conflict-changed-syrian-states-exercise-power.

2. Rami Makhluf, YouTube, May 3, 2020, https://www.youtube.com/watch?v=2RtVuyXzQ8k.

3. O. Peri and H. Varulkar, "Struggle between Russia, Iran for Control over Syria's Centers of Power," MEMRI, September 23, 2019, https://www.memri.org/reports/struggle-between-russia-iran-control-over-syrias-centers-power#_edn17.

4. Elizabeth Tsurkov, "Syrian Terror Returns to the Basements," *Forum for Regional Thinking*, September 4, 2018 (Hebrew), https://www.regthink.org/articles/%D7%94%D7%98%D7%A8%D7%95%D7%A8-%D7%94%D7%A1%D7%95%D7%A8%D7%99-%D7%97%D7%95%D7%96%D7%A8-%D7%9C%D7%9E%D7%A8%D7%AA%D7%A4%D7%99%D7%9D.

5. Louisa Loveluck and Zakaria Zakaria, "Syria's Once-Teeming Prison Cells Being Emptied by Mass Murder," *Washington Post*, December 23, 2018, https://www.washingtonpost.com/graphics/2018/world/syria-bodies/.

6. Haid Haid, "Reintegrating Syrian Militias: Mechanisms, Actors and Shortfalls," Carnegie Middle East Center, December 12, 2018, https://carnegie-mec.org/2018/12/12/reintegrating-syrian-militias-mechanisms-actors-and-shortfalls-pub-77932.

7. Carl Yonker, "Wither the Syrian Ba'th? Down, but Not Out," Dayan Center, Tel Aviv University, March 28, 2018, https://dayan.org/content/wither-syrian-bath-down-not-out.

8. *Aymenn Jawad Al-Tamimi*, December 24, 2018, http://www.aymennjawad.org/2018/12/the-shia-of-busra-al-sham-interview.

9. "Protests Erupt Again in Daraa," *Syrian Observer*, November 14, 2019, https://syrianobserver.com/EN/news/54265/protests-erupt-again-in-daraa.html.

10. After the displacement of thirty-five thousand toward the north, residents of northern Homs and south Hama fear that the regime would prevent the return of twenty-five hundred civilians to their jobs, as the regime recruits hundreds of employees from the families of proregime casualties. Syrian Observatory for Human Rights, September 17, 2018, https://www.syriahr.com/en/?p=102701.

11. "President al-Assad to Jordanian Parliamentary Delegation: Relations between Countries Must Always Be Driven by Peoples' Interests and Aspirations," Sana—Syrian Arab News Agency, 19 November 2018, https://sana.sy/en/?p=151494.

12. Kamal Alam and David Lesch, "The Road to Damascus: The Arabs March Back to Befriend Assad," *War on the Rocks*, December 7, 2018, https://warontherocks.com/2018/12/the-road-to-damascus-the-arabs-march-back-to-befriend-assad/.

13. "Bashar Asad Gives a Rare Interview to Chief Editor of Kuwaiti Al Shahed Newspaper, *Sabah Al Muhammad Al Sabah*," Twitter, October 3, 2018, https://twitter.com/smmsyria/status/1047445855287083008/photo/1.

14. US Department of State, December 3, 2018, https://www.state.gov/briefing-with-special-representative-for-syria-engagement-ambassador-james-f-jeffrey/.

15. US, Russia Discuss Peace Plan That Would End Syria's Isolation, *Al-Monitor*, May 29, 2019, https://www.al-monitor.com/pulse/afp/2019/05/syria-conflict-idlib-un-russia-us.html#ixzz5rI15V9CV.

16. For interview of both government and opposition members, see "Nasser al-Hariri: We Are Not Naive and We Will Not Wait Forever," *Syrian Observer*, November 29, 2019, https://syrianobserver.com/EN/interviews/54583/nasser-al-hariri-we-are-not-naive-and-we-will-not-wait-forever.html.

17. Faisal Al Yafai, "A Speech That Buried All Hope for Syria," *National*, October 2, 2018, https://www.thenational.ae/opinion/comment/a-speech-that-buried-all-hope-for-syria-1.776278.

18. "Jamil al-Hassan: Any and All Opposition Will Be Eliminated," *Syrian Observer*, August 2, 2018, https://syrianobserver.com/EN/features/19769/jamil_hassan_any_all_opposition_will_be_eliminated.html.

19. Bashar al-Asad, *Aletho News*, August 20, 2017, https://alethonews.com/2017/08/28/speech-by-the-president-of-the-syrian-arab-republic-bashar-al-assad-on-august-20th-2017-to-the-syrian-diplomatic-corps/.

20. Balanche 2018.

21. Sinan Hatahet, "Russia and Iran: Economic Influence in Syria, Middle East and North Africa Programme," Chatham House, March 2019, https://www

.chathamhouse.org/sites/default/files/publications/research/2019-03-08RussiaAn
dIranEconomicInfluenceInSyria.pdf.

22. Sarah Gray, "'You Know What? It's Yours': Trump Reportedly Threw His Hands Up on Syria during Phone Call with the Turkish President," *Business Insider*, December 22, 2018, http://static-ssl.businessinsider.com/trump-syria-us-troops -pullout-turkish-president-erdogan-2018-12.

23. Donald J. Trump, Twitter, December 19, 2018, https://twitter.com /realDonaldTrump/status/1075397797929775105.

24. Courtney Kube, Carol E. Lee, and Josh Lederman, "U.S. Troops to Leave Syria as President Trump Declares Victory over ISIS," NBC, December 19, 2018, https://www.nbcnews.com/news/us-news/u-s-troops-leave-syria-president-trump -declares-victory-over-n949806.

25. Donald J. Trump, Twitter, December 20, 2018, https://twitter.com /realDonaldTrump/status/1075718191253504001; Donald J. Trump, Twitter, December 20, 2018, https://twitter.com/realDonaldTrump/status/1075721703421042688.

26. "Ambassador James Jeffrey on the Future of U.S. Policy in Syria," YouTube, Atlantic Council, December 17, 2018, https://www.youtube.com/watch?v=cj099EFxwlY.

27. Ibid.

28. "Read: James Mattis' Resignation Letter," CNN, December 21, 2018, https:// edition.cnn.com/2018/12/20/politics/james-mattis-resignation-letter-doc/index.html.

29. "U.S. Envoy Brett McGurk Quits over Trump Syria Pullout," BBC, December 23, 2018, https://www.bbc.com/news/world-us-canada-46661384.

30. Brett McGurk, "Trump Said He Beat ISIS. Instead, He's Giving It a New Life," op-ed, *Washington Post*, January 18, 2019, https://www.washingtonpost.com/outlook /trump-said-hed-stay-in-syria-to-beat-isis-instead-hes-giving-it-new-life/2019/01/17 /a25a00cc-19cd-11e9-8813-cb9dec761e73_story.html.

31. "Top General Disagrees with Trump over Syria Pullout," CNN, February 15, 2019, https://edition.cnn.com/videos/politics/2019/02/15/top-us-general-votel-disagrees -trump-pullout-syria-starr-newday-vpx.cnn.

32. Mike Pompeo and David Friedman, "International Law Backs the Trump Golan Policy," op-ed, *Wall Street Journal*, May 14, 2019, https://www.wsj.com/articles /international-law-backs-the-trump-golan-policy-11557875474.

33. Micky Aharonson and Aiman Mansour, "Vladimir Putin's Surprise Visit to Syria Delivered an Unequivocal Message," *Jerusalem Post*, January 15, 2020, https:// www.jpost.com/Opinion/Vladimir-Putins-surprise-visit-to-Syria-614181.

34. Recep Erdogan, op-ed, *New York Times*, January 7, 2019, https://www.nytimes .com/2019/01/07/opinion/erdogan-turkey-syria.html.

35. Vivian Salama, "Bolton Says U.S. Withdrawal from Syria Is Conditional," *Wall Street Journal*, January 6, 2019, https://www.wsj.com/articles/bolton-says-u-s -withdrawal-from-syria-is-conditional-11546777230.

36. Bianca Britton, Isil Sariyuce, Nicole Gaouette, and Kevin Liptak, "Turkey's Erdogan Slams Bolton, as Trump Position on Syria Seems to Shift," CNN, January 9, 2019, https://edition.cnn.com/2019/01/08/politics/erdogan-bolton-syria-kurds -turkey-intl/index.html.

37. Michael Crowley, "'I'm a Big Fan': Trump Gives Warm Welcome to Turkey's Erdogan," *New York Times*, November 13, 2019, https://www.nytimes.com/2019/11 /13/world/middleeast/erdogan-trump.html.

38. Fabrice Balanche, "A Humanitarian Time Bomb in Idlib," *PolicyWatch* 3147 (June 28, 2019), https://www.washingtoninstitute.org/policy-analysis/view/a -humanitarian-time-bomb-in-idlib.

39. Interview with Russian senior official.

Conclusion. From the Syrian Civil War to the Lingering Syrian Crisis

1. See chapter 4.

2. Marc Lynch, "The New Arab Order," *Foreign Affairs*, September–October 2018, https://www.foreignaffairs.com/articles/middle-east/2018-08-13/new-arab-order.

SELECTED BIBLIOGRAPHY

Abouzeid, Rania. 2018. *No Turning Back: Life, Loss, and Hope in Wartime Syria*. New York: W. W. Norton.

Adamsky, Dima. 2016. "The Russian Intervention in Syria: Strategic Significance and Systemic Lessons." *Eshtonot*, no. 13:7–95. National Security College, Research Center. November. [In Hebrew.]

Adham, Saouli. 2020. "Hizbollah's Intervention in Syria: Causes and Consequences," in *The War for Syria*, ed. Raymond Hinnebusch and Adham Sauli, 69–82. New York: Routledge.

Ahmadian, Hassan, and Payam Mohseni. 2019. Iran's Syria Strategy: The Evolution of Deterrence. *International Affairs* 95:341–64.

Ajami, Fouad. 2012. *The Syrian Rebellion*. Stanford, CA: Hoover Institution Press.

al-Haj Saleh, Yassin. 2017. *The Impossible Revolution: Making Sense of the Syrian Tragedy*. London: Hurst.

Andrew, Christopher M., and A. S. Kanya-Forstner. 1981. *France Overseas: The Great War and the Climax of French Imperial Expansion*. London: Thames and Hudson.

Balanche, Fabrice. 2018. *Sectarianism in Syria's Civil War*. Washington, DC: Washington Institute for Near East Policy.

Batatu, Hanna. 1999. *Syria's Peasantry, the Descendants of Its Lesser Rural Notables, and Their Politics*. Princeton, NJ: Princeton University Press.

Bengio, Ofra, ed. 2014. *Kurdish Awakening: Nation Building in a Fragmented Homeland*. Austin: University of Texas Press.

Cafarella, Jennifer, and Genevieve Casagrande. 2016. "Syrian Armed Opposition Powerbrokers." *Middle East Security Report*, no. 29. Washington, DC: Institute for the Study of War. March.

Carter, Jimmy. 1995. *Keeping Faith: Memoirs of a President*. Fayetteville: University of Arkansas Press.

———. 2007. *The Blood of Abraham: Insights into the Middle East*. 3rd ed. Fayetteville: University of Arkansas Press.

Clinton, Hillary Rodham. 2014. *Hard Choices*. New York: Simon and Schuster.

Dagher, Sam. 2019. *Assad or We Burn the Country*. New York: Little, Brown.

Darwich, May. 2020. "Saudi Policies in the Syrian Crisis," in *The War for Syria*, ed. Raymond Hinnebusch and Adham Sauli, 120–33. New York: Routledge.

Duclos, Michel. 2017. *Syria: To End a Never-Ending War*. Paris: Institut Montaigne. June.

Dukhan, Haian. 2014. "Tribes and Tribalism in the Syrian Uprising." *Syria Studies*, June, 1–28, https://ojs.st-andrews.ac.uk/index.php/syria/article/view/897/746.

Esman, Milton J., and Itamar Rabinovich, eds. 1988. *Ethnicity, Pluralism, and the State in the Middle East*. Ithaca, NY: Cornell University Press.

Fulton, Will, Joseph Holliday, and Sam Wyer. 2013. *Iranian Strategy in Syria*. AEI Critical Threats Project and the Institute for the Study of War. May.

Gates, Robert. 2014. *Duty: Memoirs of a Secretary at War*. New York: Alfred A. Knopf.

George, Alan. 2015. "Patronage and Clientelism in Bashar's Social Market Economy." In *The Alawis of Syria: War, Faith and Politics in the Levant*, ed Michael Kerr and Craig Larkin, 159–79. Oxford: Oxford University Press.

Gunter, Michael. 2014. *Out of Nowhere: The Kurds of Syria in Peace and War*. London: Hurst.

Haddad, Bassam. 2011. *Business Networks in Syria: The Political Economy of Authoritarian Resilience*. Palo Alto, CA: Stanford University Press.

Hamid, Shadi, and William McCants. 2017. *Rethinking Political Islam*. Oxford: Oxford University Press.

Hashemi, Nader, and Danny Postel. 2013. *The Syria Dilemma*. Boston: Boston Review Books,

———. 2017. *Sectarianization: Mapping the New Politics of the Middle East*. Oxford: Oxford University Press.

Heller, Sam. 2016. *Keeping the Lights on in Rebel Idlib: Local Governance, Services, and the Competition for Legitimacy among Islamist Armed Groups*. New York: Century Foundation. November 29.

Heras, Nicholas A. 2014. "A Profile of Syria's Strategic Dar'a Province." *CTC Sentinel*, June, 20–24.

Heydemann, Steven. 1999. *Authoritarianism in Syria: Institutions and Social Conflict, 1946–1970*. Ithaca, NY: Cornell University Press.

Hinnebusch, Raymond. 2004. *Syria: Revolution from Above*. London: Routledge.

Hinnebusch, Raymond, and Adham Sauli, eds. 2020. *The War for Syria*. New York: Routledge.

Hinnebusch, Raymond, and Soren Schmidt. 2009. *The State and the Political Economy of Reform in Syria*. Boulder, CO: Lynne Reiner.

Ignatieff, Michael. 2013. "Bosnia and Syria: Intervention Then and Now." In *The Syria Dilemma*, ed. Nader Hashemi and Danny Postel, 45–60. Boston: Boston Review Books.

International Crisis Group (ICG). 2004. *Syria under Bashar (II): Domestic Policy Challenges*. Report no. 24, Middle East and North Africa. Amman/Brussels. February 11.

———. 2018. *Keeping the Calm in Southern Syria*, Report no. 187, Middle East and North Africa. Amman/Brussels. June 21.

Kagan, Frederick W., Ahmad K. Majidyar, Danielle Pletka, and Marisa Cochrane Sullivan 2012. *Iranian Influence in the Levant, Egypt, Iraq and Afghanistan*. Washington, DC: American Enterprise Institute and the Institute for the Study of War. May.

Kam, Ephraim. 2018. "The Iranian Military Intervention in Syria: A Look to the Future." *INSS Strategic Assessment* 20, no. 1:19–30.

Kerr, Malcolm. 1965. *The Arab Cold War, 1958–1964: A Study of Ideology in Politics*. Oxford: Oxford University Press.

Kerr, Michael, and Craig Larkin, eds. 2013. *The Alawis of Syria: War, Faith and Politics in the Levant*. Oxford: Oxford University Press.

Kerry, John. 2018. *Every Day Is Extra*. New York: Simon and Schuster.

Kershaw, Ian. 2011. *The End: The Defiance and Destruction of Hitler's Germany, 1944–1945*. New York: Penguin.

Khoury, Philip S. 1987. *Syria and the French Mandate: The Politics of Arab Nationalism, 1920–1945*. Princeton, NJ: Princeton University Press.

Landler, Mark. 2016. *Alter Egos: Hillary Clinton, Barack Obama, and the Twilight Struggle over American Power*. New York: Random House.

Larkin, Craig, and Olivia Minha. 2015. "The Alawis of Tripoli: Identity, Violence and Urban Geopolitics." In *The Alawis of Syria: War, Faith and Politics in the Levant*, ed. Michael Kerr and Craig Larkin, 180–206. Oxford: Oxford University Press.

Lesch, David W. 2005. *The New Lion of Damascus: Bashar al-Asad and Modern Syria*. New Haven, CT: Yale University Press.

———. 2012. *Syria: The Fall of the House of Assad*. New Haven, CT: Yale University Press.

Lister, Charles. 2015. *The Islamic State: A Brief Introduction*. Washington, DC: Brookings Institution Press.

———. 2016a. "The Free Syrian Army: A Decentralized Insurgent Brand." *Analysis Paper*, no. 26., Brookings Institution: Brookings Project on US Relations with the Islamic World. November.

———. 2016b. "Profiling Jabhat al-Nusra." *Analysis Paper*, no. 24. Brookings Institution: Brookings Project on U.S. Relations with the Islamic World. July.

———. 2018. *The Factory: A Glimpse into Syria's War Economy*. New York: Century Foundation.

Lund, Aron. 2013. "Syria's Salafi Insurgents: The Rise of the Syrian Islamic Front." *Occasional UI Papers*, no. 17. Swedish Institute of International Affairs. March.

Lund, Aron. 2015a. "Chasing Ghosts: The Shabiha Phenomenon." In *The Alawis of Syria: War, Faith and Politics in the Levant*, ed. Michael Kerr and Craig Larkin, 207–24. Oxford: Oxford University Press.

———. 2015b. "Media Maskirovka: Russia and the Free Syrian Army." *Syria Comment*, November 8, https://www.eurasiareview.com/10112015-media-maskirovka-russia-and-the-free-syrian-army-analysis/.

———. 2018. *The Factory: A Glimpse into Syria's War Economy*. New York: Century Foundation.

Makdisi, Ussama. 2000. *The Culture of Sectarianism: Community, History, and Violence in Nineteenth-Century Ottoman Lebanon*. Berkeley: University of California Press.

Myers, Robert. and Nada Saab, eds. 2019. *Sentence to Hope: An Aa'dallah Wannous Reader*. New Haven, CT: Yale University Press.

Neep, Daniel. 2012. *Occupying Syria under the French Mandate: Insurgency, Space and State Formation*. New York: Cambridge University Press.

Norton, Augustus Richard. 2014. *Hezbollah: A Short History*. Princeton, NJ: Princeton University Press.

O'Bagy, Elizabeth. 2012. "Syria's Political Opposition." *Middle East Security Report*, no. 4. Washington, DC: Institute for the Study of War. April.

Olmert, Ehud. 2018. *In the First Person*. Tel Aviv: Yediot Aharonot Books. [In Hebrew.]

Orion, Assaf, and Udi Dekel. 2016. "The United States on the Verge of Military Intervention against Assad?" *INSS Insight*, no. 861. Tel Aviv: Institute for National Security Studies. October 13.

Panetta, Leon. 2015. *Worthy Fights: A Memoir of Leadership in War and Peace*. New York: Penguin Books.

Pearlman, Wendy. 2017. *We Crossed a Bridge and It Trembled: Voices from Syria*. New York: HarperCollins.

Perthes, Volker. 2004. "Syria under Bashar al-Asad: Modernisation and the Limits of Change." *Adelphi Papers* 44, no. 366:5–67.

Pierret, Thomas. 2013. *Religion and State in Syria: The Sunni Ulama from Coup to Revolution*. New York: Cambridge University Press.

———. 2018. *Brothers in Alms: Salafi Financiers and the Syrian Insurgency*. Beirut: Carnegie Middle East Center. May 18.

Rabinovich, Itamar. 1972. *Syria under the Ba'th, 1963–66: The Army-Party Symbiosis*. New York: John Wiley and Sons.

———. 1979. The Compact Minorities and the Syrian State, 1918–45. *Journal of Contemporary History* 14, no. 4:693–712.

———. 1998. *The Brink of Peace*: The Israeli-Syrian negotiations. Princeton, NJ: Princeton University Press.

———. 2008. *The View from Damascus: State, Political Community and Foreign Relations in Twentieth-Century Syria*. London: Vallentine Mitchell.

———. 2017. "In Memoriam: Sadiq Jalal al-'Azm, 1934–2016." *Bustan: The Middle East Book Review* 8, no. 1:104–9.

Rhodes, Ben. 2018. *The World as It Is: A Memoir of the Obama White House*. New York: Random House.

Rice, Condoleezza. 2011. *No Higher Honor: A Memoir of My Years in Washington*. New York: Crown.

Seale, Patrick. 1965. *The Struggle for Syria: A Study in Post-war Arab Politics, 1945–1958*. Oxford: Oxford University Press.

Sosnowski, Marika. 2018. "Violence and Order: The February 2016 Cease-Fire and the Development of Rebel Governance Institutions in Southern Syria. *Civil Wars* 20, no. 3:309–32.

Tabler, Andrew J. 2011. *In the Lion's Den: An Eyewitness Account of Washington's Battle with Syria*. Chicago: Lawrence Hill Books.

Van Dam, Nikolaos. 2017. *Destroying a Nation: The Civil War in Syria*. London: I. B. Tauris.

Von Maltzahn, Nadia. 2015. *The Syria-Iran Axis: Cultural Diplomacy and International Relations in the Middle East*. London: I. B. Tauris.

Weiss, Michael, and Hassan Hassan. 2015. *ISIS: Inside the Army of Terror*. New York: Regan Arts.

Wieland, Carsten. 2015. "Alawite in the Syrian Opposition." In *The Alawis of Syria: War, Faith and Politics in the Levant*, ed. Michael Kerr and Craig Larkin, 225–46. Oxford: Oxford University Press.

Yassin-Kassab, Robin, and Leila Al-Shami. 2016. *Burning Country: Syrians in Revolution and War*. London: Pluto.

Yazbek, Samar. 2012. *A Woman in the Crossfire: Diaries of the Syrian Revolution*. London: Haus.

———. 2016. *The Crossing: My Journey to the Shattered Heart of Syria*. London: Ebury.

Zeid, Rania Abu. 2018. *No Turning Back: Life, Loss, and Hope in Wartime Syria*. New York: W. W. Norton.

Zisser, Eyal. 2001. *Asad's Legacy: Syria in Transition*. New York: New York University Press.

———. 2006. *Commanding Syria, Bashar al-Asad's in Power*. London: I. B. Tauris Academic.

Ziter, Edward. 2015. *Political Performance in Syria: From the Six-Day War to the Syrian Uprising*. New York: Palgrave Macmillan.

INDEX